THE ARROW OF JUSTICE
AND OTHER BIBLE STORIES

THE ARROW OF JUSTICE

AND OTHER BIBLE STORIES

ARYEH LEIB BRODER

authorHOUSE®

AuthorHouse™
1663 Liberty Drive
Bloomington, IN 47403
www.authorhouse.com
Phone: 1-800-839-8640

First published by AuthorHouse   02/03/2012

ISBN: 978-1-4670-0078-9 (sc)
ISBN: 978-1-4670-0077-2 (ebk)

Printed in the United States of America

INTRODUCTION

The sources of these Bible stories are the Books of Joshua, Samuel, Kings and Daniel; Midrash, classical Biblical commentators and the author's imagination.

Midrash is an orthodox rabbinical commentary from the time of the Talmud that often uses the vivid imagery of colourful stories to highlight certain character traits of the heroes and villains of the Bible.

Later Classical Biblical commentators, who flourished from the 10th to the 20th Century, adopted a more pragmatic approach with their commentaries on Biblical texts.

A number of stories in this book feature the Urim V'tumim, an artefact mentioned in connection with the garments of the High Priest of Israel but without the Torah text providing any revealing description of its appearance or function.

According to Midrash the Urim V'tumim was a slip of parchment on which was written the ineffable name of God and inserted into the garment of the High Priest behind the breastplate. Whenever, the nation was in need of Divine guidance, the High Priest would consult the Urim V'tumim which miraculously illuminated key letters in the names of the twelve tribes that were engraved on the precious stones in the breastplate. The High Priest would then interpret the meaning of the coded message.

The purpose of this book is to demonstrate the continuous relationship between mankind and his Creator and how He expects them to live and behave according to a consistent moral and religious code. If I, the author have been even slightly successful in this endeavour I must express my gratitude to both my Creator and my dear wife, Angela who gave me every encouragement and assistance in bringing this project to fruition.

CONTENTS

THE PROMISE

"Only another five minutes to go," said Mr Gabriel to his family as they stood in their garden holding their special glasses in their hands. "Remember! Don't look at the sun without these glasses and even then don't stare at the sun too long."

"But where's the moon, daddy?" asked Joel. "You told us the moon was going to cover the sun. It hasn't turned up yet. It's not going to get here in five minutes. Are you sure you got the time right?"

"Of course I'm sure."

"So where is it?"

"It's there."

"Where?"

"Next to the sun."

"I can't see it."

"Of course you can't. The moon hasn't any light of its own. It only reflects the light from the sun. At the moment it's so close to the sun that there is no reflection for us to see. But when it gets in front of the sun, it will block out the light from the sun and cause an eclipse."

"But how can it block out the light from the sun, daddy? The moon is much much smaller than the sun. You've always told me the sun is huge."

"It is. But the moon is very close to the earth and the sun is millions of miles away. You can't imagine how big the sun is. But it looks small because it's so far away."

"Well, daddy, if the sun is so big I have a problem."

"What's your problem?

"You once told us a Bible story about Joshua making the sun stand still. How did he do it?"

"Joel, leave your problem till later. For the moment concentrate on the eclipse."

*   *   *

"Well, daddy," Joel asked his father that evening as they were having supper. "The story about Joshua making the sun and the moon stand still. Is that a hard thing to do?"

"It's not easy."

"How hard is it?"

"Well, very hard."

"What's more hard, daddy? Stopping the sun or splitting the Red Sea."

"They're both very hard," he said cautiously."

"I know, daddy, but which one is harder?"

Although Mr Gabriel's knowledge of science was only elementary, he suddenly appreciated how wondrous these miracles must have been. "Why do you ask, Joel? Hard, shmard. Who cares how hard a miracle is? If God wants to do something, He goes right ahead and does it."

"I know daddy, but I'm still a bit confused."

Mr Gabriel took a deep breath. He hoped he could solve his son's next problem. "What don't you understand?"

"I can understand the reason for the splitting of the Red Sea. The Jews were in great danger. They were surrounded by Egyptians, deserts, wild beasts and water. They had nowhere to go. God had to save them. He had to produce a really big miracle. But with Joshua. Why did He make the sun stand still? Why such a big miracle?"

Mr Gabriel sighed with relief at the question. This one he felt he could answer. "You have to know your Bible to answer that. Let me tell you a story. It starts with something unusual happening to Joshua and the people. It happened something like this . . . ."

*   *   *

On the outskirts of the Israelite camp in the middle of the Land of Canaan, two sentries, we'll call them Barak and Naphtali, were on guard duty. Suddenly in the distance, they saw three men walking slowly towards them. As the men drew nearer, the sentries saw they were on their last legs. They were stumbling and falling, as if they had no strength left in their bodies.

"I wonder who they are," said Barak. "What can they want from us?"

"We'll soon find out," said Naphtali. "From the look of them, I'd say they want a drink and a rest."

The sentries drew their swords and waited in silence, until the men were only a few metres away. Then Barak extended his sword and held up his hand in an unmistakable signal. "Halt," he called out. "Who are you? What do you want? Where do you come from?"

The answer didn't make sense. The strangers spoke a language, the sentries had never heard before.

"Don't you understand Hebrew?" persisted Barak. "Who are you? What do you want?"

"Don't waste your breath," said Naphtali. "It's obvious, they don't understand us."

"And we don't understand them either," fumed Barak. "They might seem friendly enough. But one never knows. At least, let's try to get some information from them. Come along, Naphtali. You're good with your hands. Think up some sign that will help us communicate with them."

Naphtali rose to the challenge. He spread out his hands and pointed them in every direction. Then he pouted his lips and spread out his hands while raising and lowering his shoulders. To his surprise, he succeeded in conveying his intentions to the three men.

Their response was just as theatrical. They jabbed their fingers in the air and waved their hands in a curved motion in the direction of a distant mountain.

"I think they're saying they come from a long way away," said Naphtali.

"That's pretty obvious," said Barak. "They certainly haven't come from just round the corner. Look at the state of their clothes. They're in shreds. And their shoes. I've never seen so many faded colours on a piece of leather. Look how dusty their hands and faces are. They've got more sand on them than the Egyptian desert. Either they couldn't find water. Or they didn't have time to have a wash.

"I wonder what's in their sacks. If it's food, and if it's as old as the rest of their clothing. I wouldn't even give it to an Amalekite."

Naphtali pointed to their sacks and made an exaggerated gesture with his hands. "Open them up!"

The strangers opened their bags and one of them held his bag under Naphtali's nose for closer inspection.

"Take it away, quick," screamed Naphtali, almost fainting from an attack of nausea. "Your right, Barak. Even rats wouldn't eat such mouldy bread."

"Let's see this other sack," commanded Barak.

One of the men opened his sack to reveal a pale red liquid, which if it had been wine, had long lost its strength. Barak shook his head in bewilderment. "They've certainly travelled far. But why have they come here? What do they want from us? Until we get someone who understands their language, we won't have any answers." He turned to Naphtali. "Shout out for reinforcements. In the meantime, let's see if they have any weapons."

As Naphtali shouted out towards a small tent about four hundred metres from the two men, Barak, by pointing to his sword and dagger, soon made his intentions clear to the three strangers.

After nodding their heads in agreement, each one took out a small dagger from his clothing. Holding them by the blade, they handed them carefully to Barak.

"Good," said Barak, as he saw four soldiers approaching from the tent. "Let's arrange to take them to Joshua. He'll decide what to do with them."

* * *

"Now, Joel," said Mr Gabriel. "You must understand a bit of the background to what was happening at that time. Forty years had passed since the Exodus of the Israelites from Egypt and Joshua was now leader of the people after the death of Moses.

"Just before Moses died he sought permission from two nations, Bashan and Emori, to cross their borders in order to enter Canaan. Both nations refused and mobilised their armies to fight the Israelites.

"At that time, Bashan and Emori were at the peak of their military power. They were ruled by two giants, Sihon and Og who were considered to be invincible.

"Nevertheless, Moses did not back off. He fought these two powerful nations, annihilated Og and Sihon together with their armies and populated their kingdoms with the Israelite tribes of Rueben, Gad and Manasseh. Then Moses died and Joshua took over.

"On the arrival of the Israelites in Canaan, Joshua and his army immediately sent a shock wave of fear throughout Canaan.

They toppled the walls of Jericho with the sound of trumpets, then utterly destroyed the city, by razing it to the ground. Immediately afterwards they captured the city of Ai in the centre of Israel. Now they were well placed to swoop down on the rest of Canaan.

The Canaanites were desperate. How could they defeat these powerful Israelites? What tactics could they use to repel the Israelite invasion? Were these three strangers part of those tactics? The reason for their unexpected arrival at the Israelite camp had to be thoroughly investigated."

* * *

The three strangers were conducted to a large tent in the centre of the camp. There they washed their feet, drank some water and had a light meal of parched corn and unleavened bread. Then Joshua and the princes of Israel interrogated them.

The problem of language had been overcome. Joshua, being a Torah scholar of considerable repute was a master of seventy languages.

In addition, two members of the seventy elders were present to act as interpreters on behalf of the princes.

Joshua began the questioning. He looked down imperiously at the three men as they sat on low stools in front of him. "Who are you? From where do you come? Why have you come to our camp?"

"We come from a distant country," they replied. "Our journey has taken many days. We almost despaired of ever reaching you."

"You claim to come from a distant land. Yet you speak the language of the Chivites?" exclaimed Joshua. "Explain yourself."

"The Chivites!" interrupted the prince of the tribe of Simon, Nachman the son of Amihud. "They are one of the seven nations. Their main city's not far from here."

"I am aware of that," said Joshua to the prince. "Allow me to continue the questioning." He turned to the three men. "You are Chivites. How can you claim to live far away?"

"We are descended from the Chivites," came the reply. "But we no longer live in Canaan. About two hundred and fifty years ago, there was a famine in Canaan. It was so severe that many of our tribe perished. Only the wealthy were able to buy corn from Egypt. After a time even their money was used up. Some of our tribe decided to emigrate. Just over five hundred people began travelling northwards from Canaan. After a journey of forty days, we found a country where there was pasture for our cattle and grain for ourselves. But many of those travellers died on that journey. The few who survived were blessed by the Lord and prospered in their new home. We are their descendants."

"Well, princes," said Joshua. "What say you? Their story does have the ring of truth. They left Canaan the same time as our father Jacob left to go down to Egypt. And for the same reason."

"We still haven't heard why they've come here today," said Nachman. "I don't trust them. I think the whole thing is a trick. By their own tongue they admit they're Chivites. We were commanded to wipe them out." He drew his sword from his sheath and strode towards the three Chivites.

"Wait!" cried out Joshua. "You can't kill three people in cold blood."

"If they're Chivites, I can," roared Nachman. "Now let me be."

"Son of Amihud, wait!" The command of authority from Joshua was unmistakable. "You will not shed blood in my presence. We shall hear what else these Chivites have to say. After that we shall decide. Put away your sword. It's not your decision, it's our decision."

Joshua addressed the Chivites once more. "If you're honest people, you have no need to be afraid. Prove to us you're telling the truth."

"We are telling the truth. When we left our homes, we put fresh bread in our sacks and fresh wine in our bottles. That was many days ago. See how they've become mouldy and stale. Look at our clothes. They were fresh and clean when we started out. We've come a long way to meet you."

"For what purpose?"

"We wish to make a covenant with your nation. We are sick of war and conflict. We want to draw up a non aggression pact between our two nations."

"Why? If you live so far away. You have nothing to fear from us."

"You Israelites are an ambitious and resourceful people. You have a powerful God. You have destroyed Sihon and Og. You have conquered Jericho and Ai. Before long your armies will be at the gates of our cities. We wish to make peace with you now, to make an alliance with you, to trade with you."

The earnestness of the Chivites softened the resistance of the princes. They listened carefully to the rest of their words. "We know from your father Jacob that you are a peace loving people. You don't want to spend all your life in fighting wars. There will come a time when you wish to put an end to war, to rest under your vine and fig tree, to till the soil and harvest your crops. What guarantees do you have that your neighbours will not attack you? Our nation will never wage war against you and we will be your loyal ally if any nation attacks you."

The Chivites paused as though expecting an answer. Joshua, however, who was listening impassively to what they were saying, gestured with his hand for them to continue.

"We can assure you of peace," said the Chivites. "We are your neighbours on your Northern border. We shall guarantee the safety and security of that area. That is why we have come here today. For our mutual benefit."

"The men speak sense," said Joshua. "What say you, princes of Israel? Shall we accept them?"

"No," cried out Nachman. "I don't trust them. By their own words they are Canaanites. We were commanded by Moshe to destroy them. We cannot accept their treaty. Their trading and non aggression pact is nothing but a sham. They are deceiving us."

"I understand and share your reservations," said Joshua. "But negotiations are still better than war."

"Only if we negotiate with people of integrity," countered Nachman.

"That I intend to determine now." Joshua turned to the Chivites once more.

"You claim you wish to enter into a treaty with us, to become partners with us in trade and national security. That is not enough. Any treaty with us must include your acceptance of our way of life. You must accept a commitment to worship of the God of Israel."

"We would gladly accept that commitment," they replied. "The news of the victories of the Israelite nation has swept the world. Everyone has heard of the plagues in Egypt, the killing of the first born and the division of the Red Sea. Our people heard in amazement of the destruction of Og and Sichon. And on our journey to your camp, we had news of your recent spectacular victories over Jericho and Ai. You are a powerful nation. You have a powerful God. We wish to worship your God, the God of the Israelites. We wish to learn how to serve Him. Teach us how to serve Him. Show us how to perform His commandments."

Inwardly, Joshua approved of the Chivites's request. Like his master Moshe, he was always prepared to accept converts. But he could not reply hastily. First, he had to exercise caution.

"Let me warn you, Chivites. Our lives are governed by the Book of God, the Torah. A Torah life is not an easy one. Our God is very demanding. He is a jealous God. He abhors idols. Our Torah demands you remove all images from your homes and cities.

"In addition, our God is not just a God of war. He is a God of peace and compassion He is concerned with the rights of the widow and the orphan. He is concerned with justice, and honesty, in the streets and in the market places. He is concerned with morality, with the separation of men and women, of forbidding immoral marriages. He is concerned with the food that you eat and the clothes that you wear. All must be prepared according to the laws and customs of Israel.

"Will you accept the Code of our Law, our Torah?"

"We will accept," the Chivites shouted out in unison. "We shall observe your Torah. We shall smash our idols. We shall worship the God of Israel."

"Do you speak in the name of your people?"

"We speak in the name of our people."

Joshua turned to the princes. "Princes of Israel. You represent the tribes of Israel. Do you accept this nation as allies?"

"We accept," they said. "The name of God will be glorified by our alliance with this people."

"We shall accept you as allies," said Joshua to the Chivites. "We shall make an alliance between your nation and my nation, the people of Israel. But both parties to this alliance must take a binding oath. The princes on behalf of Israel. And you on behalf of your people." Joshua looked at the princes and the Chivites. "Do you understand?"

"We understand," they replied.

"Now you must swear on the most sacred object we have, the Book of our Law, the Scroll of our Torah."

On Joshua's instructions the Scroll of the Torah was brought to his tent. And the princes together with the Chivites took an oath to honour their agreement.

*   *   *

The pact drawn up between the princes and the Chivites was not fully approved by the whole of Israel. A small minority objected to an alliance with an unknown nation whose kingdom might well be within Canaan itself. Some of the Israelites remembered a similar occurrence in the time of Moses, when a foreign nation had deceived the Israelites as to the true whereabouts of their country.

These objectors soon discovered the treachery of the Chivites. Unbeknown to Joshua when the Chivites left the camp, they (the objectors) followed them. In less than a day's journey, they came across their home town, not faraway in the North across some mysterious border. Their home town was in the city of Gibeon in the heart of Canaan.

*   *   *

The objectors wasted no time in revealing their discoveries. On returning to their camp, they voiced their feelings for everyone to hear. "They're liars and cheats," they announced. "We shall inform Joshua immediately."

*   *   *

The rebel Israelites stunned Joshua with their story. "When the Chivites left our camp, we followed them from a safe distance. Occasionally, they turned round to see if they were being followed, but later they didn't even bother to check who was behind them. They seemed confident they'd completely fooled us.

"Just before sunset, they arrived at Gibeon, about twenty miles from here. The welcome they got was overwhelming. People rushed out of the city, lifted them in the air and shouted and danced with joy. All we could hear was 'welcome home and well done.' They didn't travel hundreds of miles to get to us. They've come from just around the corner. They live in Canaan. They're Gibeonites."

"We'll check your story immediately," said Joshua. "If you're right, they've cheated us. But we made a pact with them. We're stuck with them. We cannot undo that binding oath."

"What do you mean stuck with them?" the people protested. "The covenant you made with them is not valid. It was made under false pretences. The Gibeonites are liars. We shall destroy them like the rest of the Canaanites."

"No," said Joshua emphatically. "An oath was made. The name of God was used. The Torah Scroll of Moses was a witness. We cannot renege on our alliance."

"But they tricked us. They deserve to die for making us take the name of God in vain."

"No, repeated Joshua, "we cannot kill them. We cannot do away with the covenant. But we can add to it."

"What do you mean?"

"I'll explain later," said Joshua. "Now we march to Gibeon."

*   *   *

Two days later, Joshua arrived at Gibeon. He assembled his army outside the walls of the city and one of his officers addressed the Gibeonites.

"Citizens of Gibeon. We made a covenant of peace with you. But you lied to us. Send out the leaders of your city. They will not come to any harm. We shall inform them of the new terms of the covenant."

When the officer had finished his address, the gates of the city swung open. A delegation of Gibeonites hurried out to Joshua and fell on the ground at his feet. "Have mercy upon us," they pleaded. "We have sinned against you and Israel. We were afraid of your God and your army. We meant you no harm. We pray you, spare our lives."

Joshua looked down on them with contempt. "The children of Israel serve the God of truth. The children of Israel keep their word. Had you told us the truth, we would still have accepted you as converts to our Torah. Now it is too late. Our relationship can never be the same. Have no fear for your lives though. We shall keep our promise of peace towards you. But we shall fine you for the wrongs you have committed against us. Henceforth, you shall be slaves to our people. You will become hewers of wood and drawers of water. Your duties will start immediately. Now go and tell your people of the new terms of the covenant we have drawn up."

*　　*　　*

The story of the Gibeonites was not yet over. Within days, Joshua and Israel were called upon to honour their agreement with them. The other kingdoms of Canaan were furious with the Gibeonites for the alliance they had made with Israel. In a rare display of unity, they declared war against Gibeon, besieged the city and threatened to destroy all its inhabitants.

The Gibeonites, however, managed to send a message to Joshua for help.

*　　*　　*

Joshua convened a council of war meeting with the princes and informed them of the latest development in the devious and unwelcome saga of the Gibeonites. "I have received a request for assistance from the Gibeonites. This time, it does appear to be genuine."

"Genuine!" Once again Nachman exploded. "You trust those Canaanites. They tricked you once and now they're tricking you again. The whole exercise is a trap."

"He could be right," said Elitsafan the son of Parnach, the prince of Zebulun. "The Canaanites saw what happened at Ai. If we can win by strategy, so can they. We can't risk the lives of our men for the sake of these Gibeonites. They're treacherous. They're not to be trusted."

"What do you suggest?" someone asked.

"I suggest we play a waiting game. Let's wait a day or so. Let's see what happens. If the attack by the Canaanites on the Gibeonites is genuine, then both sides will be weakened. Once they start killing each other, we'll have less of the enemy to worry about."

"And if it's not genuine."

"Then we know the Gibeonites are liars. They will have violated our agreement. We can punish them as we think fit."

"Well, said," said Nachman. "At last someone is talking sense about these lying Gibeonites. What do you say, Joshua? What's your opinion?"

"Your suggestion is rejected." Joshua was not prepared to surrender to the demands of the princes. "We have no choice in the matter. We have taken an oath to help these people. Now they have asked for our help. We are morally bound to come to their rescue. This time I have checked and rechecked the story of the Gibeonites. The story they now tell is true. They are in imminent danger of their lives. We march at once. Princes of Israel! Prepare your soldiers for battle."

*　　*　　*

As the princes left to rally their troops, Joshua stood up and walked over to the side of the tent. He placed his hands before his eyes and, with all his heart, prayed to God. "O. God of Israel! I pray, please vindicate me today. Grant a complete and speedy victory to your people Israel over their enemies. Let the whole of Canaan know that you are the living God.

"Let them know that you are a God of truth and that your people are a nation of truth. Let them know that the word of an Israelite is his bond so that they will come to serve You with a perfect heart."

Joshua uncovered his eyes and composed himself. Then, picking up his shield from the back of the tent he went out to lead his army against the Canaanites.

*　　*　　*

The suddenness of all the recent events gave Joshua no time to plan any complicated strategy. He decided to boldly attack the Canaanite positions, hoping their morale was so weak they would flee before him.

The simple strategy proved effective. At the sight of the advancing Israelite army, the Canaanites fled, with Joshua in hot pursuit. But the hour was late, the sun was setting and Joshua's vital victory was threatening to elude him. Moreover, not only would the Canaanites be safe in the darkness, they could even prove to be dangerous. Unlike the Israelites, they were familiar with the countryside. There was even a possibility they could launch a successful counterattack.

Once more Joshua prayed. Not quietly this time but aloud. He raised his sword to the heavens and called out. "O,' sun, stand still upon Gibeon. And you, 'O,' moon, in the valley of Ajalon."

God, wanting Israel to win their battle quickly, responded immediately. To the amazement of the Canaanites and the joy of the Israelites, the sun and the moon stood still, the light no longer faded from the sky. Joshua and his troops continued their pursuit of the fleeing Canaanites

This miracle was swiftly followed by others.

A whirlwind whooshed down from the hills behind the Israelites and hurtled them towards the Canaanites who fled headlong along the valley of Ajalon. And from the heavens, a hail of boulders rained down and annihilated the Canaanites as they fled to Azekah. That day, Joshua and Israel won a miraculous victory over the Canaanites

*   *   *

"That is the answer to your question," said Mr Gabriel to Joel. "When we look at the miracles in the Bible, we don't ask how God did the miracle. We leave that to the scientists and physicists. We only ask why. Why did He do the miracle. At the Red Sea, God wrought a miracle to save the Israelites and punish the Egyptians. At the valley of Ajalon, God wrought a miracle to honour Joshua and the Israelites for being a nation of Truth that honours their words and commitments to others.

"Well, Joel. That's the end of the story I hoped you liked my explanation."

"Yes, daddy. I think it answers my question. Now tell me. What happened to the Gibeonites afterwards? Did they cause any more trouble to the Jewish people?"

"Yes, Joel, they did. Later in Jewish history, in the time of King David, a very serious incident took place. But that's another story."

A WIFE'S PRAYER

This account of the events that led to the birth of Samuel is based on the Book of Samuel and Midrashic insights into the thoughts and deeds of the main characters of the story.

Everyone was busy. Maidservants were scrubbing pots and pans, patching up garments, and baking bread, biscuits and cakes. Menservants were oiling bridles and harnesses, replacing worn horseshoes, repairing broken wheels and nailing down loose floor boards in wagons. In Ramatayim Tzofim in Central Israel, Elkanah, his two wives and children were preparing for their journey to the Sanctuary in Shilo.

Elkanah's wife, Peninah looked with pride at her ten children as they skipped, danced and ran around the house and the stables. "Come here Ephraim," she called out to her youngest son. "I want to hear you say your morning prayers."

From outside the stable, a small figure broke away from the group of playing children. He ran over to his mother and fell in her arms. Then, with both hands held tightly over his eyes, he rocked backwards and forwards and said the traditional words, 'Hear O' Israel the Lord our God, the Lord is One.'

"You're a good boy," said Peninah, stroking his soft golden curls. "I didn't have to help you even once. Your daddy will be proud of you." She looked towards her husband carrying parcels to the wagon. "Elkanah!" she called out. "Did you hear that? Aren't you proud of him?"

Elkanah fought hard to control his emotions. At first, he said nothing. Then he turned towards his other wife, Hannah standing in the doorway of the house. He saw the tears moistening her cheeks and his eyes hardened. "Yes, I heard him," he said, with a trace of bitterness in his voice. "He's a fine boy."

"Thank you, Elkanah! Please don't be so upset. One day Hannah will give you sons; just like I have."

*　　*　　*

After his first wife Hannah had failed to bear him children, Elkanah married a second wife, Peninah. But this marriage turned out to be a mixed blessing. Peninah not only brought ten children into Elkanah's home, she also brought strife and friction. After the birth of her first child, she began taunting and mocking Hannah for her lack of children.

At first her motives had been sincere. 'God always opens the gate of tears,' she reasoned. 'The more I provoke Hannah, the more sincere and heartfelt will become her prayers and there will be a greater chance of her prayers being answered.'

However, over the years, time had blunted her feelings and gradually, her sympathy blurred into contempt. 'If God allows her prayers to remain unanswered for so long, she must be undeserving of children,' she said to herself. 'Since I have been blessed with ten sons, I am now the mainstay of this house and Elkanah should give me the respect and status that I deserve.'

* * *

Now, on the morning of their departure to the Sanctuary in Shilo, Peninah's eyes gleamed with triumph as she cuddled her youngest son. "It won't be long now," she called loudly to Elkanah, "I'm sure God will answer your prayers at the Sanctuary this year. I'm sure God will reward Hannah for being such a good wife to you."

"That's enough," snapped Elkanah. "How many times have I told you? Don't make remarks about Hannah. No man could ask for a better wife. Hannah is better to me than ten sons."

Elkanah's passionate defence of Hannah was a knife in the heart of Peninah. 'Why does he not accept me?' she thought bitterly. 'How much longer can he love Hannah more than me? 'Every time they go to the Sanctuary, their love seems to be stronger, even though his prayers remain unanswered.' She bit her lip and rubbed her chin against the top of Ephraim's head. 'What must I do to win his love?' With mounting envy, she watched him stride over to Hannah and attempt to placate her.

* * *

Elkanah, wanting to arrive at Shilo well before nightfall, was eager to start the journey. He checked the provisions and luggage into the wagons, and then called out to the children. "Children, children! Stop fighting and get into the wagons. Nethanel, Uriel and Uzziel. You sit in the second wagon next to your mother and sisters. Paltiel, Refael, Gabriel, Michael, Gershon, Eliezer and Ephraim. You come with me."

"But Daddy?" protested the children "It's not fair."

"Do as I say. When we come back, we'll change round. But hurry! It's getting late. Look how high the sun is." He pointed to the sky and as the children looked upwards, he scooped up Ephraim in his hands and placed him in the wagon. "Now the rest of you can get on. Who wants a hand up?"

The children rushed towards him. Elkanah, with a smile on his face, picked them up and swung them in their places. "Now hold tight and count to a hundred. Then give a big shout and off we'll go. Remember Gershon! No cheating. Count in ones not tens. Right! Start counting now."

"One, two three . . . ." Elkanah helped his two wives into the wagons. "Fifty-one, Fifty-two, Fifty-three . . . ." He ran back to the house and fetched a small scroll from a cupboard. "Eighty-one, eighty-two, eighty-three . . . ." Elkanah picked up a biscuit that Ephraim had thrown on to the ground. "Ninety-six, ninety-seven.." He took his seat next to the servant driving the front wagon. "Ninety-nine, a hundred!"

The wagons lurched forward.

"We're off," the children shouted excitedly, "we're off to the Sanctuary in Shilo."

*   *   *

"Daddy? Why are we going this way?" Paltiel pointed to a rock by the road. "Last time we went on the other side of that rock."

Elkanah turned round to face his son. "You've got a good memory for places, Paltiel. We did take the other turning last time, but I want to go past the village at the end of this road."

"You want to buy something Daddy?"

"No, Paltiel." Elkanah scratched at his beard as he considered how much he should say to his son. "I want to sell something."

"I thought you were in a hurry to get to the Sanctuary."

"I am. I also want others to go too. I want to sell them the idea of going to the Sanctuary."

Paltiel looked puzzled. "Why do you have to tell them, Daddy? It says in the Torah they have to go to Sanctuary three times a year. Why don't they go by themselves?"

"They have their reasons. We have our duties. One day when you're older you'll understand." He turned round to the driver. "Be careful of the holes over this stretch of the road. We don't want any accidents."

Sensing his father did not want to discuss the matter, Paltiel looked towards Hannah sitting opposite him. "What does Daddy mean? Why can't I understand now?"

Hannah also seemed embarrassed by the question. "Sometimes, we say things that are just a guess and then it's so easy for talking to become evil gossip that can hurt someone. So it's better not to say anything at all.

"Who has not been behaving properly?" asked Paltiel. "Is it the villagers? Or is it to do with the priests in the Sanctuary?"

The shrewdness of the questions surprised Hannah. "Oh Paltiel, you're growing up so fast. I'm sure daddy will tell you all about it one day. Then he'll tell you in private; not in front of the other children. In the meantime I'd like to tell you a story about one of the judges. Who shall it be?"

"Samson!" the children all shouted out. "Tell us a story about the strong Samson."

Hannah smiled. "Very well, listen carefully. We shall begin with his father. A man called Manoah. Some time ago . . . .

The sound of the horses' hooves clicking on the hard mountain road seemed to fade away as Hannah told her story. Even Paltiel sat enthralled. He forgot all about his questions and drank in the music of her voice.

*   *   *

As Elkanah sat in the carriage he reflected on his son's remarks. Even Paltiel knows that Hafni and Phineas, the sons of the High Priest Eli, are bringing the Sanctuary into disrepute. Why do they behave with so little dignity? Why do they abuse the privileges Torah gave them?

'Of course they're entitled to certain parts of the sacrifice. Yet they act with such little respect? They sit at home and send their servant to fetch their portions for them. And the way he takes those portions! He pushes people aside, plunges a giant fork into the pot and grabs the biggest portions he can find.

It's hardly surprising that fewer and fewer people visit the Sanctuary every festival. If the priests can't see the holiness in the sacrifices, how can the people be expected to have respect for them?

Yet the people have a duty to attend. And it's my duty to persuade them to go to the Sanctuary; despite the presence of Hafni and Phineas.'

*   *   *

"Daddy? Did you hear the story about Samson? The children's voices broke into Elkanah's thoughts. "When I grow up I'll also be strong and fight the Philistines; just like he did."

Elkanah smiled at Paltiel. "You don't have to fight to be a good Israelite. There are other ways. Look! See that village at the end of the road. Come with me. Let's see how many people we can persuade to follow us to the Sanctuary in Shilo."

*   *   *

The villagers extended a warm welcome to Elkanah and his family and listened courteously to his suggestion to go to Shilo for the coming Festival. However, after he had finished speaking some of them objected to his invitation to go to Shilo.

"As long as Hafni and Phineas are in charge of the Sanctuary, I'm staying at home," said one villager. "Don't tell me they represent God. All they care about is themselves. I'm not going to the Sanctuary to line their pockets—and stomachs—at our expense."

Others, however, were persuaded by the sincerity of Elkanah's request. Hurriedly, they packed a few personal belongings into sacks and followed Elkanah and his family to Shilo.

*   *   *

As Elkanah and his family rode slowly through the gates of Shilo, he told them about the proud history of the city. "Can you imagine that hundreds of years ago, Joshua walked along this path? Do you know that the children of Israel are living where they are today because of what Joshua did here?" The children all listened attentively. "Joshua assembled all the elders of Israel in Shilo and cast lots to decide which tribe should live in which part of Israel."

"And we were given Ramatayim Tzofim, near the Sanctuary," said Paltiel.

"Yes, we're Levites. We have to live near the Sanctuary."

"Daddy, I like Shilo," said Gabriel. "It's such an exciting place. Look! There are so many people and so many animals. I've never seen so many sheep and cows in a town before. Why can't we live in Shilo? Something must always be happening here."

Elkanah laughed. "I'm very happy in Ramatayim Tzofim. If God decided we should live there, it must be the best place for us. As for all those animals you see, they're going to be used in the Sanctuary. That's why it's so busy here." He nudged the driver and the wagon came to a halt. "I'm getting off here for a moment. I want to find a place for us to stay before it gets dark. I won't be long."

Elkanah stepped down from the wagon and walked over to a small house at the side of the road. He knocked at the open door, waited for a reply and smiled broadly when a man came to the doorway. "Shalom! Peace unto you, Jacob! How are you?"

"Elkanah! I knew you wouldn't let us down." Jacob was delighted to meet his old friend again. He seized Elkanah's hand and shook it vigorously. "Nothing will keep you away from the Sanctuary. Not even . . ."

"Not even a wagon-load of ten lively children," said Elkanah, hugging his friend before he could utter any slander. "Can I bring in the children? They're tired and hungry."

"Of course. Bring them in. They'll all eat and sleep here." He turned and called to his wife. "Tsiporah! Elkanah and his family have arrived. Bring out some fruit. Put drinks on the table. Bake a few cakes. They must be starving." He waved his hand to the children in the wagons. "Come on in. Make yourself at home."

$$* \quad * \quad *$$

On the following day, amid a crowd of people, Elkanah and Jacob waited to enter the Sanctuary. The sun had just thrust its head above the horizon and, at the entrance to the Sanctuary, a gentle breeze ruffled the screen of fine linen that hid the altar from the gaze of passers-by. "A perfect day to celebrate the Festival," said Jacob to Elkanah. "May God give you everything you desire."

"For myself, I'm like our father Jacob. I have everything. But for others. There's so much to ask for. If only God would give them the desire to come more often to the Sanctuary."

"You can't complain about the number of people here today, Elkanah. It's crowded. I can hardly move," said Jacob, gently pushing away the calf gnawing at the heel of his shoe.

"But only with local people. Where is the rest of Israel? Where are the people from the North and the South? When did you last see someone from the tribes of Rueben and Gad?" Elkanah pointed towards the silver hooks supporting the curtain around the Sanctuary. "Those hooks are four hundred years old. They go right back to the time of Moses. "I wonder what Moses would have done if he were alive today?"

"What do you mean?" His friend looked at him sharply.

"Was the Sanctuary designed to last forever? Or was it only for use in the desert? Look Jacob! There's only one entrance to the Sanctuary. Everyone and everything have to go through it. Priests, Levites, Israelites, sacrifices, wood, wine, flour and oil."

"You want to see a change, Elkanah?" Jacob asked cautiously. "You want to change the commands of the Torah."

"I don't intend to change the commands of the Torah. It is the elders who have to find a way within the Torah. They did this with Boaz and Ruth. They found a way of permitting Boaz to marry Ruth although she was born a Moabite."

"But not everyone agrees with them."

"They only disagree because they don't have the chain of tradition going back to Moses; the tradition that tells them that a woman from Moab can marry into the Israelite nation. Boaz and his Law Court did have that tradition. This is the trouble. Tradition gets lost."

"But the Sanctuary is different," Jacob argued. "It's too holy for us to interfere with."

"No, I disagree. Because it's holy, we have to find a way. You see with the present system everyone is crowded together. Men and women should be separated. Yet there is only one entrance? How is it to be done properly?

"There's another thing Jacob. Crowds lead to arguments. We can't blame the priests for everything that goes wrong in the Sanctuary."

"It was all right in Moses's time," said Jacob, as people emerged from the Sanctuary and the crowd lurched forward a few more feet.

"Yes, but Israel has grown tenfold since the time of Moses. Besides when Moses was there to supervise there were no problems. Now it is different. You can see for yourself." Elkanah shook his head sadly. "Unfortunately, there's no one with the authority to do something about it. We need a prophet to guide us; or a king."

"One day God will show us the way," said Jacob hopefully. "Perhaps in your son's lifetime, someone will arise and do something about it."

"In my son's lifetime," thought Elkanah. "Pray that it be Hannah's son too."

Jacob did not hear the words, but the look in Elkanah's eyes conveyed his feelings. "Amen," he said quietly to himself.

*   *   *

Elkanah offered his sacrifice in the Sanctuary and brought part of it back to Shilo to share with his family. As in previous years, he gave a double portion to Hannah.

This time, however, more than before, Peninah was enraged by his favouring of Hannah. She believed her ten sons made her superior to the barren Hannah. She should receive the double portion. Peninah's fury erupted as a volcano and her spiteful words reduced Hannah to tears.

Elkanah vainly attempted to comfort Hannah. Again and again he repeated the words. "I am better to you than ten sons."

Hannah refused to be comforted. Peninah's merciless goading had driven her to the abyss of despair. She rose from her place, walked purposefully through the streets of Shilo and, in the early afternoon, entered an almost deserted Sanctuary. With tears flowing freely down her face, she composed herself for prayer and protest—to God.

*   *   *

Hannah's prayer, unlike the custom in those times, was lengthy, silent and directed to God—not his ministering angels. No sound emerged from her moving lips as she stood, almost motionless, at the rear of the Sanctuary.

Her prayer was born of faith and bitterness. God had denied her the precious gift of motherhood. The Lord of Hosts had been unwilling to entrust her with even one precious soul from his vast treasury of souls. From the depths of her heart, she pleaded and protested for justice and mercy.

*   *   *

Not far from Hannah, on the chair by the door post of the inner sanctuary, sat the High Priest of Israel, Eli, the father of Hafni and Phineas. As usual, he wore the eight splendid garments of his High Office including the breastplate with its twelve precious stones on which were engraved the names of the twelve tribes of Israel.

*   *   *

Behind the breastplate was the Urim V'Tumim, a slip of parchment bearing the Divine name of God. Miraculously, whenever God's advice was required on behalf of Israel, the Urim V'Tumim illuminated key letters in the breastplate. The meaning of the message would then be interpreted by the High Priest.

Joshua had used the Urim V'Tumim when dividing the land after the conquest of Canaan. The tribes of Israel had consulted the Urim V'Tumim before their civil war with the tribe of Benjamin in the days of the Judges. Later in Jewish history, Saul and David would also make use of its supernatural properties.

Significantly, the Urim V'Tumim could only be used by the leaders of the nation on behalf of the nation. Yet on this occasion, Eli believed he was justified in using the Urim V'Tumim. Although lacking full prophetic powers, he sensed the spiritual state of Israel had reached a turning point. He felt the imminent presence of a saviour; the birth of a child who would grow up to redeem Israel from its ignorance and lawlessness; a saviour who would free the Sanctuary from the web of evil spun by his own sons, Hafni and Phineas.

Hannah, the woman praying in so irregular a manner, could well be the mother of that child. She might need help with her prayer, thought Eli. As High Priest, he could raise her prayer to the throne of God himself. Eli, on behalf of Israel, decided to consult the Urim V'Tumim.

*   *   *

Eli's request to the Urim V'Tumim drew an immediate response. Four letters in the breastplate—**H, K, R, S**—twinkled brightly and Eli had to decide the order in which to arrange them.

Eli looked puzzledly at Hannah. Her method of prayer was so unusual. What did the letters indicate? Were they a sign of approval; or rejection? Had this woman been drinking too heavily from the wine of the festival and was she now showing disrespect to the Sanctuary? Or was she the woman whose son would, once more, guide Israel along the paths of Torah and righteousness? Would this son indeed restore glory and holiness to the Sanctuary? Would God also use him to uproot his own household? How should he interpret the letters?

Hannah, totally immersed in her prayer, ignored the presence of the watching Eli. The full strength of her feelings had been brought to the surface by Peninah's cruel, relentless provocation. In silent outrage, she expressed her despair and resentment at God's decree of childlessness.

Hanna's prayer was not born of selfishness. She desired a child not merely to fulfil her instinct for motherhood. She desired a child who would serve both God and Israel. She concluded her prayer with the following words.

"O. Lord of Hosts. If only You will look upon the affliction of your maidservant. And You will remember me and not forget your maidservant. And You will give to your maidservant an upright son. Then I shall give him unto the Lord all the days of his life; and no razor shall touch his head."

*   *   *

Eli finally finished juggling the letters of the breastplate and made his decision. The order of the letters was **S K R H** and when the correct vowels

21

were inserted it would be pronounced **SiKoRaH**: the Urim V'Tumim had spoken; the woman was a drunkard.

Eli reacted immediately. "How long will you remain drunk?" he accused Hannah. "Remove your wine from you."

"No, my lord," replied Hannah, "Do not be deceived by my aggressive demeanour. I am perfectly sober. I have drunk neither wine nor strong liquor. But I am bitter and I am pouring out my soul to God. I beg you, do not look upon your maidservant as a woman with no virtue; for it is from aggravation and despair that I have spoken until now."

Eli looked at her dumbfounded. These were not the words of a drunken woman. She was sincere and righteous. He must have decoded the message of the Urim V'Tumim incorrectly. Hastily, he rearranged the letters of the breastplate.

*   *   *

This time Eli produced the word **KeSaraH**; the meaning—**LIKE SARAH**. Like Sarah, this woman was praying for a child. Like Sarah, from her would be born the salvation of Israel.

Eli, however, did not wish to embarrass Hannah by revealing his awareness of her desire for a child. His words (in Hebrew) only hinted at the request she had made to God. "Go in peace. The God of Israel will grant the request you ask of Him."

*   *   *

The words of Eli being a Divine decree, winged their way into Hannah's heart.

Miraculously, she was transformed, her face radiating an air of expectancy and fulfilment. She returned to Elkanah and informed him of her encounter with Eli, the High Priest of Israel.

Overjoyed, they returned to Ramatayim Tzofim, knowing that their nightmare was over. Before long, Hannah would give birth to a son.

The rays of Eli's blessing to Hannah extended far beyond the boundaries of the Sanctuary and Shilo. 'Like Sarah,' had been Eli's interpretation of the letters of the Choshen and like Sarah, he had blessed Hannah.

Thus, as the birth of Sarah's child Isaac was accompanied by an outbreak of other long awaited births, so too was the birth of Hannah's child. God visited Hannah and opened up the gates of motherhood throughout the land.

Thus when Hannah gave birth to her child, hundreds of other woman also gave birth and miraculously, each of these mothers believed their sons destined to be the saviour of the Torah in Israel. Each one called their babies Samuel—he is identified with God.

*   *   *

From the moment of Samuel's birth, Hannah and Elkanah made his cradle into a mini Torah school, educating him to fear God and observe the teachings of the Torah.

Samuel's progress was exceptional. At the age of two, he had mastered every detail of the sacrificial service. He was ready to serve his apprenticeship in the Sanctuary.

*   *   *

To fulfil their promise of dedicating their son to God for the rest of his life, Elkanah and Hannah took Samuel to the Sanctuary. But Elkanah, before placing him into the care of Eli, decided to bring an offering. This decision, taken for the best of motives, almost claimed the life of Hannah's son, Samuel.

Elkanah, in order to demonstrate the act of religious slaughter to the young Samuel, wanted to slaughter the offering himself. Some of the priests, however, objected. "Slaughtering is the duty of the priest," they said. "Hand over the offering to us."

Elkanah protested. "I want to teach my son about slaughtering. I want to show him myself. Please allow me to show him how it's done."

The priests were adamant. "No. That's not possible. It's the duty of the priest. We cannot allow a stranger, a non priest, to perform such a holy command."

Elkanah knew the priests were incorrect in their ruling; the priests did not have exclusive rights to perform the slaughtering of an offering. He—even an Israelite, a non priest—was perfectly entitled to slaughter it. However, not wanting to make a scene in the Sanctuary, he put down his knife and prepared to hand over his offering to the priests for slaughtering.

Then Samuel intervened. "Father! These men are speaking against the Torah. Of course you're allowed to slaughter the offering."

Elkanah looked embarrassed. "Samuel! Keep quiet! These men know what they're doing."

"No father. They do not know." Samuel's fear of the Torah was greater than his fear of man. He was not prepared to stand by quietly and accept an incorrect decision. "Torah says anybody can perform the slaughtering of an offering."

The priests looked at the small child in amazement. "How dare you argue with the priests in the Sanctuary?" They picked Samuel up and, with Elkanah and Hannah following closely behind, took him to Eli for judgement.

$$*\quad*\quad*$$

Despite Samuel's tender years, the priests insisted that Eli treat him according to the full rigours of the Law. "This boy must be punished for contradicting his teachers. There is only one punishment for such a sin. We demand you put him to death."

"I am fully aware of the Law," said Eli. "But first I must hear the evidence. Just because he's a child does not mean we can dispense with the formalities of justice. Present your case."

One of the priests stepped forward and informed Eli of the details of Samuel's impudent behaviour.

"Is that a true account of what took place?" Eli asked Elkanah. "Did your son behave in that way? Remember you are in the Sanctuary. You are in the presence of the God of Judgement. Are the priests telling the truth?"

Elkanah, not knowing what to say, nodded dumbly in agreement.

"This is a serious matter." Eli shook his head in dismay as he looked at the small child clutching Elkanah's hand. "Samuel! You might know the Laws of sacrifices but you certainly do not know the Laws of good manners. Respect for one's teachers is the same as respect for God. Disrespect for one's teachers is the same as disrespect for God.

"Even the sons of Aaron were punished for such a sin. Nadav and Avihu were put to death in the Sanctuary because they had no respect for their teachers Moses and Aaaron. Samuel! You have committed a serious sin. I am compelled to pass the full judgement on you. I decree . . ."

"No! No! Do not kill the child." Hannah, who had been listening in horrified silence to the words of Eli, could contain herself no longer. She broke through the ring of priests surrounding Eli and Samuel, and flung herself at Eli's feet. "Spare him! Please spare my son. He is only a child."

"Spare him?" Eli thundered. "Why should I spare someone who has no respect for his elders? Respect for others takes precedence over Torah."

"But he can be taught the laws of respect for others," Hannah pleaded. "That is why I brought him to the Sanctuary today."

The power of the sincerity and protestation that had overcome the Divine decree that she should be childless now penetrated the heart of mind of Eli the High Priest.

"Wait!" Eli said to the priest who wished to remove Hannah from before his judgement chair. "Let the woman be." Eli looked at Hannah. "Tell me! Who are you? Where have I seen you before?"

"I am the woman who prayed in the Sanctuary for a child and this boy was given to me. In every way, my prayer has been fulfilled. Samuel has been blessed with outstanding talents. He is intelligent and he learns well. He will learn the laws of respect for others. "I beg you. Your prayer gave him life. Do not take away that life. Forgive him. Permit him to stay in Shilo. Teach him the duties of a Levi in the house of God."

'Like Sarah,' Eli said to himself. 'That is what the Urim V'Tumim said about this woman. Now God has handed over to me the task of making sure that her son grows up as an Isaac.'

"Come here!" Eli said to Samuel. "Your mother prayed to God and He answered her prayer. Now she is praying to me. Can I be less gracious than God? I shall answer her request. I will teach you the laws of the Sanctuary and I will teach you the laws of respect for others. You will live with me here in the Sanctuary and I will bring you up to be a faithful servant to God."

*　　*　　*

The decision was wise and prophetic. Through Samuel, the glorious heritage of Torah was restored to Israel, the monarchies of Saul and David were established and the Temple was built in the reign of King Solomon.

DOEG THE EDOMITE

According to the Talmud, Doeg the Edomite was responsible for estranging Saul from David and bringing about the destruction of Nov.
Various reasons are suggested by the Midrash for his title 'the Edomite.' The following story is based upon one of them.

The lamb was unaware of the shadow of death stalking the hillside. Grazing contentedly only yards from the pine forest at the top of the hill, it failed to notice a wolf's paw emerge from the nearby undergrowth. When the rest of the flock moved downhill towards fresh pastures, the lamb remained alone.

As the distance between the lamb and the flock increased, the wolf in the forest crouched low to the ground, steadying itself for attack. Suddenly the wolf straightened up. It hurled itself forward. With lightning speed, it buried its jaws into the neck of the lamb.

The sound of pounding paws and the momentary bleat of a lamb alerted the shepherds at the far side of the flock. "Hey! What's going on there?" The chief shepherd, Menachem shouted out to the other two shepherds with him. "Who's in charge of that section? Where's Naphtali? Quick! See what happening to the lamb. Then go and find Naphtali."

The sight and sound of the approaching men frightened the wolf. It dropped the lamb from its jaws and retreated to the safety of the forest.

"Too late!" One of the shepherds arrived at the top of the hill. He looked down in dismay at the dead lamb at his feet. "Doeg will be furious. Where's Naphtali? Naphtali! Where are you?"

"Here I am. What's going on?" A yawning figure rose from the long grass by the edge of the forest. "What's all the fuss about?"

"That's what all the fuss is about." The shepherd pointed to the carcass of the lamb. "If you hadn't been sleeping, this wouldn't have happened. Come along we'll have to report the matter to Doeg. You'd better have a good excuse. But knowing Doeg, I don't think it will make any difference."

*   *   *

In the crude shepherd's hut at the foot of the hill, Doeg looked up from the Torah scrolls he had been studying. He stared impassively at Naphtali.

Doeg's red hair and complexion betrayed his foreign origins. After Saul's conquest of his birthplace, Edom, he had converted to Judaism and dedicated himself to the study of the Torah. Remarkably, before long, his mastery of Jewish Law was recognised throughout Israel. Despite his non-Jewish background, he succeeded in attracting numerous pupils to his classes in Torah.

A man of outstanding talents, Doeg had been appointed by Saul as adviser on domestic and foreign affairs as well as chief herdsman over his vast herds of sheep. He was fiercely loyal to his master Saul and prepared to go to any lengths to protect his person and property. Under no circumstances would he tolerate any lapse in the high level of duty expected from the king's servants.

"I have heard the charge against you," said Doeg. "One of the king's sheep has been killed and you were on duty at the time. Is the accusation correct?"

Naphtali nodded dumbly. He knew the futility of reasoning with Doeg.

"Sleeping while shepherding is a serious matter! With the king's flock it is even more serious. Even without the loss of a sheep, you would be punished. You will pay twofold for your negligence. You will compensate King Saul for the loss of his sheep. You will also be punished. He turned to Menachem. "Give him forty lashes."

Menachem, shocked at the harshness of the verdict, was unable to restrain himself. "Have mercy on him. His wife gave birth to his third child only ten days ago. The circumcision was a difficult one. The child cries all night. He is unable to sleep."

Doeg looked coldly at Menachem. "Are you questioning my orders? Do you disagree with my verdict? Do you feel I do not know all the facts of the case?" Menachem did not answer.

"Good, but don't think I am not aware of your feelings for your companion. I will be present when you carry out the punishment."

*   *   *

In the small grass clearing just outside his tent, Doeg scrupulously supervised the whipping of Naphtali. While two men firmly held Naphtali's wrists around the stump of a tree trunk, Doeg counted out the strokes. Whenever he felt that Menachem's whip came down too lightly, he insisted on an extra lash.

After ten lashes, Menachem was unable to contain himself any longer. "Surely he's been punished enough. He'll never repeat his mistake."

"Continue!" Doeg commanded.

As Menachem raised his whip to bring it down on Naphtali's back, the sound of galloping hooves attracted the attention of Doeg and the shepherds. A rider on a foam-flecked horse was thundering towards them.

Within minutes, he arrived at the clearing and without ceremony, alighted from his horse. "I have an urgent message from King Saul," he informed Doeg. "He needs your presence immediately. The Philistines have gathered at Aleh. They have a giant soldier who is taunting our soldiers. Our morale is sinking fast. We fear a Philistine attack is imminent. King Saul has given instructions. Leave everything. Go to Aleh."

Doeg beckoned to one of the men holding Naphtali's wrist. "Seth! Fetch my horse. I leave immediately." He turned to Saul's messenger. "Tell me about this giant Philistine. You say he is tall. Have you seen him? How much taller than King Saul is he? Which city does he come from? What is his name?

"No, I have not seen him. They say he is at least three heads taller than King Saul. He comes from the city of Gath. His name is Goliath."

"One man can hold an entire nation to ransom," reflected Doeg. "Where is the fighting spirit of the army of the Lord?"

No one answered and the silence was broken by the return of Seth with his master's horse.

"Menachem!" Doeg commanded. "Finish the punishment. Remember the sentence was forty lashes."

As Doeg mounted his horse and rode swiftly away with Saul's messenger, Menachem brought the whip crashing down on the floor. "That man might be descended from Abraham and Isaac. But he has also the blood of Esau flowing through his veins. We are the descendants of Jacob. Release him," he commanded the men. "Rub oil in his back. Give him water. Let him rest in the shade."

"Naphtali! Forgive me." Menachem said, helping him to the side of the clearing, "and promise me one thing. Never again will you sleep when guarding the sheep."

*   *   *

Inside the royal tent in the valley of Aleh, King Saul, fully aware he had a personal duty to respond to the challenge of the giant Philistine, strode restlessly up and down as he talked to Abner, his Commander in Chief and Doeg.

"Why has no one accepted my reward for defeating the Philistine?" he demanded of Doeg. "Has everybody been informed of the honour and wealth that will come to the man who defeats Goliath? How can it be that no man in Israel is tempted to become the saviour of Israel and marry my daughter?

"Patience, your majesty, replied Doeg. "Someone is bound to accept your offer."

"If no one comes forward today," said Saul. "I will fight him myself."

"No, your majesty," said Abner. "If no one comes forward. I will fight him. We cannot risk the life of the king of Israel."

"Noble words, Abner. But I won't risk the life of my best general. I will fight him."

"Neither of you will have to fight him," said Doeg. "Your reward will find the man. I can assure you there will be a response. Listen! Someone is approaching the tent."

"Permission to enter," the voice of the sentry rang out in the tent.

Abner looked at Saul who nodded briefly.

"Enter!" commanded Abner and two soldiers escorted a young shepherd into the tent.

One aspect of the newcomer's appearance, his ruddy complexion, matched Doeg's. But there the similarities ended. The young man, glowing with the fresh air of the countryside, was a picture of vigour and vitality, his eyes sparkling with a fire of good will and optimism. On the other hand, Doeg had the look of the scholar with the dust of books and benches in his nostrils, his narrowed eyes reflecting the single mindedness and cruelty of his character.

The three men bowed low to Saul and waited for permission to speak.

"What is your mission?" Abner demanded.

One of the soldiers spoke. "This lad requested to be taken to the king. He claims he has an urgent message for him."

"Very well," said Abner. "Leave the lad here and return to your posts."

The three men instantly recognised the young man as Saul's personal minstrel and armour bearer. For a moment, they stared at him with a mixture of hope and curiosity. Then Saul broke the silence. "David! What are you doing here? Your father requested you stay at home a few days to help with the sheep."

"Yes, your majesty. But later my father requested me to return with supplies for my brothers who are serving in the army."

"Why are you being escorted by the soldiers? Carry out your father's request and return home. A battle with the Philistines is imminent. Now I require warriors not minstrels. What service can you offer me now?"

David shrugged his shoulders disarmingly. "I hear the king is offering great wealth and his daughter as a bride to anyone who defeats the giant Philistine. I seek that reward."

"Anyone who defeats Goliath is deserving of such a reward. He will be the saviour of Israel." Saul hesitated as though digesting the significance of his words. "Tell me David. Why would you risk your life to fight this giant Philistine? Are you so discontented with your portion that you want to throw everything away?"

"No, your majesty. I wish to better myself. I am the youngest and most insignificant of eight siblings. My portion in my father's estate will be minimal. I am tempted by the reward you are offering for defeating this Philistine." David was a consummate actor. When Saul had appointed him as musician to relieve his moods of depression, he had concealed his true strength and character; his passion for truth and justice and his unswerving sense of trust and belief in God, the God of Israel. Instead, he had skilfully projected an image of naiveté and unconcern.

One of the three men was not deceived by David's performance. Doeg believed there were hidden depths to David's character. He perceived, swirling behind the display of innocence and good humour, a powerful current of ambition. David did not appear to be the type of person to throw away his life. He had too much to live for. He could well defeat Goliath. In addition, Doeg felt that David's personality, good looks and physique could well make him into a contender for the throne of Israel.

Doeg was only too acutely aware of Saul's mental instability and the voices of discontent sweeping through Israel. David's victory over Goliath would undoubtedly be a defeat for the Philistines. It might also be a mortal blow to Saul and himself.

"Your majesty," said Doeg, "your offer of a reward was only made today. It might be better to wait until another challenger, a seasoned warrior, accepts your offer. This lad is a shepherd. He is inexperienced in warfare. The dangers on the battlefield are different from the one in the meadows. Consider the consequences if he fails in his fight with Goliath. Not only might it deter a more capable soldier from coming forward, but the smell of Jewish blood in the Philistine nostrils might lead them to a full scale attack. We cannot allow the fortunes of the nation to rest on such slim and untried shoulders. I say we wait for someone else to come forward."

"So far no one has come forward," said Abner. "The longer we wait, the more the advantage is given to the Philistines, Your majesty! May I ask him a few questions."

Saul nodded.

"First, let me extend you a welcome," said Abner, holding out his hand to David.

As David grasped his hand, Abner slowly tightened his grip and was surprised at the response he met. This was not the hand of a feeble minstrel. The hands and fingers that were so adept at strumming a harp possessed a strength that easily matched his own.

"You realise the importance of this contest with Goliath," said Abner, on releasing his hand from David's iron grip. "Ideally, either the king or one of his generals should accept the challenge. On the other hand, were they to lose, the consequences would be catastrophic. The Philistines would shoot over the fields of Aleh like an arrow from a bow. Our soldiers would be slaughtered.

"With you it's different. You're unknown. Were you to lose, the Philistines would react with indifference. However, if you win, and please God you do, the effect upon our soldiers would be exhilarating. They'll shred the Philistines to pieces.

"But the odds against you winning are high. I wouldn't like to sacrifice a Jewish life, needlessly.

"Now tell me, what are your chances of defeating this giant? What experience do you have as a warrior?"

"I've fought against wild animals," said David. "I've killed a bear and a lion when they attacked my father's flock of sheep."

Abner carefully considered David's response. Was he exaggerating, or telling the truth? Would his bubble of bravado burst on the battlefield at the first swing of Goliath's sword? Or was he indeed a fearless fighter, worthy of representing Israel? "Do you realise what you are up against with Goliath? Do you know how tall and powerful he is? From this distance he looks small and vulnerable. When you get close up it will be a different story. Doeg is right in one respect. The battlefield is different from the meadow. Tell me! When you see a ten-foot giant towering over you, will you keep your nerve? Goliath is a seasoned warrior. He is strong and well protected. His reach is immense. You need confidence and ability to defeat him in single combat. What makes you think you can kill him?"

In response to Abner's searching questions, David knew he could no longer conceal his true character. He felt compelled to reveal something of his personal strength and absolute faith in the power of God. "When a bear carried off a sheep from the flock, I seized it by its beard and fought it face to face. Your servant has killed both a lion and a bear. This Philistine is an animal and he will be treated as an animal. He has reviled the armies of the living God."

The impassioned words of an inspired David rang out in the royal tent. "God who saved me from the lion and the bear, He will save me from the hand of the Philistine."

The power and confidence of David's words electrified the three men. At the last minute, Israel had found its champion, a man of God and a man of war. Saul now fully supported David's right to challenge Goliath. "You may go! And may God be with you. But first, we must equip you for battle." He stripped off his armour and attempted to put it on David.

David refused. "I need speed and mobility to beat Goliath. I will go as I am."

"The lad is right," said Abner to Saul. "He could never hope to beat Goliath face to face. He must outmanoeuvre him. Armour would weigh him down. Let him go as he is." Abner turned to David, "may God be with you."

* * *

As Saul, Abner and Doeg accompanied David to the edge of the valley, a sense of expectancy swept the camp. After forty days of taunting by Goliath, the movements of the four men could have only one possible meaning.

Earlier that day David, after returning from his father with provisions for his brothers, had loudly enquired from Saul's soldiers about the reward for defeating Goliath. He had made the whole camp aware of his interest in the proposed marriage of Saul's daughter to the conqueror of Goliath. Now this same lad, David, was being escorted by the leaders of Israel towards a confrontation with the giant Philistine.

* * *

There was a growing feeling that soon the stalemate was to be broken. Soldiers hastened to the edge of the valley to secure a prime position for viewing an epic contest.

Without trace of nerves or excitement David, armed with only a shepherd's staff, sling and pouch, strode to the brook in the middle of the valley. There he bent down and carefully selected five smooth stones from the running waters. He put them in his pouch and advanced to meet Goliath.

David's smooth, fluid movements mesmerised Saul, Abner and Doeg. The minstrel had been unmasked and the true David emerged; a warrior, a leader and—to the rising concern of both Saul and Doeg—a future king of Israel.

Outwardly Doeg appeared calm, but, in reality, his mind was in turmoil. Were David to be a contender for the throne of Israel, he could not have chosen a better theatre to establish his claim. The setting was perfect; the valley of Elah, his stage; the armed forces of Israel, his audience; and the drama to be played out; a conflict of life and death.

Doeg stared pensively across the valley. He saw the shimmer of heat rising from the spears of the massed Philistines forces; and Goliath, with sparks of sunlight glinting from his helmet, hurling fresh insults at the Israelite soldiers. He heard the rustle of leaves on the pistachio trees at the edge of the valley, and felt a cool westerly breeze ruffling the hems of his garments. For a brief moment, he allowed his imagination to hold sway over his emotions.

"If only I had the power of a Moses," he mused, "I could raise my staff in the air and the earth would swallow up this Philistine. Or if I had the powers of a Samuel, I could hurl bolts of lightning at him and reduce him to ashes. A miracle is needed and whoever brings that miracle will be honoured by all Israel. God always helps the underdog. He helped Joseph in Egypt. He helped Saul after his tribe was almost wiped out.

Doeg snapped himself out his daydreams. "Will He help Israel through David?" he said to himself, "and if He does, will this David topple Saul from his throne? Will he contest the monarchy? His ambitions have to be checked."

Doeg and David were no strangers to each other. In fact Doeg had introduced David to Saul as a minstrel. Doeg, aware of David's descent from Ruth and Boaz, an elder of the tribe of Judah, now believed that his illustrious ancestors could well serve as a stepping stone to the throne.

Doeg, however, was determined to undermine his progress. As David strode across the valley of Elah towards Goliath, he fired the first arrow from his quiver of Torah knowledge.

"Your majesty should prepare himself for a new son-in-law," Doeg said casually to Saul.

"A son-in-law? A husband for my daughter Michal?" Saul suddenly recalled his impulsive promise. "But who is this lad? Is he fit to marry my daughter?"

"Your majesty," said Doeg, "you ask if this lad is fit to marry a princess. Better ask, is he fit to marry a Jewess."

"What do you mean?"

"He is descended from Ruth the Moabite. Her conversion to Judaism is indisputable. Her marriage to Boaz is not. Torah clearly states that neither an Ammonite nor a Moabite shall enter the congregation of God. Ruth is a Moabite. Her marriage to Boaz is invalid. David is illegitimate."

"Doeg!" protested Abner, "you do Boaz and Ruth an injustice. Your interpretation of the verse is unsound. Only the males are forbidden. The females are permitted to intermarry."

"Abner," said Doeg smoothly, "when interpreting the words of the Torah, do not allow your imagination—and loyalties—to run away with you. Torah clearly mentions the Moabite race. Both males and females are included. No argument can deny that conclusion."

"You have not taken into account the conclusion we can derive from other Torah verses," replied Abner. "Your decision is rather hasty, and in my opinion, incorrect."

"You question my authority?" retorted Doeg.

"I do not question your authority. I question the substance of your reasoning."

"Do not play with words, Abner. I . . ."

At that moment Saul intervened. "A battlefield is not the place to determine Jewish law, Doeg. It is also not the place for creating division among ourselves. This issue will be settled in the house of study. I have a feeling there will soon be other matters to occupy our minds."

*   *   *

In the middle of the valley, Goliath impatiently awaited his first challenger. To his relief, he saw, in the distance, a figure heading towards him from the lines of the Israelite forces.

"So Saul has at last found his courage," Goliath smiled down to his armour bearer. "By Dagon, when I hold up his head at the end of my spear, the whole of Israel will see who is the true god. I only hope our boys catch them before they run into their rabbit holes."

With the sun directly opposite him, Goliath had difficulty in focusing his eyes on the approaching figure. Then, to his amazement, at a distance of about one hundred metres, he saw a fresh-faced youngster; without armour and with only one weapon in his hand—a shepherd's stick.

At the sight of David, Goliath lost his composure. He felt he was being treated as a clown by the Israelites. He went white with rage. "Am I a dog that you come out to battle me with sticks? The gods of the Philistines will destroy you and feed your carcass to the birds of the field. Come to me."

David, detecting a hint of uncertainty in the words of Goliath, seized the initiative. His fearless response rang out over the valley. "You come against me with a sword and a spear. I come against you in the name of the Lord of Hosts, the Lord of the armies of Israel that you have reviled.

"This day, God will deliver you in my hand. I will remove your head from you. And I will leave your carcass in the field for the birds of the heavens and the beasts of the land. Then all the land will know that there is a God in Israel. And this entire people will know that it is not through the sword and spear that God delivers. The battle is unto God. And He will deliver you into our hand."

Goliath had expected the challenger to come forward and meet him on his terms. Now his advantage was lost. It had shifted in favour of the Israelite. Knowing the Philistines had also heard David's words, he felt compelled to advance and fight.

Goliath, was heavily weighed down with armour and arms; one hundred kilograms of chain mail on his chest, an iron helmet on his head, shin guards on his legs, a brass metal plate on his shoulders; and in one hand a spear as long as a weaver's beam. In front of him, with extra protection and weapons, was his armour bearer with a three sided shield. Despite Goliath's ten foot stature, very little of his person was exposed to an attack. Only his eyes and forehead were vulnerable, well beyond the reach of an opponent's sword.

Sweating profusely and breathing heavily from nervous tension, Goliath lumbered forward to meet David.

David unflinchingly met Goliath's charge. Standing his ground, he quickly took a pebble from his pouch, placed it his sling and whirled it faster and faster around his head.

When barely twenty-five metres separated the two men, David released one end of his sling. Too fast for the eye to follow, the loosed pebble flew through the air and, with the power of a javelin, struck Goliath on his forehead.

Like a slaughtered ox, Goliath sank lifelessly to the ground. His armour bearer fled.

With quick nimble strides, David ran to the prostrate body of Goliath. He drew the giant's sword from its scabbard and holding it in both hands, raised it high in the air. Then, with every Israelite and Philistine eye glued to his outstretched arm, David sent Goliath's sword scything down to the ground.

A deathly hush fell on the valley, as the two opposing armies awaited the sign that signalled the end of the dramatic encounter.

Finally it came.

David put down the sword and, with both hands, picked up the severed head of Goliath. Holding it high in the air, he turned the face, first towards the Israelites, then towards the Philistines.

"For the Lord and for Israel!" Saul's command to charge was drowned in the cheering, shouting and whooping of the Israelite soldiers. Like lions they charged across the Elah Valley towards the enemy that had taunted them. Like startled deer, the Philistines fled before them.

*   *   *

David's triumph over Goliath catapulted him to wealth, honour and fame. He became the idol of the nation. Throughout the country, wherever he went, the maidens of Israel showered him with coins and sang his praises, 'Saul has slain in his thousands, David in his tens of thousands.'

Although David won the hearts of Israel, he failed to win the trust and friendship of Saul. Indeed, Saul, alarmed at the prospect of living in the shadow of so popular a son-in-law, was persuaded by Doeg to postpone David's marriage to his daughter. However, after the court of Samuel the prophet confirmed that a Moabitess could convert and marry an Israelite, David did eventually marry his daughter Michal.

Sadly, David's stay in the palace of Saul was brief and stormy. Regarded as a threat to the monarchy, his fame and popularity proved to be a handicap with the king and his courtiers. Forever plagued by the brooding melancholia of Saul and the poisonous intrigues of Doeg, his relationship with Saul slowly deteriorated. Within weeks, the slayer of Goliath was looked upon as a traitor to Israel.

Fortunately, during this time, David succeeded in making one close friend, Saul's son, Jonathan. Through Jonathan, David discovered that Saul's patience with him had finally snapped and his life was now at risk. Without arms or provisions and accompanied by only four trusted servants, David fled from the wrath and sword of his father-in-law, Saul.

For two days the five men hid in the inhospitable woods and forests of Israel, desperately seeking refuge from the relentless hot pursuit of Saul and his men. On the third day, a Shabbat, David, weak from hunger and exposure, was compelled to seek sustenance for himself and his companions.

Knowing that Saul would not pursue him on Shabbat, David made his way to the one city that he felt would be free from the clanging of swords and the tramping of soldier's boots; the city of peace, where the Sanctuary was established; the city of priests, Nov.

*   *   *

Fourteen years after the Children of Israel came to Canaan, Joshua established in Shilo the Sanctuary with the Ark of the Covenant. Later, in the time of Eli the High Priest, the Ark of the Covenant was captured by the Philistines and Shilo destroyed. After these tragedies the Sanctuary and its remaining vessels were transferred to Nov, a small town just north of Jerusalem in central Israel.

In the Sanctuary, there are a number of differences between the weekday and the Shabbat service. One is the additional Shabbat offering; another is the exchanging of the week-old Shew Bread for fresh ones.

The Shew Bread, was 'loaves' of unleavened bread, four inches thick, each one weighing about four kilograms. They were displayed in two columns, six loaves high, on the golden table in the Tent of Meeting, the enclosed part of the Sanctuary.

Every Shabbat, four priests removed the old twelve loaves of Shew Bread together with their bowls of frankincense and, at the same time, four other priests replaced them with fresh loaves and spices.

The old Shew Bread were placed on a table outside the Tent of Meeting and, after the incense was offered on the gold altar in the Tent of Meeting, they were permitted to be eaten by the priests.

Six of the Shew Bread were allocated to the ordinary priests; the other six went to the High Priest.

*   *   *

David, after leaving his companions in a small wood just outside Nov, pulled his tattered cloak over his face, cautiously entered the city and went to the clearing directly in front of the Sanctuary. There he waited for an opportunity to send a message to the High Priest of Nov, Achimelech the son of Achitachav.

A constant flow of people on their way to the Sanctuary passed by the motionless, unrecognisable figure of David, but only when a priest passed by, did David make his move.

"I need your help," David called out to the priest.

The priest stopped, turned round and looked sharply at David's ragged figure. "What do you want? I'm due back immediately in the Sanctuary."

"I have an urgent message for the High Priest, for Achimelech the son of Achitachav."

"The High Priest? The High Priest is fully occupied on a Shabbat," said the priest preparing to walk away. "I am unable to help you."

"Wait!" David commanded in a tone that demanded attention. "Tell the High Priest that you have an urgent message from the son of Jesse. He must see him without delay."

"Who are you? Why should I give a message to the High Priest? Why are you dressed like this on the Shabbat?"

"You're right to ask questions," said David raising his cloak from his face and staring into the eyes of the priest. "But at the moment, there are no answers. Say, you have an urgent message from the son of Jesse."

For a moment, the priest stared defiantly at David, then a look of recognition and compliance came into his eyes. "I'll fetch him immediately."

*   *   *

Late on that Shabbat afternoon, the High Priest of Israel, Achimelech the son of Achitachav stood in prayer by the Tent of Meeting preparing himself spiritually for the evening offering, the final sacrifice of the day. Next to him and all around the curtains in the courtyard of the Sanctuary, other priests, Levites and visitors to the Sanctuary stood in fervent prayer to their Creator.

A priest entered the Sanctuary, looked around until he spotted the figure of Achimelech, the High Priest, then walked quickly over to him.

"I have a message for you," he whispered. "From the son of Jesse."

Achimelech spun around to face the priest. "The son of Jesse? Today? Where is he? What does he want?"

"He is waiting outside the Sanctuary."

"David? Here on a Shabbat? There must be something wrong." Achimelech hastened from his prayers in the Sanctuary to meet David.

One of the visitors, swaying and praying by the curtain of the Sanctuary, overheard some of the conversation between Achimelech and the other priest. With his curiosity further aroused by the sudden departure of the High Priest from his service in the Sanctuary, he went over to the priest who had brought the message from David. In his excitement to discover more information he was less guarded than usual in his manner of speech and a hint of an Edomite accent was apparent in his words. The person enquiring about Achimelech's unusual behaviour was Doeg.

*   *   *

"David! What are you doing here?" Achimelech was astonished both by David's sudden arrival and his dishevelled appearance, the look of strain and fatigue in his face and the marks of thorns and thistles on his arms and legs. "How did you get here? How could you have arrived on the Shabbat? Where are your Shabbat garments?"

"I'm here on a matter of national security. Saul has entrusted me with a mission that demands the utmost secrecy." David sought to avoid implicating Achimelech in an act of rebellion against Saul. He felt his dire circumstances justified this explanation of his extraordinary behaviour. "It's a matter of the greatest urgency. It even overrides the Sabbath."

"I must soon return to the Sanctuary for the evening sacrifice. Why do you wish to see me?"

"I need advice. I must know how to continue with this mission. I must consult the Urim V'Tumim."

*   *   *

The Urim V'Tumim was a slip of parchment bearing the Divine name of God that the High Priest inserted within the folds of his garments just behind the sacred breastplate. Inset in this breastplate were twelve precious stones on which were engraved the names of Abraham, Isaac, Jacob and the twelve tribes of Israel. Whenever God's advice was sought on behalf of Israel, the Urim V'Tumim, miraculously but cryptically, illuminated key letters in these names.

The meaning of the coded message could only be given by the High Priest. Furthermore, only the king or his representatives could consult the Urim V'Tumim on matters of national interest.

*   *   *

Achimelech had no hesitation in complying with David's request. David, in his official capacity of a leading general in Saul's army, had often made use of its miraculous powers. "Ask what you will. But make haste. I must return to the Sanctuary."

David put a series of questions to the Urim V'Tumim and as the letters on the breastplate lit up, Achimelech interpreted their meaning.

The response of the Urim V'Tumim satisfied David. He appeared more at ease. His cheeks regained their colour and some of his old sparkle returned. "At least I know that for the next few days, God will be guiding my footsteps. Whatever happens, if I live or die. I know it is the will of God. Now, Achimelech I have a further request to make. I require food and weapons for myself and my men."

"You left Saul without arms or provisions?"

"As I said, the matter is urgent. It is a life and death issue. Saul insisted I leave immediately. I left his home in Gibeah without warning or preparation. Now we must have food to continue our journey."

"David, I cannot help you. There is only holy food and Shew Bread in Nov. They are both sanctified foods. Only priests may eat them."

David's face sagged at this news. He had not eaten for three days. He was almost at the end of his reserves of strength. "We have no choice. Give us some of the sanctified food."

Achimelech was reluctant to accede to David's request, but felt he had no choice. Admittedly, David's circumstances would permit a violation of the code prohibiting holy food to a non-priest, yet he still wished to minimise the degree of the transgression. "Tell me David. Are you and your men ritually pure?"

"Achimelech! We are all pure. For the last three days, my men and I have had no contact with any unclean object or person. Give us some of the Shew Bread."

"You leave me no alternative, David. You can have my portion of the Shew Bread. Wait here."

"And a weapon," David begged. "I need a weapon to defend myself."

"There is only one weapon in the Sanctuary. Will you accept the sword of Goliath? It hangs in its sheath in the Tent of Meeting as a sign of thanksgiving to God. By rights, it belongs to you."

David nodded and Achimelech returned to the Sanctuary to carry out his requests.

* * *

Doeg did not immediately inform Saul about the events in Nov. Even by his standards, the passing on of such unsolicited information would have been an act of gross slander.

The strain of silence however, weighed heavily upon him and a few weeks later he had the opportunity to unburden himself.

Saul, during a brief respite from his pursuit of David, delivered a lengthy tirade against his officers and courtiers. He accused them of failing to co-operate with him in his efforts to locate David, of conspiring against him and withholding information from him. He commanded them to inform him of David's recent movements and his whereabouts.

No one responded except Doeg. He told Saul he had been present in Nov when Achimelech and the priests had given David food and weapons in his flight from Saul.

Doeg, the man who had urged Saul to display clemency to Agag, king of Amalek, showed no compassion when implicating the priests of Nov in a conspiracy against Saul. He mentioned neither David's famished condition nor the plausible story David had told Achimelech. Doeg clearly implanted in the receptive mind of Saul an image of mutiny and rebellion against the monarchy.

In the light of Doeg's damning information, Saul had no choice. He summoned Achimelech and the senior priests to his palace in Gibeah.

*   *   *

Achimelech and eighty-five priests were escorted by a group of soldiers from Saul's personal bodyguard into the temporary court room set up in the banqueting hall of Saul's palace. Then, they were lined up in three rows in front of Saul who sat on his throne at one end of the room.

Saul opened the proceedings. "Achimelech the son of Achitachav! I have heard from a reliable source that you and your priests assisted the son of Jesse recently. Is the report true?"

"Yes, your majesty."

"You don't deny the charge." Saul was immediately angered at the casual manner in which the question had been answered. "Be careful with your answers. Your life and the lives of your priests depend upon them."

"There is nothing to deny, your majesty. There is also nothing to hide. I gave David assistance because I was not aware he had become an enemy of your majesty."

Saul was incredulous. "You were not aware the son of Jesse was a fugitive from justice? You were not aware that I was pursuing him as a traitor to the State."

"No, your majesty. I was not aware."

"I issued a proclamation to the whole of Israel that the son of Jesse was a traitor. And you claim you were not aware."

"Yes, your majesty."

"Tell me, son of Achitachav. How many visitors come to the Sanctuary every day?"

"About four thousand."

"And on Shabbat?"

"About eight thousand."

"And no one informed you that the son of Jesse was a fugitive?"

"The Sanctuary is a place of Prayer and Service. We do not converse about other matters."

"Pious words, son of Achitachav. We shall soon see if your deeds match your preachings. We shall soon see if you have nothing to hide. Now tell me what happened on the day that the son of Jesse came to Nov."

"He sent a message to the Sanctuary that I should see him."

"Who took the message?"

"One of the priests."

"A priest. Why did he assist the son of Jesse?"

"As I said before. We were not aware of your decree about David."

"Thousands of people go to the Sanctuary and no one had heard my decree. Not one priest was aware of the son of Jesse's treachery?"

"Yes, your majesty." Achimelech said feebly. "No priest was aware of David's treachery."

"How did you respond to this message?"

"I went to see him."

"Remind me son of Achitachav. On what day of the week did this incident occur?"

"A Shabbat."

"A Shabbat. The busiest day of the week."

"Yes, your majesty.

"So on the busiest day of the week, you, the High Priest, responded to a request from the son of Jesse, an ordinary Israelite, to leave your duties in the Sanctuary in order to see him."

"Yes, your majesty. I had a message saying the matter was urgent and there appeared to be something wrong. I assumed there was a good reason that David could not enter the Sanctuary."

"Did you enquire about the reason?"

"No."

"You just left all your duties and rushed outside? Would you have acted in the same way to any other person?"

"I know David. He is a leading general in your army, your majesty. The matter was obviously serious."

"What happened next?"

"I went out of the Sanctuary and saw immediately there was something wrong. David was dressed in old, torn clothing. He also appeared to be suffering from hunger. I asked David how he had travelled on the Shabbat to be at the Sanctuary."

"What did the son of Jesse say?" Saul would only refer to David by his father's name.

"He said he was on a secret mission on behalf of your majesty. It was both urgent and private. Even his servants who travelled with him were unaware of the mission and his final destination."

"So why did he come to you?"

"He needed advice from the Urim V'Tumim."

"You gave him the advice he sought?"

"Yes, your majesty."

"Did you give him any other form of assistance?"

"David was without food or weapons. He had been travelling for three days without sustenance. I supplied him with some loaves of Shew Bread and the sword of Goliath."

Saul had prepared himself well for the trial of Achimelech and the priests. So far, he had rigorously controlled his emotions. Now he went on the offensive. "Tell me, son of Achitachav, why did you give the son of Jesse, Shew Bread?"

"There was no other food."

"No other food? In an entire city there was no other food apart from the Shew Bread."

"We are priests, we only eat holy food. Only holy food is available in Nov. Holy food would be forbidden to a non-priest, like David."

"Is not Shew Bread also sanctified food?"

"Its degree of holiness is somewhat less than Holy Food."

"Tell me, son of Achitachav. What is the significance of the Shew Bread?"

"Your majesty, Shew Bread represents the gratitude of Israel to God for the sustenance he gives to Israel."

"Why are the priests privileged to eat such holy food?"

"Because they, as the descendants of Aaron, have been chosen to represent God, the living God of Israel."

"So only priests are privileged to eat this sanctified food?"

"Yes, your majesty."

"Yet you chose to give it to a non-priest. Do you regard the son of Jesse so highly? Do you regard him as equal to a priest?"

"He was famished, your majesty. He hardly had the strength to stand."

"But he still had the strength to carry the Shew Bread and the sword of Goliath that you gave him."

Achimelech looked at the king in stony silence.

"Tell me! Son of Achitachav, Why did you give him the sword of Goliath?"

"As I said before. He required a weapon to complete his mission."

"But why the sword of Goliath? Why not another weapon?"

"We are a tabernacle of peace, not war. We do not possess weapons."

"In that case, son of Achitachav, what was the sword of Goliath doing in the Sanctuary?"

"The sword of Goliath represents the miracle that God wrought for His people Israel, through his servant David."

"To whom does that sword belong, son of Achitachav?"

"To the people of Israel."

"Yet you gave it to the son of Jesse?"

"In my opinion, your majesty, David's circumstances justified my giving him the sword of Goliath."

"In your opinion. You hold very dangerous opinions, son of Achitachav. Especially your opinion regarding the son of Jesse. I note you hold him in high regard. You gave him Shew Bread. You gave him the sword of Goliath. You also gave him the services of the Urim V'Tumim. Surely you know the Urim V'Tumim is to be used only on behalf of the king for matters of national interest. How did you have the effrontery to use the Urim V'Tumim to seek advice for a commoner?"

"David told me he was acting on your behalf, your majesty. He was engaged on a special mission."

"On a special mission? And you believed him?"

"I had no reason to doubt his word. Besides it was a Shabbat. No man tells lies on the Shabbat."

"Today is not Shabbat. So one does tell lies." Saul's eyes narrowed as he spat out the words. "Are you a fool, son of Achitachav? You believed his story that I sent him on a secret mission? What do you take me for? A monster? Or a simpleton? Would I send out someone on a secret mission, without food or weapons, just two days before Shabbat? Would I send out the son of Jesse on a secret mission? Next to me, he is the most recognisable man in Israel? Every man, woman and child in Israel recognise the man who slew Goliath. Every Philistine recognises the man who slew Goliath. Could I send out the son of Jesse on such a mission? Son of Achitachav! You're either a fool? Or you are a rebel?"

In the crowded courtroom, Saul's courtiers, officers and soldiers listened in silence to the drama being played out before them. Each one was aware there could be only one outcome to so biased a trial.

Saul's two generals, Abner and Amasa looked gravely at each other. Their years of comradeship in Torah study and the fields of battle had created a bond of mutual understanding between them. They prepared themselves for the inevitable verdict.

"Son of Achitachav!" said Saul. "You have been grossly negligent with two laws. The laws of the priesthood and the laws of the monarchy. You have grossly abused your office as High Priest.

"You gave Shew Bread to a commoner.

"You gave away the sword of Goliath after being entrusted with it on behalf of Israel.

"You used the Urim V'Tumim on behalf of a commoner. "You and your fellow priests have abused their position as priests to God. Your duty is to promote peace. Instead you have sown discord and strife. On those accounts alone you are deserving of punishment.

"But you did more than that. You acted treacherously towards the monarchy. You gave support to an enemy of the monarchy, an enemy of Israel. I cannot accept your claim that the entire city of Nov was unaware of my decree against the son of Jesse.

"Son of Achitachav! Your story is a lie. You and your priests rebelled against the king. You must know according to the law of Torah, a king is not permitted to surrender the respect that is due to him. "Your sin is so severe it merits only one means of atonement.

"Son of Achitachav, I sentence you and your fellow priests to death. The sentence will be carried out immediately. Abner, Amasa, I instruct you to carry out the sentence."

Abner and Amasa stepped forward and stood in front of Saul's throne. They bowed low to the ground, then Abner spoke. "Your majesty! We are soldiers, not executioners. We cannot carry out this order." Both men withdrew their swords from their sheaths and placed them on the ground in front of Saul.

"The sentence stands," declared Saul. "These men will be executed for treason. Doeg! You are the principal witness against these men. Torah demands you carry out the sentence."

*   *   *

Doeg carried out Saul's sentence of death. Without assistance, he executed the High Priest, Achimelech the son of Achitachav and eighty-five of his fellow priests. He then went to the city of Nov and executed the rest of its inhabitants.

Some priests, however, managed to avoid the sword of Doeg. One of them, Evyatar, seized the Urim V'Tumim and fled to join David and his small band of fugitives in the hills and forests of Israel.

The news of Doeg's merciless massacre of the priests swept Israel. Wherever he went, he was pointed out as the butcher of Nov. Men and children shouted abuse at him in the streets. His friends shunned him. His pupils in his Torah academy lost respect for him. No longer prepared to accept his authority, they sat in contemptuous silence throughout his lectures. He lost his ability to expound the words of the Torah and made mistakes in his teachings.

When sleeping, he had nightmares of the massacre. He saw his bloodstained arm rising and falling on the bodies of the priests of Nov. He heard, again and again, the wailing of women, the crying of children and the terrified snorting of cattle.

Frightened to close his eyes, he lay awake in his bed at night, denying himself the precious balm of sleep. Soon his appetite was impaired and his lust for life destroyed. His health slowly deteriorated and his body became a living skeleton.

Saul regretted his association with the man who incited him to wipe out an entire city of men, women, children, together with their cattle and sheep. He expelled Doeg from the palace.

*   *   *

Doeg died, at the age of 34, unloved and unlamented.

Our wise men of blessed memory) tell us that Doeg was one of the four laymen who forfeited their share in the world to come.

'*Saul's Last Battle*' is a semi-fictional account of the last twenty-four hours in the life of King Saul. The events take place in the north of Israel, on and around Mount Gilboa.

The surprise ending, however, is based upon a Midrash.

SAUL'S LAST BATTLE

The Philistines mobilised in the Jezreel Valley. Fully recovered from David's slaying of Goliath, they confidently prepared for the conflict with the Israelites.

At the northern edge of the valley, archers loosed arrow after arrow at rows of pumpkins crudely painted as bearded faces with bushy eyebrows. Horsemen, brandishing swords, thundered at breakneck speed towards melons set on poles, then with expert flicks of their wrists, sliced them in two. White robed priests marched up and down the valley displaying omens of victory. Foot soldiers practised sword fencing, spear hurling and hand to hand combat. At the same time, they loudly boasted of the unspeakable cruelties they would inflict on the bodies of Saul and his son Jonathan. The sense of Philistine supremacy was overwhelming.

In a large tent, in the centre of the camp, stood a statue of the Philistine sea-god Dagon, a grotesque figure, half man, half fish. Outside the tent was a queue of Philistines waiting to offer prayers and gifts to their god.

"This time it won't be us running away at the end of the battle." A veteran Philistine soldier spoke to a youth barely thirteen years old. "Mark my words, boy! You're going to see a famous victory tomorrow. I wouldn't like to be in Saul's shoes when our boys get hold of him."

The youth looked up in awe at the soldier who had deigned to speak to him. "This will be my first battle," he said proudly.

"You're lucky to be in on this one. You'll never have a better chance for victory."

"Why's that?"

"Where's David the son of Jesse?" the soldier asked. "Where's the man who slew Goliath? He may be an Israelite, but by Dagon he's a brave fellow. I wouldn't like to face him in battle. Take him away and the Israelite army will fall to pieces.

"But what about Saul? Saul's no coward and he's still a powerful warrior. Look what he did to the Ammonites. And look at what he and Jonathan did to our armies over the last few months."

"Saul!? Saul's finished. He must know he needs their God on his side. So what does he do? He wipes out all the Israelite priests. And he spends half his time and energy in hunting down David, the only man who has a chance of defeating us. The man is a maniac. How can such a man be a leader? You see boy! That's what it's all about—leadership. Now watch me carefully, son. I'll lead you to your first battle. And to your first victory."

The old soldier spat in the air away from the wind, then bent down to peer closely at the ground. "The omens are good, boy. Don't always rely on the omens of the priests. Sometimes you have to make your own." He slapped the youngster hard on his shoulders. "The gods are with us. Tomorrow night you won't be wearing those old rags. Tomorrow night, you'll have fine warm Israelite wool around your shoulders. Believe me! You won't have to pay for it."

He looked up and saw that their turn had come to enter Dagon's tent. "Come on! Let's go in to Dagon together. You'll hear what a Philistine soldier says before going into battle."

*　　*　　*

Saul had mobilised his forces on Mount Gilboa at the other end of the Jezreel Valley. They included a small standing army of three thousand hand-picked men—and conscripts from all the tribes of Israel, from Dan in the North to Judah in the South.

The inexperienced recruits were given a brief, rudimentary training in the arts of warfare. They were taught how to wield a sword, hurl a spear, sling a shot and shoot an arrow from a bow. They also performed the menial tasks in the camp; cooking, guard duty and construction work.

*　　*　　*

On a tree-covered slope halfway up the mountain, a group of conscripts from the tribes of Dan and Ephraim were preparing timber for the coming battle; felling trees and making logs in order to roll down the mountainside for a defence against the Philistine chariots.

In the bright afternoon sunshine, two men swung their axes against a giant fir tree. Facing each other, six feet apart, they took turns to sink their axes deeper and deeper into the trunk of the tree. Stripped to the waist, sweat glistening on their bodies, their arm pistoned backward and forward piling up wood chips around their feet.

"Fall down!" One of the men urged the tree. "I can't go on much longer."

"We'll soon be there."

"You said that five minutes ago."

"You're not hitting hard enough."

Four more blows of the axe and the tree finally groaned its signal of defeat.

With renewed vigour, the two men intensified their assault on the tree and, as it crashed down on to the mountainside, collapsed exhaustedly on to the pine-riddled ground.

"Why do they work us so hard? Don't they know we have to fight a war tomorrow?" The Ephraimite, his face glowing like hot coals, lay on his back, drinking in huge gulps of air as he spoke. "We need time to rest."

His companion took time to answer. Eventually he replied. "That's just the point. They can't afford to give us too much time to rest. When we rest, we think. And when we think, we ask ourselves questions that only have awkward answers."

"What sort of questions?"

"Like what chance we have of surviving the battle with the Philistines. I don't know about you, but I'm scared stiff."

"You don't look it."

"I know how I feel."

"In that case you shouldn't be here. You know what the law is. 'The man who is afraid and soft-hearted should return home from the battlefield.'"

"Don't get me wrong. I may be scared. But I'm not faint hearted. Even Moses was frightened before fighting the giant Og. Before a battle, it's natural to be frightened. I'm sure David was before fighting Goliath."

"Don't you believe it. I saw him fight Goliath. I've never seen such confidence in a person. Besides you can't compare him to Moses. David is a natural warrior. He'd already killed a lion and a bear by himself. If only he were here now. Why doesn't Saul let him fight with us? I can't believe he's a traitor."

"Saul is putting personal interest before national security. Doesn't he realise, if the Philistines win this battle, the whole country will be under their thumb? I agree with you. We need a man of vision and power. At the moment, only David can save Israel." In an idle gesture, he picked up a stone from the mountain floor and showed it to his friend. "What have I here?"

"A stone from the mountainside," was the puzzled answer.

"No, you're wrong. This is not a stone. It's a missile. In the proper hands, it can kill. It's a dead Philistine. That's what I mean by vision. One has to look beyond the boundaries of the three dimensions. One has stop thinking about themselves and start thinking about the bigger picture. Saul no longer has that ability. Saul is only concerned with his own petty interests. He has become obsessed with destroying David. He doesn't realise that, at the same time, he is destroying himself; and also destroying Israel."

"He wasn't always like that. When do you think this change in Saul started?"

"I think it started with the death of Samuel. Samuel's death shattered Saul's confidence. He thought every one was conspiring against him. Samuel was a great prophet. He was an inspiration to all Israel. Had he lived he would never have allowed Saul to wipe out the priests of Nov. If he were alive today, Saul and David would be standing shoulder to shoulder fighting those Philistines."

"I see you've lost confidence in Saul. Why are you here then?"

"I'd no choice in the matter. I was conscripted to fight the Philistines. It seems to be the lot of my tribe to forever clash with the Philistines.

"Now let me ask you another question." He pointed towards a giant boulder standing about fifty metres from where they were lying. "What do you see over there, a giant boulder?"

"No, I see more than that." The Ephraimite was not going to be tricked a second time. "I see a mangled chariot, a host of dead Philistines. I see the Philistines fleeing like a pack of frightened jackals."

"Where is your vision? We've already killed all the Philistines with the stones. We don't need the boulder as a weapon of war. We need the boulder to build. There lies the foundation stone for the Temple, the place of worship where all the tribes can gather and pray as one nation."

The Ephraimite looked at him uncomprehendingly. "You're mad!"

"We're all mad. We're fighting a war we can't hope to win. Where are our weapons? Where is our armour? What chance do we stand against a sword, a spear or an arrow? Only one man can turn the war in our favour. Who knows he may even be fighting with the Philistines. If only David was fighting with us. We're all mad."

*   *   *

From one of the upper slopes of the North east face of Mount Gilboa three men looked down at the Philistine forces in the Jezreel Valley; Saul,

King of Israel, his commander-in-chief, Abner, and his senior general Amasa.

Saul was ill at ease. He pursed his lips, clenched his hands and stared fixedly ahead with a hint of panic in his eyes.

In contrast, Abner appeared relaxed and confident. He spoke with conspicuous self-assurance as he assessed the prospects of the Israelite army in the coming battle with the Philistines. "Chariots are not the ideal vehicle for mountain warfare. If we sit tight on Gilboa, the Philistines will be disadvantaged. Tell me Amasa! Where are the likely places of their advance?"

Amasa pointed to a number of paths at the foot of the mountain. "We've stationed some of our best troops there. For the last four days, we've been training a regiment of conscripts in anti-chariot combat. They have ropes, timber, chains and an arsenal of giant boulders. The chariots can only advance on a narrow front. If we can hold them in the early stages of the battle, they'll all pile up on each other. That's when we order a counter attack.

"If we rout them in this battle, we crush them for good. The time has come to take the fight to the enemy."

Both men looked towards Saul for some comment. But there was no response. He appeared to be oblivious of the conversation taking place between his two generals. He stood in silence, as though mesmerised by the distant clouds of dust thrown up by the whirling wheels of the Philistine chariots. Suddenly, he whirled round to confront Abner. "Where are they? Why have they not yet returned? I told you Abner. Send only your most trustworthy men. These men have deserted me. They have deserted Israel.

"Patience, your majesty. They will soon be here. Remember, they had to make a detour to avoid contact with the Philistines." He pointed to a place just beyond the line of the Philistine chariots. "See, where they had to go."

"Do not belittle my intelligence, Abner. If they had good news they would have been here by now. Good news breaks down the strongest of barriers." Saul turned away from the two men and began walking towards the royal tent that had been set up in a clearing further up the mountain.

"Wait your majesty! Your physician requested me to be sure you were accompanied at all times.

"A physician dictates to the king of Israel," said Saul. "I ask you Abner. Who sits on the throne of Israel, the king or his physician?"

Abner shrugged his powerful shoulders in a gesture of helpless resignation. With Saul in this mood, it was pointless to argue. Besides he felt there were times when it is essential for a man to be alone. As he watched Saul return to his tent, he ruefully stroked his beard. "No one would believe he's changed so much in so short a time. Remember Amasa, when the ark of God was stolen by the Philistines. They had the effrontery to take out the stone tablets of the Ark of the Covenant. Goliath held them up for everyone to see. Saul rushed up to him, jumped up, snatched the tablets from his hands and ran away. Where is his courage now? Where has his confidence gone? If he was well, there's not a man in Israel to match him. I'd even include David in that assessment."

"I agree. Saul has become a shell of a man. And our soldiers know it. We must try to hold them together. But I fear it's an impossible task. If only Samuel were alive, we might have persuaded him to support Saul in this battle."

"Samuel is dead. The past is buried. We have to rally the troops. What is more important, we have to rally Saul. Come Amasa! Let's find the physician. He may be able to help."

*   *   *

Inside the royal tent, Saul looked down with horror at his hands shaking uncontrollably with fear. "Samuel!" He cried out in anguish. "Help me! Answer me!"

No voice, no sound calmed his fears and Saul sank even deeper into the pit of despair. Again he called out the name Samuel, but again his words met with silence.

Saul was desperate to draw back Samuel from the world of the spirits to be at his side. He created in his mind, an image of Samuel, an image with as much substance as possible. He visualised Samuel's face, Samuel's hands and the simple cloak he always wore.

To intensify this image, he focused on the last occasion he had seen Samuel, the moment when Samuel had travelled to Gilgal after Saul's defeat of Amalek.

Saul hoped to make the image so real that it would be possible to reach across the barrier that separated the world of the living from the dead; to draw back Samuel to the world of flesh and blood; to beg him for forgiveness and help.

But instead of drawing out a living Samuel from his recreation of the past, Saul was swept along by the vividness of his own imagination. Against his will he was drawn back to the incident in Gilgal when he had been rejected as king over Israel.

*   *   *

Saul saw himself, after the triumph of his defeat of Israel's archenemy Amalek, standing proudly and upright in the plains of Gilgal. Samuel was striding towards him and Saul assumed Samuel would congratulate him for a swift and decisive victory.

"Blessed are you unto God," Saul said to Samuel jubilantly, "I have established the word of God."

"Established the word of God? What is this sound of sheep in my ears? What is the sound of the cattle that I hear?" Samuel unhesitatingly rebuked the man he had anointed king over Israel for failing to carry out God's commands.

"It is the people that brought them from Amalek." Saul attempted to excuse himself. "They spared the best of the sheep and the cattle. They want to offer them as a sacrifice to God. They . . ."

"Wait!" interrupted Samuel. "I will tell you what God told me last night."

With fear in his heart, Saul waited for Samuel to speak.

"Even if you are small in your own eyes, you are the head of the tribes of Israel. God has anointed you to be a king over Israel. It is God who sent you on this mission.

"God instructed you. 'Go, destroy Amalek. Fight him until he is utterly destroyed.'

"Now why did you not listen to the instruction of God? Why did you pounce on the spoils of war? Why did you do evil in the eyes of God?"

Saul tried to justify his actions. "I did listen to the voice of God. I did go on the path He sent me. I did utterly destroy them. I have taken Agag, their king prisoner. They are finished as a nation. Never again will they pose a threat to the people of Israel.

"As for the sheep and the cattle, it was the people who took from the spoil—but only to bring as a sacrifice to God in Gilgal."

"Does God wish for sacrifices as much as listening to His voice?" Samuel rejected Saul's argument. "Obedience is better than sacrifice. Listening is better than the fat of rams. Your abundance of excuses is itself a sin. You have rejected God. Now God rejects you as king."

Saul, devastated by Samuel's blunt words, cried out with passion. "I have sinned. I have sinned against God. I have sinned against your command. I feared the people and I listened to their voice. Forgive my sin. Return with me and I will bow down to God."

Saul's confession, however, came too late to avert the decree of God. His failure to carry out the royal duty of destroying Amalek, forfeited for him and his family, the throne of Israel.

"I will not return with you," said Samuel. "You have rejected God. And He rejects you as king over Israel."

Samuel's dire words were enforced by a vivid symbol of doom and destruction. As he turned away from Saul, he took his cloak in his hands and tore it in two. "God has torn the kingdom of Israel from you this day. God is giving it to someone better than you . . . ."

*   *   *

'Someone better than you.' The image of the past faded away but the words of the dead Samuel still rang through Saul's head. In the royal tent on Mount Gilboa, an image of David now flashed through his mind. He saw David being greeted with ecstasy by the people after his victory over Goliath. He saw the maidens of Israel showering David with gold coins and heard them singing, 'Saul has slain in his thousands, David has slain in his ten thousands.' 'Someone better than you.' Again and again the refrain ran through his mind until Saul exclaimed loudly. "I have sinned! How can I atone for my sin? O,' God, show me how to repent."

Saul's frenzied crying brought an immediate response. Two men, Abner and the king's personal physician, burst into the tent and rushed to Saul's side. The physician, a short stocky man with a straggly beard, rudely grasped Saul's shoulders and with a surprising display of strength for such a small person, shook him rudely backwards and forwards. "Your majesty, there is no cause for alarm. I am here by your side. Here! Drink this." He took a small water bottle from a pocket in his clothing and offered it to Saul. "This will make you feel more at ease."

Saul snatched the bottle from the physician's hand and hurled it to the ground. "What Israelite eats or drinks on the day of a battle. On the day of a battle, I fast. How can we expect victory if we flout God's laws? I shall neither eat nor drink until the battle with the Philistines is over."

"They will not attack today," Abner said. "If the attack is to come, it will come tomorrow. There is no need to fast today. For the sake of your men, I bid you drink."

"For the sake of my men, I will not drink. I will not go back on my word. Now leave me!" Saul strode over to the side of the tent, picked up a spear and arched his back as though preparing to throw it at the two men. "Leave me. I wish to be alone."

"Your majesty," said Abner, keeping a wary eye on the spear, backed away from Saul, "if it is your royal wish, we shall leave."

Saul did not reply. He merely tightened his grasp on the raised spear and the two men retreated from the tent.

*   *   *

Outside the tent, a despairing Abner spoke to the physician. "How can he fight a battle in that condition? How can he inspire his men to follow him when he treats them like his enemies? Is there nothing we can do to help him?"

"Very little. Saul is suffering from a disease of the mind. It began in Gilgal when Samuel rejected him as king and favoured David instead. Saul, when left alone, becomes quickly depressed. He starts recalling his past mistakes."

"Amalek?"

"Certainly Amalek. Nov as well. He feels guilty at having wiped out an entire city of priests. Of course, he believed at first that they assisted David when he fled for his life. Only later he had doubts. He has the death of hundreds of priests on his conscience. His guilt is tearing him in two and there is no Samuel to guide him."

"So only Samuel can help him." Abner said thoughtfully.

"Or someone or something that will give him the answers he requires."

"Who knows? Perhaps the messengers he sent may bring back information." Abner stared down at two men who had just emerged from a dip in a lower plain of the mountain. They appeared to be heading towards them. Soon Abner recognised them as the men sent by Saul to David and Evyatar for information from the Urim V'Tumim.

*   *   *

The Urim V'Tumim was a slip of parchment bearing the Divine name of God that the High Priest inserted within the folds of his garments just behind the sacred breastplate. Inset in this breastplate were twelve precious stones on which were engraved the names of the twelve tribes of Israel. Whenever God's advice was sought on behalf of Israel, the Urim V'Tumim, miraculously but cryptically, illuminated key letters in these names. The meaning of the coded message could only be given by the High Priest.

After the massacre at Nov, Evyatar, the priest had taken the Urim V'Tumim and joined David in his flight from Saul. Surprisingly, they had been given shelter by one of the kings of the Philistines.

*   *   *

Abner knew the messengers should be taken to Saul immediately. He steeled himself to confront an enraged and unpredictable Saul. Approaching

55

the entrance to the royal tent, he called out. "Your majesty, the messengers have returned. May we come in?"

Some mumbled reply emerged from the tent which Abner optimistically understood as permission to enter. He beckoned to the messengers and they entered the tent.

Inside the tent, Saul looked with scorn at the two messengers. "I see you have finally returned," he said, in a voice heavy with sarcasm. "Did you obtain the information I require?"

The older of the two messengers, Nachman, acted as the spokesman. "We succeeded in reaching the camp of David the son of Jesse. We conveyed your requests to him."

To Saul, the name David was like a red rag to a bull. He could contain himself no longer. "The son of Jesse, the betrayer of Israel! He is not for us. He is for the Philistines."

Abner intervened. "Your majesty, you do him an injustice. If the circumstances were right he would be your loyal subject. Even now it's still not too late to make peace with him. His presence would boost the morale of the army. His army of six hundred men could turn the tide of battle in our favour."

"Enough of this treason," roared Saul. "That son of Jesse will never fight alongside me. Now tell me Nachman. What are his intentions? Will he fight against us?"

"He enjoys the full confidence of one of the kings of the Philistines. Achish of Gath looks upon him as a trusted friend. He is eager for him to join his forces against ours."

Saul relished Nachman's words. "So this is the man who would be king of Israel. He is a trusted ally of the Philistines. This is the will of God? That my kingdom is given to a traitor? I find comfort in your words Nachman. Now tell me. The other Philistine kings. What do they think of him? Do they trust him?"

"No, your majesty. They refuse to allow him to fight. They ordered Achish to withdraw all Israelite forces from their ranks."

"What does the son of Jesse himself want? Whose side is he on?"

"We spoke to him personally. He assured us he will not fight against his own people. He was happy the other kings rejected him"

"But had they accepted him," said Saul sharply, "he would fight against us?"

"No, your majesty," Abner could contain himself no longer. "He is loyal to Israel."

"He is loyal to himself. As long as he lives he will be a danger to the kingdom. Do not be misled by his cloak of piety. When the battle with the

Philistines is over, we shall pursue him once more. Next time he will not escape me.

"Now Nachman," Saul abruptly changed the subject. "Tell me about my other request. Tell me about the answer you received from the . . . ." To his horror, Saul found he was unable to finish the sentence. His mouth refused to form the words Urim V'Tumim.

Another nightmare from his past had come back to haunt him. Saul suddenly recalled the destruction of Nov; the massacre of an entire city of priests for aiding and abetting David to escape; the pitiless slaughter of entire families; men, women and children, sheep and oxen.

The Urim V'Tumim. The words hovered on Saul's tongue. In panic, he buried his face in his hands and tried to blot out his feelings of guilt and remorse. Vainly, he tried to justify the action he had taken. 'The priests of Nov were guilty of treason. I acted properly. I acted in the interests of the nation. With the priests, I had to be resolute.

'Yet with Amalek I showed mercy. I spared Agag. And I spared the best of the cattle.' Saul's self-confidence was steadily crumbling; the inconsistencies in his behaviour were tearing him apart.

'But,' Saul asked himself, 'was I resolute at Nov? Or was I vindictive? Was I right to order the slaying of all those priests because of my jealousy of that son of Jesse?'

"Your majesty!" Abner broke into Saul's troubled thoughts. "We have urgent matters to attend to in the camp. With your permission, we would like to finish this report."

With a superhuman effort, Saul steeled himself to finish his question. "Did Evyatar listen to your request? Did he consult the Urim V'Tumim on my behalf?"

"Yes, your majesty. Evyatar gave us every assistance."

"The message? What message did he receive?"

"There was no reply. The Urim V'Tumim was silent to your request."

"No reply?" The answer bewildered Saul. He turned away from the two men, mumbling to himself in despair. 'The Urim V'Tumim is the servant of the king. Why does it not answer my request? Where shall I now turn? The fountains of prophecy have dried up. The tellers of dreams are silenced. I am abandoned by the Urim V'Tumim. Whom can I call? Samuel would have helped me. And Samuel is dead.'

"Your majesty," Abner said. "The men of Israel are still loyal to you and your son Jonathan. We will defeat the Philistines." He turned to the two men. "You have done well and you will be rewarded for your efforts. However, I expect one further duty from you before the battle with the Philistines.

"What you have seen and heard these last few minutes will not, under any circumstances, be repeated. Swear that to me. Swear that to me in the presence of the king of Israel. Swear it to me. Now!"

"We swear. We will not repeat a word of what was just said."

"Good. Now return to your quarters and get some rest. You will need all your strength tomorrow."

As the two messengers left the tent, Saul turned towards Abner and placed his hand on his shoulder. "No king could ask for a better general, Abner. But I must have guidance for the battle with the Philistines. No one answers me. Neither soothsayer nor prophet. For heaven's sake Abner. Surely there must be someone in my kingdom who can help me."

As though hiding a feeling of guilt, Abner avoided looking directly at Saul. "After the death of Samuel, you gave instructions to rid the country of witches and wizards. To the best of my ability I carried out your instructions. Yet rumours persist. It is claimed there is someone in your kingdom that possesses supernatural powers."

Saul failed to notice the hesitancy in Abner's voice. Momentarily his face brightened. "Supernatural powers! Abner, take me to see him tonight."

"This medium is not a man. She is a woman—a witch. Somehow she remained alive. But to go tonight when the Philistines will attack tomorrow?"

"That's why we must go tonight. I must know about the coming battle. Tell me Abner. Where does she live?"

"About ten miles to the north of Mount Gilboa. In the village of Endor."

"Abner, I must see her. Who can take me to Endor?"

"I used to live near that village. I know the district well. I could take you there without being detected."

"It would be madness to go to Endor at this time." Amasa objected. "Our scouts have reported the movement of the Philistine army. They encamped first at Shunem and then moved on to Jezreel. They are now less than five miles away from our position. The whole area between us and Endor is swarming with Philistine troops."

Abner looked at Amasa. "I know it's madness. But to stay here and fight while the king's in this mood? That's also madness. We have too few choices left. We must act fast. This is what we must do. Find ordinary clothing for the three of us to wear. Arrange to have three horses prepared and saddled at the foot of the mountain. Get hold of sackcloth and muffle their hooves. I guarantee we can avoid the Philistine sentries. Besides, they won't expect anyone to be making such a journey by night. Amasa, hurry!"

*   *   *

A shrill, cold wind swept across the eastern face of Mount Gilboa. Dust-clouds eddied wildly along the rows of tents and horses neighed bitterly as, huddled together for warmth, they vainly protested against the cold of the night.

An hour after nightfall, three men emerged silently from the royal tent and strode to the perimeter of the Israelite camp where they gave careful instructions to the guard. Then swiftly descending the snake path to the foot of the mountain, they mounted the horses awaiting them.

Under a canopy of stars, fleeting wispy clouds and a moonlit sky, Abner and Amasa accompanied a disguised Saul to a ramshackle hut on the outskirts of a nearby village, the home of the witch of Endor.

*   *   *

Bang! Bang! "Open up! Open up!" Abner's insistent shouting and knocking eventually brought a response. Through a crack in the door, he saw a light growing steadily brighter.

"Who is it?" a voice rasped through the door. "What do you want with an old woman at this time of night?"

"We are here on urgent business. Open the door!"

"Who are you? What are your names?"

"Our names are not important. My friend is sick. He has a troubled soul. We heard you can help him. Let us in."

"All right, all right," grumbled the witch as she fumbled with the bolt, swung the door open, and held up a lantern to look at her visitors.

Never before had she seen a man as tall as Saul. Her scrawny neck craned sharply upwards to see his face. She stared at him in disbelief. "Who are you?" she asked again, looking suspiciously at the scratches in Saul's legs where his ill-fitting clothing had failed to protect him from the thistles and thorns of the mountainside. "What do you want from me?"

"My friend needs help. Let us in."

Abner's commanding tone silenced the witch. Backing away from the door, she beckoned the men to follow her. "Come inside and sit down quickly. Otherwise, there'll be a hole in my roof every time he moves his head." She pointed to the floor. "Sit here while I stoke up the fire and make him a drink. He has ice in his heart."

"I need no drink," said Saul, squatting on the floor with his two companions. "I need advice."

"Advice! You come to me, an old woman at this time of the night and ask for advice."

"It is not your advice I seek."

"So why come here and disturb me."

"Because only you can make contact with the soul I am seeking. I seek advice from the dead."

"From the dead!" shrieked the witch, her eyes ablaze with fear. "You must know what Saul has done. He has destroyed the witches and wizards from the land. You have come to spy on me. You wish to trap me. You wish to kill me."

"I wish you no harm. I swear you are in no danger. All I need is your help."

The simple appeal in Saul's voice aroused the sympathy of the witch. "Swear it to me."

"I swear it. No harm will befall you over this matter."

For a moment the witch hesitated. Then, finally convincing herself of the sincerity of Saul's oath, she placed a few logs on the fire, tightened the black scarf around her head and sat down in front of the men.

From a pocket in her dress, she withdrew a small bone. "This human bone has supernatural powers. It can recall the spirits of the dead. Now listen carefully. Do not question anything I do. It is dangerous to interrupt the spirits of the dead."

The witch raised the bone close to her eyes. "Soon you will witness many strange things. But remember! Only I can see the form of the spirit. Only he," she pointed to Saul, "can hear what the spirit is saying.

Outside the hut, the wind that had swept down from Mt. Gilboa was battering the door. It found a multitude of cracks and crevices in the flimsy timber and, whining and whistling fanned the embers in the hearth into flames that cast dancing shadows on the wall behind the seated men.

Swaying gently from side to side, the witch spoke softly to Saul. "Concentrate on this bone in my hand. Concentrate on the spirit you are seeking. Whom are you seeking? Whom should I call from the other world?"

With his eyes fixed hypnotically on the polished surface of the bone, Saul started speaking. "I seek the spirit of Samuel. Raise up for me the spirit of Samuel."

In spellbound silence, Abner and Amasa watched the witch urge the spirit of Samuel to appear before her. "He is coming towards me," she whispered. "I see him . . ." Her voice tapered away. With fear in her eyes, she saw the spirit rising headfirst from the other world. "Only for a king will a spirit rise like that," she said angrily to herself. "You have deceived me. You are a king. You are Saul, king of Israel."

"Do not be afraid," said Saul. "I have sworn to you. I will keep my oath. Tell me what you see."

Saul's sincerity reassured the witch. "I see a god arising from the earth."

"His appearance?" demanded Saul. "Describe him to me."

"He is an old man. And he wears a cloak."

"A cloak! The cloak of Samuel," Saul bowed low to the ground and waited for the spirit to speak.

A voice thundered in his ears. "Why did you disturb me to bring me up?"

The harsh words of the spirit unnerved Saul. He had to force himself to speak. "I am distressed. The Philistines are about to fight me. God has departed from me. He no longer answers me. Forgive me for disturbing your rest. There is no one to guide me. I have asked the prophets. I have asked the tellers of dreams."

Saul did not mention the Urim V'Tumim. Although unable to see the spirit of Samuel, he was suddenly overwhelmed by a dazzling flood of light from the world of truth. At last, he perceived his soul free from the shadow of vanity and self-interest. He agonised at the magnitude of the sin he had committed.

How foolish had he been at Nov. Why had he fallen into the web of lies and deceit spun by Doeg the Edomite around the priests of Nov? Why had he allowed his obsession for David to cloud his judgement? How could he have slaughtered an entire town of innocent people?

Saul was engulfed by a feeling of remorse and shame. Not the shabby shame of shattered pride, but the noble, cleansing shame of self-reproach. For Saul, in the presence of the all-seeing eye of the spirit of Samuel, the Urim V'Tumim had become his badge of bigotry and guilt. He could not bring himself to utter its name.

Saul composed himself. "I am calling you to tell me what I shall do."

"Why do you ask me?" was the brusque answer. "God has departed from you. He is with your enemy. He will do with you as I have spoken. God has torn the kingdom from you and given it to your friend David, since you did not listen to the voice of God and satisfy His anger with Amalek. Therefore, God will do this thing against you this day."

"Have I no choice?" cried out Saul. "Must I die in the battle tomorrow?"

"You have a choice. You may flee the field of battle and live. But then you forfeit your share in the world to come.

"Or you may fight. And God will deliver you with Israel into the hand of the Philistines. But tomorrow, you and your sons will be with me."

Saul was devastated by Samuel's dire prediction. Overwhelmed by fear, hunger and fatigue, he fell to the floor in a mood of black despair.

Immediately, the witch rushed to his side. "He needs food. Let me give him something to eat."

"No," Saul forced the words from his lips. "I shall not eat this day."

"The woman is right." The hitherto silent Abner asserted his authority as Commander-in-Chief of Saul's army. "Tomorrow we fight the Philistines. You must eat before returning to camp." He turned to the witch. "Hurry! Prepare food. Boil water. Slaughter a young calf. Tomorrow we lead Israel into battle."

Dawn was not far off when Saul and his two companions departed the hovel of the witch of Endor. Thanking her profusely for her generous hospitality they set off immediately to return to the Israelite camp on Mount Gilboa.

*   *   *

Just before mounting his horse, Abner let out a quiet, startled cry. "Wait! I must return to the hut. One of my keys must have slipped from my belt."

Amasa looked at him suspiciously. "Don't be too long. If you can't find it immediately, then leave it. We can't risk riding back in the morning light. Hurry!"

Abner returned to the hut, knocked gently at the door and was immediately admitted by the witch. He went over to the place where he had been sitting and picked up his key from off the floor. "I had to return for a minute," he said simply.

"I understand. I expected you. Take care, Abner."

For a brief moment, Abner took hold of the witch's hands and squeezed them gently. "Good-bye, mother," he whispered. Then turning quickly, he left the hut to rejoin his companions.

*   *   *

That day, as the sun rose over the horizon, the Philistines attacked. With chariots and archers, they swiftly penetrated the easier slopes of the mountain from Jezreel.

After the chariots lost their impetus on the higher ground, the archers wreaked havoc on the demoralised Israelites who fled before them.

Saul and his sons perished in battle and the jubilant Philistines seized and displayed their bodies as trophies of war.

Saul, however, did not live or die in vain. His achievement of uniting the tribes of Israel led eventually to the downfall of the Philistines and the consolidation of the kingdoms of Judah and Israel.

David cursed the mountain that had failed to protect Saul and his son Jonathan. He eulogised them with the immortal words.

"The beauty of Israel is slain in the high places. How are the mighty fallen!"

Sources:
Samuel Book 1: ch. 28-31

THE BROKEN PROMISE

Harry Gabriel recognised the look in his son's eyes. Without any doubt, he was going to ask him a question. "What's on your mind, Joel? It's not like you to be shy. I know you want to ask me something."

"Yes, daddy."

"So go ahead and ask. If I can't give you an answer, don't worry, I'll tell you."

"Can you tell me something about the Gibeonites? We were learning about them in class the other day. I remember you promised to tell me something more about them."

"Something more? Refresh my memory. What have I told you already?"

"You told us all about Joshua and the Gibeonites and after he found out they tricked him, he made them work for the people of Israel. You also promised to carry on the story later. So can now be later?"

"That's a funny sentence. But I understand what you're saying. First, let me ask you a question. Who do you think was the greatest hero we ever had?"

"Judah Maccabeus?"

"Not bad. Try someone else."

"Samson."

"Good. Carry on."

"David."

"You're getting warm"

"Bar-Kochba?"

"I don't know how you jump from David to Bar-Kochba. I said you were getting warm with David. That should be a good clue."

"I don't know. I give up. Please tell me."

"Harry Gabriel! You always speak in riddles," Harry's wife, Jacqui joined in the conversation. "We can be here all night trying to work out he is. Who is he?"

"Yes, daddy," piped in Joel. "Who is he?"

Harry refused to be hurried. "I'll give you some clues. In his time, the only weapons the Jewish people had were just two swords and two spears. Can you imagine? Only two people in the whole of Israel had proper weapons to defend themselves. The rest had to make to do with shovels, pickaxes, hay forks; and, if they were lucky, bows and arrows. But even then their arrows had no metal tips. Just hard solid wood.

"On the other hand, their enemies, the Philistines were fully equipped with all the weapons of war; chariots, swords, spears, bows, and arrows with vicious iron tips."

"How come?" asked Jacqui.

"I know it sounds corny. But the Philistines ruled Israel with an iron fist. They kept a tight control over all iron tools and weapons. The Israelites were not allowed to have their own iron works. If a person wanted to have his plough or sickle sharpened, he had to go to a Philistine smithy. And they charged a fortune for sharpening the Jewish tools."

"Come along. Let's start the story," said Jacqui impatiently. "So who had the two weapons?"

"You give up too easily. I'll give you one more clue. Think of the king before David."

"Of course! It must be Saul," said Jacqui triumphantly.

"And the other one must be his son Jonathan," added Joel.

"Right. They were the only ones who had proper weapons. And it was only by a miracle they got them. But that's another story. Now let's start this story."

"We shall start at a place called Gilgal where Saul had assembled thousands of Israelites to organise a Jewish army against the Philistines. Naturally, the Philistines did not want Saul to establish a kingdom so when they heard about this large gathering at Gilgal, they raised a huge fighting force and set out from Gaza, where they lived, to wipe out Saul and punish the Israelites for rebelling against them.

The Philistine forces were divided into three armies. One of them headed for Gilgal.

SAUL'S CAMP

In Israel, not far from Gilgal were two major towns, Geva and Michmash. A road ran between these two towns and, on each side of this road, stood two massive rocks. The one to the South was called Botsas and the one, directly opposite it, to the North, was called Seneh. Each rock, on the side facing the road was smooth, steep and impossible to climb, whereas; on the other side a gentle slope led down to a clearing not too far away from the summit.

Saul had encamped in the clearing to the South, behind the rock called Botsas, with only his son Jonathan and six hundred loyal men. The thousands of Israelites who had flocked to Gilgal to support him had disappeared. On hearing about the huge Philistine army heading towards them, they deserted and fled to the safety of the nearby hills.

Behind the other rock Seneh, to the North was a Philistine garrison, normally manned by about fifty Philistines. They guarded the road to the North of Israel and reported any attempts by the Israelites to break the stranglehold of Philistine domination.

Not far from the garrison, about a couple of miles to the north, one of the Philistine armies had encamped and was preparing for its campaign against the Israelites.

*　　*　　*

Saul's son, Jonathan was becoming impatient at kicking his heels for so long. "We cannot stay here for much longer," he said to his armour bearer, Naphtali. "The Philistines are sending their soldiers throughout Israel. There's no one to stop them. You know how vicious they can be. We must get out of here and fight them."

Naphtali, who had left his ageing parents and his two younger sisters at home, was also eager to end their siege. "I agree. We must take the fight to the Philistines. But to go by the path into their camp would be suicide."

"I have an idea," said Jonathan. "I know my father would never agree to it but it's worth a try. Let's first go to the top of the rock, and then we can work out a plan."

*　　*　　*

At the top of the slope, Jonathan and Naphtali looked out across the panorama of the Israeli countryside, at the valleys criss-crossed with neatly harvested green fields; and at the hilly slopes covered with vines and olive groves. "Why should the Philistines plunder our crops and labour?" said Jonathan angrily. "I swear to you, Naphtali. One day, our people shall be free. Today, we shall take the first step to freedom."

There was very little vegetation on the rocky surface at the top and Jonathan had to walk about fifty metres to his right in order to reach a solitary tree that overlooked the road running between the two rocks.

Jonathan looked across to the opposite rock. "If we could make a bridge, we could attack the Philistines. But it would take too long and be too obvious. No. There must be another way. "Come," he said to Naphtali. "Let's see what we can find."

The two men began walking along the edge of the top of the rock. Suddenly, Jonathan stopped and looked excitedly across the road. "See there's another tree. Naphtali! Give me some stones."

Naphtali somewhat surprised at this request, nevertheless soon found a few stones and handed them to Jonathan.

"Good, now let's mark the spot," said Jonathan as he threw the stones onto the road directly beneath the tree.

Naphtali shook his head in puzzlement. "Those stones are going to help us climb that cliff face? I don't see how."

"Tonight you will see what a few stones can achieve," said Jonathan. "We leave two hours before daybreak. Be ready. Take with you all my weapons and one other thing—a long sturdy rope. It has to reach the ground from that tree.

*   *   *

Two hours before dawn, two figures stealthily left the group of sleeping soldiers and climbed up the slope of the rock towards the tree they had seen earlier in the day.

Naphtali whispered to Jonathan. "I can see how we climb down. But . . . ."

Jonathan smiled as he unwrapped an object he had been carrying. "This will get us down—and take us up."

In the dim moonlight before dawn, Naphtali peered hard at the object. "What is it?" he asked.

"It's called a grappling iron. See! It has a handle and four hooks. When it is wrapped around a tree or some other fixed solid object it acts like an anchor."

"Who told you about it? Where did you get it? It's made of iron. How did the Philistines let you get hold of it?" The questions tumbled out of Naphtali's mouth.

As the two men approached the tree, Jonathan explained. "A few months ago, a group of acrobats came to entertain us at our house. They used this tool to do some amazing climbing tricks. I offered to buy it from them. But naturally, they refused. This tool was their livelihood. The farmer does not sell the plough with which he tills the soil."

"So how did you get hold of it?"

"I said that I would like such a tool. And I would be prepared to pay any price for it. Four weeks later, they came back with one specially made for me."

"It must have cost a fortune."

"It helps to be a king's son sometime," smiled Jonathan. "The beauty of this hook is that after you've climbed down, you can release it with a flick of the wrist. I'll soon show you how it works. First we have to tie the rope to the handle of this hook."

*   *   *

Jonathan carefully placed the grappling iron around the base of the tree and pulled tight the rope he had attached to it. "First we climb down the rope to the road. Then we will show the Philistines how Israelites can fight. Let's climb down."

Ten minutes later, both men stood on the road between the two rocks and looked up towards the end of the rope. "Now to bring it down, safely," said Jonathan.

Jonathan took hold of the rope and by flicking his powerful wrists up and down sent up a ripple in the rope to the hook. "Good, it is no longer clinging to the base of the tree. Now, if we stand at an angle and pull sharply, it should come down."

Jonathan and Naphtali moved down road for about 10 metres, and then stopped. "This is far enough, said Jonathan. "Let's hope it works." He pulled gently at the rope and to his delight felt it was free.

"Stand well back."

Jonathan tugged sharply at the rope and within seconds, the hook, with a loud metallic bang, landed on the road.

Immediately, Naphtali ran to the hook, picked it up and handed it to Jonathan.

"Now for stage two," said Jonathan.

*   *   *

The two men walked up the road till they came to the cluster of stones that marked the location of the tree on the other rock. "This time it won't be so easy," said Jonathan. "There's no guarantee I'll find that tree straight away. And each time that hook hits the ground; it's going to send out signals that someone is there. Our only hope is that the Philistines are so confident they're safe, they won't bother to send out a search party at this time of night. "Here goes!"

Jonathan, standing well back from the rock face, took hold of the rope about two metres from the handle and swung the hook powerfully round his head. At the tenth swing he released the hook and watched it soar into the air. To his delight, it landed on the top of the rock.

"Let's see if it's found that tree," said Jonathan. Slowly he pulled the rope towards him and to his concern it encountered no resistance. Three seconds later, the hook landed heavily on the road.

"We'll have to try again," said Jonathan. "But this time from a different angle."

Once more Jonathan swung the hook powerfully round his head. And once more it landed on the top of the rock.

Slowly he pulled the rope towards him and, as before, three seconds later, the hook landed heavily on the road.

At the fifth attempt, the hook found the tree.

"Thank God!" cried Jonathan, as he tested the strength of the anchorage. "Now we can start stage two."

DAYBREAK

The Philistine garrison was housed in a makeshift building on a high mound in the centre of the clearing. Access to the building was by a narrow pathway that—on its Northern side ran from the front entrance of the clearing; and on the Southern side extended to the far end of the clearing where Jonathan and Naphtali had just arrived.

From its rear and its sides, the garrison building was virtually inaccessible because of the steepness of the mound. From its front, the only access was via the pathway that only had sufficient space for two people at a time. There was no wall to the edges of the path. There was only a sheer drop on each side.

"This is our strategy," said Jonathan to Naphtali, as they arrived at the bottom of the clearing within sight of the Philistine camp. "When the Philistines see us they will have two choices. They can either say, 'Wait there Israelites until we come down to you.' Or they can say, 'Come up here and fight.'

If they say, 'Come up here and fight.' we shall accept their invitation. Because that will be a signal from God that He will deliver them into our hands.

*   *   *

Dawn was breaking when Jonathan and Naphtali suddenly appeared to the Philistines at the foot of the pathway on the Southern side.

"Where did they come from?" said an astonished Philistine soldier as he caught sight of the two Israelites. How did they get there? They couldn't have climbed that rock."

"So the Israelites are creeping out of their holes," laughed another Philistine from inside the garrison building. "We'll soon teach them a lesson. How many are there?"

"I can only see two. But how did they get there? How did they get past the guards? There's only one entrance to the camp."

"I say, we go down and fight them," said the second Philistine.

"No!" The sergeant of the garrison called out sharply. "It's a trap. An Israelite wouldn't risk his life to fight a Philistine. We'll stay here. Tell them to come up to us."

"Come up here and fight," a Philistine called out.

Jonathan looked at Naphtali. "Now we take the fight to the Philistines."

Jonathan boldly strode up the path to the Philistine soldiers who had drawn their swords and were waiting nervously for the battle to begin.

"Kill that Israelite!" the sergeant called out.

The first soldier rushed forward—directly on to Jonathan's sword.

"Kill him," shrieked the sergeant.

Another Philistine rushed forward and Jonathan slew him as well.

Jonathan rapidly advanced up the slope towards the garrison headquarters. As he felled the Philistine soldiers, they either tumbled down the slope at the edge of the path or were slain by Naphtali with a pick axe.

After some twenty Philistines had been killed, the remaining soldiers in the garrison refused to believe that only two men were fighting them. They convinced themselves that an army of Israelites and foreign mercenaries had penetrated their defences. Fearful for their safety and frightened to admit their cowardice, they shouted out to each other.

"The Israelites have hired the Amalekites to destroy us!"

"They have tricked us."

"They have wiped out our army".

"We are surrounded by the Israelites"

In wild disarray, the Philistines stampeded down the path towards the entrance of the clearing.

Panic and fear had destroyed all military discipline. No longer did they operate as a fighting unit. Each man was concerned only with himself. Ignoring the orders of their Commanding Officer to stand and fight, they ran blindly along the narrow path way to the entrance of the camp. Whoever got in their way was rudely pushed over the side of the pathway to tumble down the slopes to the rocks below.

SAUL'S CAMP

In the meantime, the fighting in the clearing had not gone unnoticed. The secret watchers that Saul had placed on the Northern side of the rock had signalled by trumpet that the Philistine garrison was being routed.

Saul reacted immediately. He counted his remaining men and, on discovering that Jonathan and Naphtali were missing, prepared for battle against the Philistines.

"Listen carefully, O' men of Israel," Saul announced to his army. "Today, God is going to deliver the Philistines into our hands. But before God can fight for us, we must purify ourselves. Today we battle for God and on the day of battle we fast and repent. Remember! Do not forget this. Today, we do not eat. This day we fast."

Saul looked down at his troops and delivered a final ominous word of warning. "Let no man break this fast. For whoever eats this day, shall surely be put to death.

"Now, follow me into battle." Saul raised his spear high into the air. "We fight for God against the Philistines. Follow me!"

* * *

As the Philistines fled into the safety of a nearby wood, Jonathan signalled to Naphtali to stop.

"Let them run. Let them go the Philistine camp. Let them spread the news that Israelites are no longer fodder for Philistine swords and spears. We can achieve more by letting them live. Let their imagination do our fighting. We'll wait here till my father comes with his troops. From the noise we made and the sound of all those signals, we won't have to wait too long."

Jonathan and his armour bearer did not have wait too long for reinforcements to arrive. Some ten minutes later, Jonathan jumped on his horse that had been brought by one of his servants, and set off in hot pursuit of the fleeing Philistines.

THE PHILISTINE CAMP

The Philistine army had encamped about three miles to the north of the garrison with confidence and high spirits. Anticipating a swift and decisive victory, they only regarded their campaign as an opportunity for sword play, archery practice and looting and harassment.

Accompanying the Philistine warlords and senior officers were their wives and mistresses; and, in order to make an immediate profit from their certain victory over the Israelites, groups of merchants and traders. All looked forward eagerly to a share of the booty, woollen and linen garments, grain, silver and gold; and the most prized possession of all, Israelite slaves.

In the camp also, were scores of Israelite slaves who had been captured on previous Philistine raids. Forced to do all the menial tasks in the camp, they spent all their time in back-breaking tasks; fetching water, chopping wood and attending to all the needs of their masters.

So confident were the Philistines of their supremacy over the Israelites they did not consider these slaves as being any threat to their safety. Arrogantly believing that their domination of Israel would never be broken, they permitted these slaves to roam unguarded around their camp.

The presence of all these different elements in the camp generated an atmosphere that was more carnival than military. No one expected anything but a total rout of the Israelite forces.

A few hours after sunrise, the first survivors of the garrison rushed into the camp. In no uncertain terms, they broadcast the outcome of their battle in the garrison headquarters.

"Flee! Flee! The Israelites are fighting back. They've a huge army. They've thousands of armed soldiers. They've bribed the Amalekites and the Moabites to fight for them. Get out of here at once. Run for your lives."

The news spread like wildfire throughout the camp and immediately, the mood changed from picnic to panic. Everyone became concerned with his own flight to safety. All traces of self control were thrown away as the Philistines fled in despair and confusion, leaving behind a rich assortment of prize possessions that included—pack horses and camels for transporting their expected plunder and, even more important, weapons of war and destruction, swords, spears, arrows and shields.

The first people to make use of these abandoned weapons were the Israelite slaves. Quickly they seized the opportunity for freedom and revenge. They separated themselves from their panic stricken masters to form themselves into a fighting group, then, using the captured weapons, they fell upon anyone isolated from the fleeing Philistines.

*   *   *

Saul and his army of six hundred men were soon reinforced by those Israelites who had deserted his ranks at the first sight of the Philistine invaders. Sensing that the tide of fortune had miraculously turned in their favour, at the first sound of Saul's battle cry, they swiftly descended from their hiding places in the surrounding hills and harassed the retreating Philistines from all sides.

Jonathan astride his horse was particularly devastating in the slaying of the Philistines. Together with the rest of Saul's army, he pursued them into a nearby forest and relentlessly scythed them down.

But the day's effort was beginning to take its toll of his strength. The time was late in the afternoon and Jonathan had had no respite for over twelve hours.

In addition, since leaving the camp in the middle of the night he had nothing to eat. The only thing that kept Jonathan going was the excitement of the battle and the adrenaline flowing through his veins.

Without warning, the consequences of his superhuman effort suddenly overwhelmed him. As the pangs of hunger set his head reeling, he felt himself slowly slipping from off his horse.

*   *   *

In the forest, the dates on the trees were dripping in honey. But none of Saul's men, although also famished, attempted to taste it. They strictly observed the oath that Saul had placed on them.

Jonathan shook his head violently to keep himself awake. Then, since he was not aware of the oath made by his father, he stretched out his spear to a nearby date tree and coated its end with a thick layer of honey. He put the spear in his mouth and swallowed the honey.

The effect was immediate.

Jonathan revived. Miraculously, his eyes lit up and his strength returned. With renewed vigour, he prepared himself to continue the battle with the Philistines.

"You should not have eaten that honey," said a voice.

Jonathan looked round in puzzlement at the Israelite soldier who had rebuked him. "What have I done wrong?" he asked.

"Your father imposed an oath on every one fighting today. We are all duty bound to fast on the day of this battle. You have violated that oath."

"My father imposed an oath!?" Jonathan was astonished at his father's action. "Look round at the people. See how they are weak from hunger. My father has stained the land. He has undermined a great victory with such an oath. If only we could all have eaten, our victory would have been twice as decisive."

*   *   *

As night fell, Saul ordered his soldiers to return to camp and after they had eaten and rested, he ordered the High Priest to use the Urim V'Tumim to determine whether they should immediately pursue the Philistines

*　　*　　*

The Urim V'Tumim was a slip of parchment bearing the Divine name of God that the High Priest inserted within the folds of his garments just behind the sacred breastplate. Inset in this breastplate were twelve precious stones on which were engraved the names of the twelve tribes of Israel. Whenever God's advice was sought on behalf of Israel, the Urim V'Tumim, miraculously but cryptically, illuminated key letters in these names. The meaning of the coded message could only be given by the High Priest.

. Furthermore, only the king or his representatives could consult the Urim V'Tumim on matters of national interest.

The High Priest carried out the king's request but to Saul's amazement the Urim V'Tumim refused to respond. None of the letters were illuminated.

Saul was furious at the failure of the Urim V'Tumim to deliver a message. He realised that only a major sin would prevent the Urim V'Tumim from responding to a request from a High Priest on behalf of the monarch of Israel. "Who has committed a sin? Who has violated the oath? Who ate today?" he demanded of the people.

No one answered. Although, some of the people were aware that Jonathan had eaten in the woods, no one spoke. No one would inform on the man who brought about such a triumph for Israel.

"We shall soon discover who is responsible," said Saul. "We shall cast lots to see who the guilty person is. First we shall divide into two groups. In one group shall be the whole of Israel. In the other group shall be Jonathan and myself.

"Achiyah!" Saul addressed the High Priest. "Cast the first lot. Between Israel on one side. And Jonathan and myself on the other."

Achiyah cast the first lot; Saul and Jonathan were chosen.

Saul did not hesitate. "Cast the second lot," he ordered.

A hushed silence descended over the people of Israel as Achiya cast the second lot. Everybody was only too aware of the tragic consequences that would follow the outcome of this lottery.

"High Priest! Call out the name of the person chosen," Saul demanded. "Who has been chosen?"

Achiya picked up the lot and looked at it with disbelief. "Jonathan has been chosen," he said quietly.

The 'lot' has spoken," said Saul. "We must obey the command of the 'lot'. Jonathan has sinned and Jonathan shall die. The sentence will be carried out immediately."

"I am ready father," said Jonathan. "I have sinned. I ate of the honey in the forest. I am ready to die."

"No! No!" With one voice, the people of Israel shouted out. "No! No! Jonathan shall not die. Shall Jonathan, who has brought about such a great victory this day, die? God forbid that even one hair of his head shall fall to the ground for today he has fought with God."

Saul looked around him helplessly. Instinctively he knew he was powerless to fight the will of the people. Against his will he had to accept their verdict. On this occasion, the king had been vanquished and so Jonathan was redeemed and did not die.

*   *   *

"What has this story got to do with the Gibeonites, Daddy? Joel asked his father. "You haven't even mentioned them yet."

"I know. But the story of Jonathan and Saul teaches us something important in regards to the Gibeonites. It teaches us that a king cannot do what ever he wants. Whatever decree he makes must have the approval of the people. If the people are not happy with his decree, they can make him change his mind. So, if the people let a king's decree go through, this means they are happy with that decree. In that case, they have to accept the consequences of such a decree

"What do you mean by that, Daddy?"

"You'll soon see what I'm talking about. In the meantime, let's get on with the story."

THE GIBEONITES

About thirty years after the deaths of Saul and Jonathan, during the reign of King David, there was a drought. For three years in succession, no rain fell and the people of Israel became desperate for lack of food and drinking water.

Prayers for rain were said regularly and special sacrifices were brought in the Sanctuary. Fast days were held and vast amounts of charity were distributed among the poor. But the drought did not stop. Each day as the sun blazed down from a clear blue sky, more and more people suffered and died from thirst and starvation.

Finally, David decided to consult the Urim V'Tumim. He went to the Sanctuary and requested the High Priest to use the Urim V'Tumim to discover the reason for such a prolonged and deadly drought.

The answer astounded and alarmed him. The Urim V'Tumim informed him that Israel was being punished for the massacre of the priests of Nov by King Saul and for the effect it had on the Gibeonites.

David was only too painfully aware that Saul, believing the priests had committed treason by assisting him when he had been a fugitive, had ordered the execution of the Priests through one of his officers, Doeg. Now he was shocked to learn that the present disastrous drought was related to that tragedy.

Israel was not only being punished for the death of the priests, they were also being punished for the consequences of that massacre; the loss of the livelihood of the Gibeonites who had acted as hewers of wood and drawers of water for the priests of Nov.

*   *   *

Israel had to accept responsibility for that loss since many years earlier, Joshua had made a covenant with the Gibeonites in which he and the princes of Israel guaranteed their safety against attack and promised them a livelihood by acting as hewers of wood and drawers of water for the community. Although this covenant had obtained by deception, nevertheless, once it had been accepted by Israel, it became binding upon them and their children.

*   *   *

David acted immediately upon the information he had received from the Urim V'Tumim. He summoned the Gibeonites to his palace.

David's Palace

Ten representatives from the Gibeonites, all shabbily dressed and emaciated, stood in front of David seated on his throne. Like their ancestors of old who had tricked Joshua, they appeared to be in a state of extreme poverty and starvation. However, unlike their ancestors on this occasion, they were genuinely in distress.

David addressed them. "I understand you have a grievance against the people of Israel. What is your complaint?"

One of the Gibeonites stepped forward. His ragged clothes hung loosely upon his feeble body and heavy, deep, black lines encircled his eyes "Your majesty. Our grievance is against Saul and his family. We have no complaint against the people of Israel."

"Yet the nation of Israel is suffering through your grievance. First, tell me about your complaint against the family of Saul. Then we can try to lift this curse hanging over the heads of the people."

"Look at me," said the Gibeonite. "I have the body of a man of seventy. Yet I am only thirty five years old."

"Everybody is suffering from this drought," said David.

"I am not the victim of the drought," said the Gibeonite. "I am the victim of the massacre of the Priests of Nov."

"Explain!" commanded David.

"I was five years old at the time of the massacre. I was in Nov when Doeg, may his name be cursed, entered the city to wipe out all its inhabitants."

The Gibeonite hesitated as though fearful of recalling painful memories.

"Go on," gestured David. "Tell us what happened."

"I was in a house in the centre of the town with a friend. We had just finished chopping firewood in a nearby forest and we were bringing it into the house.

"Suddenly we heard the noise of shouting and screaming coming from the outskirts of the town. My friend went white. 'Quick! he said. They must have found the priests guilty of treason. Saul has come to punish them. We don't want to get caught.'

We both ran out of the house but I slipped on a loose piece of wood and badly sprained my ankle. I managed to get up but I could hardly walk. 'Hurry! said my friend. You must get out of here.

"I can't walk."

"I can't wait for you,' he said and he ran for his life.

"By the time I got up and tried to hobble away, the noise of the shouting and screaming got louder and louder. It was almost on top of me. I could hear the words so clearly. Women were shouting out frantically, 'Let my baby live! Please, please don't kill my husband! Have mercy!

"But the cries for mercy fell on deaf ears.

"Suddenly I was seized round my arms by a man. Never had I been held so tightly before. I thought he was going to squeeze the breath out of my body."

"Doeg?" asked David.

"No, someone else. I found out later that Doeg had brought his henchman to assist him. But they didn't do any killing. They blocked all the entrances and exits to the town and seized the priests. Only Doeg by himself murdered everyone he could find there.

"How did you survive?" asked David.

"When Doeg came towards me with his blood stained sword, I shouted out, 'I am not a priest. I'm a Gibeonite! Do not kill me! I am a loyal supporter of king Saul.'"

"A Gibeonite, a loyal supporter of King Saul?" Doeg snarled at me. "You deserve to die. But King Saul only commanded the wiping out of the priests of Nov. Torah law decrees you live. Let him go," he ordered the man.

"The man released me and I hobbled away as fast as I could.

Since that dreadful day, every time I close my eyes, by day or by night, I see Doeg's evil face. I see his bloody sword and I see the corpses of the priests lying in the streets. I still hear the screams of the dying and the wounded. Never shall I forget the heart rending appeals for mercy by the wives of the priests.

"Your majesty, you ask me to forgive. You ask me to have mercy. What mercy did Saul and Doeg have on that day? They murdered my masters. They stripped away my livelihood. They robbed me of my childhood. I can never forgive them.

"But these events happened thirty years ago," said David. "Why do you persist with this vendetta?"

"Those events are as fresh today as they were then. I cannot forget. I cannot forgive."

"Today Saul is dead," said David." Doeg is dead. Why should Israel suffer?"

"Israel allowed the massacre to take place. No one objected. No one protested. All Israel must bear the blame. We cannot forgive them."

The courtiers surrounding the king listened in horrified silence to the Gibeonite's account of the massacre of Nov. Some shifted uncomfortably from one foot to another. Others bit their lips and screwed up their eyes in a vain attempt to blot out the nightmarish scenes described by the Gibeonite.

"What do you seek from Israel?" asked David. "Compensation? We shall compensate you handsomely if you will forgive Israel and bring this drought to an end."

"We do not seek money. We seek justice. We demand the punishment of those who carried out this crime."

"Punishment of those who carried out this crime!?" cried out David. "As I've already said, Saul is dead. Doeg is dead. There is no one alive left to punish."

"But Saul's descendants live. Not one of them protested at Saul's decision to exterminate the priests of Nov. They must bear the responsibility for that crime."

"What exactly are you seeking?" David asked.

"In Torah it says, 'A life for a life. Only life can compensate for life. When you rob someone of his livelihood, you take away his life. Give us seven of Saul's descendants. Put their lives into our hands. Then we can forget. Then we can forgive."

David thought carefully before he replied. As King of Israel he had the power of life and death over his people but the request from the Gibeonites could not be easily resolved. If he handed over the descendants of Saul, he could be accused of acting out of self interest; of ridding himself of possible rivals to the throne of Israel. On the other hand, hundreds of people were dying every day because of the drought and he, as king, was responsible for ensuring their safety and well-being. He had no doubts that the drought was caused by the actions of Saul at Nov but—in order to stop the drought—was he permitted to sanction the death of a few selected people in order to ensure the survival of his nation.

"This is a hard thing you ask for, Gibeonite," said David. "I cannot take such a decision alone. I must consult with the Urim V'Tumim. I must seek advice from my counsellors. Come back tomorrow and you will have my decision."

The following day the Gibeonites returned to hear David's verdict. It was short and to the point. "We accept your case against Saul and Israel. The heavens themselves bear witness to the injustice you have suffered. Israel is being punished for the sin we have committed against you by violating the covenant of Joshua.

"We shall hand over to you seven of Saul's descendants. Do with them what you will."

Two days later it began to rain.

*   *   *

"Well Joel," said Harry. "That's the end of the story. Remember! Don't make promises and always keep your word."

"I'll try Daddy," said Joel, "but I shan't promise."

Harry smiled.

The capture of Jerusalem by King David and his army is recorded in the Book of Samuel but the details of this conquest are unclear. This story is based upon the commentary of Gersonides, the 14th century rabbinical scholar, mathematician and philosopher.

THE BLEMISHED HERO

Harry Gabriel could not tear himself away from the books littering his table. He had just started learning about a new character in the Bible and was totally absorbed in every word.

At times like these he would continue his studies for hours on end, without interruption. Food, drink and sleep were studiously forgotten as he delved deeper and deeper into the character of his subject.

Meals could be served, telephones ring, door bells buzz and hordes of children stampede through corridors and rooms. Yet Harry Gabriel was oblivious to their presence.

For Harry the learning of Bible took over every fibre of his being. No sound, disturbance or distraction could distract him.

Mrs Gabriel had once remarked to her husband. "You know, Harry. When you're learning Bible, I could pick you up in your chair, put you in a lorry, have you deposited in Heathrow Airport and send you anywhere I fancy.

"You're probably right," Harry would say. "But I'm sure there must be some way of getting through to me."

"I'm working on it," said Mrs Gabriel.

Eventually, Mrs Gabriel found a way of getting through to her husband and, used it with great effect. Desperate for her husband to have supper with the rest of the family, she took the bold step of shouting out loudly. "For the sake of family unity, leave everything and come to the table. Supper is ready. The family is waiting!"

To her surprise, Harry closed his Bible and immediately followed her to the dining room. "Family unity!" he kept murmuring. "Nothing stands in the way of "Family unity! By the way, Jacqui," he said to his wife. "Who taught you that?"

"You did. When you told us the story about Achitophel. So let's get started on the supper. I want the children in bed at a sensible time."

At the end of the second course, Harry expressed his appreciation for Jacqui's cooking. "I must admit there's a time for everything, including closing a Bible. That was really a wonderful meal, Jacqui."

"Thank you, Harry, I appreciate that. Now, since the way to a man's heart us is through his stomach, I wonder if you can do us a little favour."

"Of course, dear. Anything you ask. Up to half my kingdom and it is yours."

"I'll leave your half kingdom for some other time. Besides I wouldn't know what to do with it. In the meantime, I couldn't help noticing how engrossed you've been with your books over the last few days. Can we share some of your learning?"

"After such a supper, how can I say no. Over the last few days, I've been learning about someone whom some Rabbis considered to be a bit of a villain."

"And other Rabbis. What did they think of him?"

"They regard him as a saviour of Israel."

"A bit of a contrast."

"There's always two ways to look at things."

"So let's hear something about him. How did he live? How did he die?"

"Yes Daddy!" the children piped in. "How did he die?"

"You know what?" said Harry. "That's a good place to start the story. The last day of his life. The day that he died. And it was not a natural death."

"Who killed him?" asked Joel. "How did he kill him?"

"Hold on," said Jacqui. "We don't even know the name of the person. Already you want to know who killed him. Come on, Harry! Who are we talking about?"

"We're talking about King David's most famous general, Joab."

JOAB

Like wildfire the news spread throughout Jerusalem. Adonijah, David's first born had been executed by royal command.

King Solomon had wasted no time in securing his throne against usurpers. Almost immediately after burying his father David, Solomon had ordered the slaying of his own brother, Adonijah—and on the most flimsy of excuses.

Adonijah had wanted to marry one of David's ex wives and Solomon interpreted this request as an act of rebellion against his authority as King of

Israel. Without delay, he ordered Benaiah the son of Jehoiada, his military commander and chief judge to execute him as a traitor to the kingdom.

Joab was at home when he heard the news of Adonijah's execution. At first he could not believe that the thirteen year old Solomon could act so swiftly and decisively. Then reality set in. He looked at his wife with dismay. "Solomon has inherited his father's passion for blood, I can see. He won't stop at Adonijah. My name is on his list. David gave him clear instructions about me. 'Do not let him go peacefully to his grave'. All my life I've lived by the sword. And now the sword will follow me to the grave."

"Joab," said his wife, tearfully. "Put your sword away. You cannot fight an entire kingdom. The less blood now, the better. Go to Solomon and ask for mercy."

"Women always believe that everything can be settled with a smile and an apology. I'm afraid it's too late to ask for mercy. Solomon will never forgive me. He knows I was a supporter of Adonijah. But let me assure you of one thing. I have no intention of taking on Solomon and his army. You're right my dear. My days of swordsmanship are over. Instead, before I accept the inevitable, I shall fight Solomon with my head."

"What do you mean?"

"I have no time to explain. And for your own safety, it is better you know nothing of my immediate plans. All I know is I must not be captured here."

"Where are you going?"

"I cannot tell you. Who knows they might arrive here at any moment and force you to tell them where I went."

Joab took a long cloak from a peg in the wall, wrapped it around his head and shoulders and walked swiftly to the front door of his house. He turned briefly and looked tenderly at his wife. "Goodbye! I will not see you again. Do not over grieve for me. Marry again, as soon as possible." Briefly he squeezed her hand. "May God always watch over you and spare you from any more grief and sorrow."

With the sound of his wife's sobbing in his ears, Joab cautiously opened the door, looked round at both sides of the road and, on seeing it deserted, strode purposefully along its dry dusty surface. As he reached the end of the street and turned the corner, three heavily armed figures entered his house.

Joab, believing his pursuers were unaware of his intentions, was determined to avoid arrest before reaching his goal. Therefore, to make his way across the city, he kept well away from all the main roads in Jerusalem, choosing only the smallest paths and streets where he ran the least risk of detection. Eventually, he arrived at a large open space packed with people;

men, women and children from all over Israel. Joab had arrived at his destination.

Joab, still keeping his face and shoulders covered, vigorously pushed and shoved his way through the masses of people blocking his path.

"Hey! Shouted a man. "What do you think you're doing? We've been waiting here for hours. Take your turn like the rest of us."

Joab ignored the man's objections. He pushed him rudely aside and continued to batter his way through the crowd.

Another man objected to Joab's queue jumping. As Joab tried to push him aside, he stood his ground. "Don't push me. You're not getting past. Who do you think you are?"

Joab did not answer. He merely seized the man's wrist, squeezed it slightly, and prepared to hurl him aside.

The man, as tall and as broad as Joab himself, felt as if his wrist was held in a powerful vice. "Only one man in Israel has such strength and power," he said. "You must be Joab . . ."

"You do me no favours by mentioning my name," said Joab, as he put one hand over the man's mouth. "My life is in your hands. I beg you to remain silent."

The man nodded his head in agreement and Joab released him.

"My name is Simon," said the man. "I served under you in the campaign against Absolom. You saved my life on that occasion. I had been separated from the rest of my company and was about to be attacked by four of Absolom's soldiers. Singlehandedly, you despatched them one by one. I've never seen before or after such a display of swordsmanship and bravery. I had no chance at the time to thank you properly. You disappeared too quickly. Now I would like to repay that debt."

"Help me get through this crowd. That's all I ask."

With Simon's help, Joab made his was through the crowd till he passed through the curtained entrance leading to the final stage of his journey, the courtyard of the Sanctuary containing the copper altar that offered asylum from Solomon's pursuing soldiers.

Israelites were only allocated a small section of the Sanctuary courtyard. They were not permitted to enter the sacrificial area around the copper altar that stood immediately in front of the Holy of Holies. Only priests were permitted in that area.

Joab, although an Israelite, strode boldly into the sacrificial area and headed for the altar. "Where are you going?" shouted out a priest as Joab put his foot on the ramp leading to the top of the altar. You're not allowed to go up there."

At this stage, Joab had no intention of being deflected from his goal of asylum. "Stand aside!" he ordered the priest blocking his path.

"I will not stand aside. Israelites are not permitted in this part of the Sanctuary. You will be severely punished for trespassing in the holy places of the Sanctuary."

"Enough of this talk," snapped Joab. He rudely pushed the priest aside and sprinted up the ramp to the altar.

"Stop him!" the priest shouted out. "He is a trespasser. He is defiling the altar."

His cry was in vain. Joab reached the top of the ramp and seized the decorative horns that protruded from the altar. He threw off his cloak and shouted out for all to hear. "I claim asylum! Tell King Solomon, I claim asylum!"

*   *   *

Clutching the horns of the altar, Joab composed himself for a long and arduous ordeal. He was confident however that the matter would be settled before nightfall. His presence was a profanity in a Holy place. All ceremonies in the Sanctuary had come to a halt. His case would be treated with the utmost urgency.

Joab knew he would be executed. But to protect his family he wished to establish the reason for his execution.

Were he to be regarded as a rebel against the king, he would be executed without trial and all his assets confiscated. He would then be buried in a shameful manner and his family left penniless.

On the other hand, were a Court of Law to declare him guilty of the crime of murder, and then execute him, his property would be inherited by his heirs.

In addition, Joab wanted to be free of the curses that King David, believing he had treacherously slain Abner, the general of Saul, had placed on him at the time.

From the high vantage point at the top of the altar, Joab had a commanding view of all approaches to the Sanctuary and, every now and then, he anxiously scanned the curtained entrance for the first signs of Solomon's soldiers.

Before long his patience was rewarded. Three people marched imperiously through the crowd of curious bystanders gathered at the entrance to the Sanctuary and headed directly towards the ramp of the copper altar.

*   *   *

"Joab! Come down immediately! I have a warrant from King Solomon for your execution." The command came from Solomon's chief justice and Commander of his armed forces, Benaiah the son of Jehoiada. Two judges from the Supreme Court accompanied him and all three stood at the foot of the ramp, looking up at Joab.

"What is the charge against me?" demanded Joab.

"You are accused of the unlawful killing of Abner and Amasa. There are many witnesses who saw you carrying out this slaying. King Solomon had decreed you are guilty and be executed."

Instantly, Joab felt a sense of relief that no charge of treason would be brought against him for his support of Adonijah. But the curse of David still hung over his family and descendants. He had to protect them.

"King Solomon has found me guilty?" said Joab. "He has found me guilty without a trial? I demand the right to defend myself. These charges are false." Joab was fully aware that Solomon's greatest ambition was to build the Temple, a house of God dedicated to the highest spiritual values of the Torah. For this reason, Solomon's father David had been denied the honour of building the Temple. He had been considered to be a 'man of blood', someone whose reputation as a warrior did not fit in well with the House of God being a symbol of peace and friendship.

This symbol of peace and friendship was so important that in the subsequent building of the Temple, the sound of clanging metal, with its association with warfare and battle, would not be heard in the Temple courtyards.

Joab knew that Solomon would never tolerate the shedding of innocent blood in the Sanctuary, especially by the altar. His unwarranted death in the Sanctuary could easily destroy Solomon's ambition of building the Temple.

The two judges looked uneasily at Benaiah. They did not wish to be involved in an attempt to coerce Joab to come down from the altar. Solomon would be furious at any attempt to thwart his ambitions.

"You shall have your trial Joab," said Benaiah. "These two judges will question you about your motives for slaying those two men, Abner and Amasa." Benaiah beckoned to the younger of the judges. "Benjamin! Commence the proceedings!"

"Joab!" Benjamin called out. "Do you admit to the killing of Abner and Amasa?"

"I do. But I had good reason to do so."

"That is the purpose of this trial," said Benjamin. "To determine your motive. Was your slaying of these men, an act of murder without justification? Or was there a good reason for taking their lives? Joab! Are you ready to explain your actions?"

"I am."

"First let us establish a few facts," said Benjamin. "These facts will—in my opinion—demonstrate your motives were sinister and evil. Is it true, Joab that at the time you killed Abner he was the commander in chief of the armed forces of the Northern Tribes of Israel, the tribes that had been loyal to the late King Saul."

"Yes."

"And you were the commander in chief of the armed forces of King David."

"That is correct."

"Can you confirm that at that time, the political situation in Israel was as follows? After the death of King Saul there was a strong possibility that the Northern tribes would accept David as their king."

"That is also true."

"Now tell me Joab! In the event of the two armies merging whom—in your opinion—would have become the Commander in Chief of the united army. You or Abner?"

"You cannot limit the answer to those two possibilities."

"What other possibilities are there?"

"With all respects to your position, my learned judge, you might be an expert on Jewish Law. But you do not understand military matters. An army functions best when it receives its orders from officers with whom they are familiar. Were two armies to merge I would recommend retaining both Commander in Chiefs as joint leaders."

"Are you saying you could have worked alongside Abner?"

"Yes."

"But say David did not agree with you. Imagine David would have appointed Abner as Commander in Chief. Would you have accepted such a situation?"

"The question is academic. David never considered such a possibility and I never thought about such a matter. Besides, I always accepted David's decisions."

Benjamin looked at Joab incredulously. "I find it hard to believe that you would have meekly given up your position as Commander in Chief had David ordered it. No! That does not ring true. Abner was a threat to your position. You murdered him out of jealousy and fear; jealousy of a man who was your superior in Torah and military skills; and fear of losing your position as Commander in Chief of David's army."

"No" said Joab defiantly. "That is a lie. I had too much respect for Abner and David to kill him for such a reason."

"So tell us Joab! What your reason for killing Abner?"

Joab replied with venom in his voice. "I killed him as the avenger of the blood of my brother, Asahel. Abner killed my brother, Asahel in cold blood."

"In cold blood? You claim that Abner killed Asahel in cold blood?" Benjamin sounded most perplexed. "The slaying of your brother by Abner can hardly be called cold blood."

"That may be your opinion," said Joab "It is certainly not mine."

"In my opinion Abner did not kill Asahel in cold blood," said Benjamin. "It is common knowledge that your brother was pursuing Abner, at the time. He sought to take Abner's life. Abner was being pursued. Your brother was a pursuer and Abner was entitled to save his own life."

"But not at the expense of the life of my brother, Asahel." Joab spat out the words. "Abner murdered my brother, Asahel. Abner could have easily defended himself against any attack from my brother. Abner was no ordinary warrior. He was a fighter without equal. He could even have defeated Goliath had Saul given him permission to go. Abner was a murderer. He killed him with one thrust of his sword. Why? Why did he have to kill him? He could have disarmed him. He could have even wounded him. Abner had the skills to defend himself without killing my brother. No! Abner murdered my brother. He took his innocent life. And I, as the avenger of Asahel's blood, took the life of Abner."

Benjamin looked almost helplessly at Benaiah. "I cannot pursue this matter," he whispered to him. "There is insufficient evidence to assume that he is not telling the truth. He might well be innocent of the murder of Abner."

"In that case Joab," said Benaiah, "we shall drop the charge of the murder of Abner. We find you innocent of the cold-blooded murder of Abner. We shall now proceed to the second case. You are accused of the unjustified slaying of Amasa.

"Joseph!" he ordered the other judge. "Continue with the trial!"

"Joab!" called out Joseph. "You are accused of the cold-blooded murder of Amasa. Do you plead guilty or not guilty to the charge?"

"I am innocent of the crime of murder."

"But you do admit to the taking of his life."

"I do. But he was deserving of such a punishment."

"We shall see," said Benjamin. "We shall be the judges of his actions. Not you. We shall decide whether your motive for his killing was justified or not.

"Joab! At the outset, let us establish a few facts. I am going to ask you to answer a few questions about the events leading up to the death of Amasa."

Joab nodded his head in agreement. "Go ahead. I have nothing to hide. Yet, there is one favour I must ask of you first."

"A favour?" queried Benaiah.

"Yes a favour. I have been standing by this altar for the last four hours and I am anxious as you for the matter to be settled one way or the other. I beg you. I am parched from the heat of the sun and from the smoke of the sacrifices. Please let me have a sip of water."

Benaiah turned to look at the High Priest who was standing nearby, anxiously waiting for the trial to be concluded so that the Temple Service could be resumed as quickly as possible. "May he have a sip of water in the Temple?"

"Normally not," replied the High Priest. "But these are not normal times. I feel that in his case he may have some water to restore his strength and enable him to continue with the trial." He beckoned to one of the priests standing in the courtyard, listening to the verbal duel between Joab and his interrogators, and instructed him to fetch some water for the parched Joab.

The priest quickly did as he was instructed and Joab, after drinking from the water he brought him, indicated to the judge, Joseph to continue with the trial.

"Let us confirm a few facts at the outset, Joab," began Joseph. "At the time of your killing of Amasa, were you the Commander in Chief of King David's army?"

"No."

"Why not?"

"King David had appointed Amasa."

"The same Amasa who led Absolom's army in revolt against King David's army?"

"That is correct. Amasa was now the Commander in Chief of King David's army."

"In other words, you were demoted from your position as Commander in Chief of King David's army and Amasa was appointed in your place."

"Yes."

"You must have felt a strong sense of resentment at Amasa's appointment as Commander in Chief, a position that you had held for many years."

"Of course, I was upset at Amasa's appointment. But I did not resent him for his position. King David had ordered his appointment. I had too much respect for King David to harbour any resentment at Amasa's appointment. I have always accepted King David's authority and his decisions. King David in his wisdom had ordered Amasa to lead the campaign against the rebel Sheba the son of Bichri and I was willing to accept orders from him."

"Yet you killed him. You killed Amasa in cold blood. You pretended to offer him the hand of friendship. Instead you extended to him the hand of treachery and cunning. You murdered him with one thrust of your sword. You left him lying by the wayside to die cruelly and painfully, without dignity or honour. Your violent, inhuman action was the action of a person consumed with loathing, resentment and revenge. There can be no justification for your barbaric deed."

"I did not slay Amasa out of resentment," countered Joab. "Amasa was guilty of an act of treason. He had violated the trust of King David. He had failed to carry out his orders."

"Explain your words, Joab," demanded Joseph. "How was Amasa guilty of treason?"

"King David had appointed Amasa to raise an army to defeat the rebel, Sheba the son of Bichri who was a danger to the stability of peace and security in Israel. It was imperative that this threat should be removed as quickly as possible. Yet Amasa failed to appreciate the urgency of the situation. Amasa was commanded by King David to raise an army within three days. Amasa failed in this task. Three days had passed and no army was raised by Amasa. His actions were not befitting of a leader of Israel. He was guilty of treason against King David. He was a traitor to the interests of King David and Israel. A traitor has to be executed. That is the Law and that is the practice of Israel. I felt honoured to act on behalf of King David and Israel—to execute a traitor and to save Israel and King David from the rebel Sheba the son of Bichri."

Joseph looked hesitantly at Benaiah. "There does appear to be an element of justification in his argument," he whispered. "I need time to consider how to continue with the questioning."

"There is no time," replied Benaiah. "I will take over the questioning."

"Tell me, Joab," demanded Benaiah. "Are you aware of the reason for Amasa taking longer than three days to muster an army?"

"Whatever the reason, there can be no justification for such a delay in carrying out the orders of the king of Israel."

"You seem to have forgotten the Law, Joab. There is a justification. If the people are engaged in a matter of extreme urgency, then that matter takes precedence over the call to arms."

"No matter is more important than to the call to serve one's king and country. Amasa was guilty of treason. I executed him as a traitor."

"Joab!" chided Benaiah. "There is one matter that does take precedence over the call to arms. It is a matter that is the very soul and life force of our nation Israel. Even the king himself has to accept its priority of place in the affairs of the kingdom and State. That matter is the study of Torah. Amasa was delayed in raising an army because the warriors of King David were engaged in the study of Torah. David's army was about to fight their own flesh and blood. A civil war was about to take place. It was imperative that David's army knew the rules of engagement under such circumstances. They had to learn Torah.

"Joab!" announced Benaiah. "You had no justification in finding Amasa guilty of treason. Amasa acted according to the Laws and practices of the King and of Israel. We, therefore find you guilty of the charge of murder. You murdered Amasa in cold blood and King Solomon, as king over Israel, has decreed you must pay the full penalty. Come down from the altar. Confess to your crime and accept your punishment."

"I will not come down," countered Joab. "I will not accept a second punishment."

"A second punishment?" queried Benaiah. "Explain yourself. When were you punished for this crime?"

"King David has already punished me for slaying Abner. He cursed me. He cursed my father's house. He cursed my children. He condemned them to lives of illness, shame and pain; to lives of bodily impurity; to leprousy; to deformed limbs; to death in battle and to hunger and starvation. That punishment is worse than death. I will not accept a further punishment. I am innocent of the murder of Abner. The curses of David are unjustified. Tell King Solomon! If he wishes me to leave the safety of this altar, he must remove those curses from me and my children."

"King Solomon cannot help you in this matter. A curse cannot be removed."

"But it can be transferred. Tell King Solomon to accept my curses on to his own family."

"You expect King Solomon to condemn his own family to such curses. No man would willingly do so."

"Those are my conditions," insisted Joab. "If King Solomon wishes to avoid bloodshed and further desecration of the Sanctuary, he must remove David's curses from my family and children."

Benaiah had been instructed by Solomon to avoid at all costs the shedding of innocent blood in the Sanctuary. He had established Joab's guilt but he would have to wait a bit longer before executing him according to Solomon's command. "Very well, Joab," said Benaiah, "I will put your request before King Solomon. Before the day is done, we shall return with his decision."

* * *

The silence in the Sanctuary was unearthly. It seemed as if heaven and earth were holding their breath—waiting for the last moment of the drama in the Sanctuary to unfold.

Birds did not sing. The cattle awaiting slaughter did not low. No breeze ruffled the curtains at the entrance to the Sanctuary and the priests stood still, as though frozen to the ground.

Joab too was silent. He was aware of the need to complete the Sanctuary service before sundown and his presence at the altar was delaying the bringing of the afternoon sacrifice.

Joab closed his eyes and thought bitterly about the events that had brought him to this tragic end. After his death, how would he be remembered? Would he be regarded as a cold-blooded murderer or a lion hearted warrior?

Joab briefly let go of the horns of the altar and held up his hands to heaven and God. "Let my legacy to Israel be my good deeds," he prayed. "Let me be remembered for the battles I fought on behalf of David and his people. Let me be remembered for securing David's kingdom. Let me be remembered for the conquest of Jerusalem."

Joab closed his eyes and recalled the exploits that had secured Jerusalem for King David and Israel.

JERUSALEM

For just over three months David and his army had laid siege to the city of the Jebusites, the city that from the time of Joshua, had defied all attempts at its conquest; the city that, being strategically placed in the heart of Israel, divided his country into two; the city that—because of its height and situation—would give him absolute control and dominion over the central part of Israel; the city that would enable David to weld the tribes of Israel into a united and powerful nation.

David had to conquer Jerusalem. But how was he to achieve this? The city was surrounded on all sides by natural and artificial barriers, by insurmountable hills and by thick walls of massive stones. Only one point of access to the city existed; an entrance that was heavily guarded by what appeared to be an indestructible and impassable force, the blind and the lame.

The blind and the lame was the name given to two rows of wooden mechanical figures. Protected from rocks and stones by a metal, mesh curtain, they had been placed at the entrance to Jerusalem and equipped with razor sharp swords that whirled around in a circle of death of destruction. No one could pass them. Swords or spears either bounced off them or were sliced into pieces.

These mechanical sentries were powered by water flowing from a lake on the top of one of the hills on which Jerusalem then stood. At a point fifty metres below the level of the lake, the strength of this flow activated the rapid movements of the blind and the lame.

Two hundred metres from the walls of the city a temporary tent had been set up for David and his commanding officers. Alongside this tent, David and Joab, pacing up and down together, conferred with each other.

"Joab," said David, "the Jebusite defences are too strong for us. We're getting nowhere with this siege. Our men cannot scale the walls and hillsides. And they certainly can't get past the blind and the lame. Yet we must take Jerusalem. I feel we are destined to conquer it and establish it as our capital. But how? There must be a way. And this I promise you, Joab. Whoever dams up that stream of water and renders those accursed blind and lame powerless, that man will become the leader of my army.

"Tell me again, Joab! What happens when you hurl heavy rocks and stones at them? Perhaps we can find a weak link in their defences."

"Our men have to go round a sharp corner before they see those infernal blind and lame," said Joab. "And the passageway in front of them is so short they don't have the chance to smash them with rocks and stones. Besides they're protected by an iron mesh curtain."

"So tear down the curtain or climb over it," argued David. "As long as they keep a safe distance from the blind and the lame, they should be perfectly safe. Surely they're stuck to their places. They can't chase you away."

"They can attack us. They're on wheels. They can be propelled forward and attack our men. Besides, our men are exposed to attack from above. The Jebusites are quite fond of throwing rock and boiling oil down on our men. In that confined space they wouldn't stand a chance."

"Joab! I cannot continue to expose our men to such dangers. I am calling off the siege of Jerusalem."

"No!" said Joab firmly. "We shall find a way. Give me three more days."

"My commanding officers have had three months to find a way, Joab. Another three days will achieve nothing. I've had enough and the men have had enough. Look at them. They're restless and bored. They've lost their drive and interest. Look at what they're doing now. They're behaving like a bunch of schoolboys."

Joab looked towards the men grouped around a small grove of trees about one hundred metres from where they were standing. They had stripped off their armour and weapons and were competing in sporting activities.

"Watch me!" shouted out one soldier. "Watch how high I can jump."

The soldier sprinted towards a tree in the grove and as he passed beneath it he jumped up and attempted to touch one its branches that was about two and a half metres from the ground. His fingers failed to touch the branch and he fell to the ground.

"Watch me," shouted out another man. He too sprinted towards the tree and leaped up to the branch. "I touched it. I touched it," he shouted triumphantly.

"Touching it is nothing," said a third man, Naphtali. "The game is to hold on to it.

"Show us how to do it," someone said mockingly.

"I will," said Naphtali quietly.

Naphtali walked back until he stood at a distance of about ten metres from the branch of the tree. Then he closed his eyes momentarily, clenched his fists; raised them to his face and shook them slowly while concentrating on his task

The men around him fell silent as Naphtali leaned forward slightly and started his run. At one metre before the branch, he reached his full speed and with outstretched arms, launched himself high into the air. Both his hands firmly grasped the branch above him and as he fell to earth, the weight of his body bent the end of the branch down to the ground.

Naphtali landed lightly on his feet and, while still holding the branch, crouched low to the ground. "Now watch this," he called out to his admiring companions.

Naphtali released the branch from his hands and as it sprang back violently into the air, a small object was hurled into the sky, high over the tree. A score of eyes followed its curved aerial path until it eventually came to rest on the head of a soldier resting on a grassy patch not far from the tree.

Immediately the soldier sprang into the air; his hair and face covered with twigs, mud and broken eggshells from the bird's nest that Naphtali had dislodged from the branch. "Who threw this nest at me?" he shouted angrily.

Naphtali ran to the soldier's side. "It was an accident. I didn't realise there was a bird's nest in the branch. I apologise."

"That was no accident," roared the soldier. "You did it on purpose. I'm not going to be made a laughing stock by you, Naphtali."

Joab was watching the minor drama with amused interest, but, at the same time, felt something ticking away at the back of his mind. Suddenly he realised the importance of what he had seen.

"Your Majesty!" he said excitedly to David. "That bird's nest is the key to the conquest of Jerusalem."

"A bird's nest? A bird's nest is the key to the conquest of Jerusalem? We're going to overpower the Jebusites by hurling bird's nests at them? Joab! What are you talking about?"

"You saw the way that bird's nest was thrown into the air. You saw the power you can get by bending a branch. Imagine the branch was thicker and longer. Imagine it was a tree. Not three metres long. But thirty metres long. The power you could get from that tree would throw more than a bird's nest into the air. It could hurl a man—a fully-grown man and his weapons—anywhere you care to place him. It could even place him on top of those walls over there. It could even place him by the lake used by the Jebusites to control their blind and lame monsters."

"Joab! You have a powerful imagination. But we are two hundred metres away from the walls of the city. Do you propose planting a tree a bit nearer and coming back in fifteen years time?"

"No, your Majesty. I don't. The trees are in place already. Around the other side of the city there are a number of cypress trees within ten metres of the walls. Some of them are higher than the walls. What's more I've climbed one of the trees and saw clearly the terrain at the top of the wall. It's flat and grassy. A man could land there without injury."

"You propose using a cypress tree as a catapult to land our men inside their city?"

"Yes."

"Joab! You're mad."

"And when you volunteered to fight Goliath; that was not madness. I volunteer to be the first one to be catapulted into enemy territory."

"Joab! Show me the trees you are talking about. But before you do it. Put a stop to the fighting going on down there."

Joab pulled out a trumpet from his tunic and blew three loud blasts. Immediately, the fighting stopped and the men lined up in orderly rows awaiting further instructions from their platoon commander, Joab.

*   *   *

"Let me say at the outset that I know exactly how you are feeling," said Joab to the assembled soldiers. "We all expected a quick and decisive battle to conquer Jerusalem. It hasn't turned out that way. The blind and the lame have—so far—proved too strong for us. But King David believes and I also believe that it is our destiny to conquer Jerusalem; to establish a city that will unite all Israel into one nation. We shall defeat Jerusalem. We shall defeat the Jebusites. And we shall defeat the blind and the lame. This is our plan . . . ."

*   *   *

Two hours after this meeting, David's army assembled again—outside one of the walls of Jerusalem—opposite the entrance guarded by the blind and the lame.

Row upon row of soldiers in full battledress lined up parallel to this wall of the city. All were equipped with bows and arrows, swords, spears and shields.

From the wall of the city, a sea of faces looked down at David's men and as the news of this gathering of David's army spread throughout the city, more and more Jebusites gathered at the wall.

Weavers left their looms, tailors threw down their scissors and needles, tanners ran away from their skins and hides, sentries and watchers on the other walls of the city abandoned their posts and most of the officers supervising the flow of water to the blind and the lame joined the throng gathering at the wall of the city

At the centre of each of the rows of David's soldiers, two men raised a trumpet to their lips and trumpeted out a long, loud and steady blast. Immediately the men on each side of them stepped four paces sideways so that a gap appeared in the ranks of each row.

The trumpeters blasted out another long note on the trumpet and, from the rear of the rows, David, accompanied by two of his generals, Ittai and Abishai began to walk slowly through the gap till they reached the front of the assembled army.

The trumpet was sounded a third time and Ittai called out to the crowd of curious and anxious Jebusites peering over the walls of Jerusalem. "We wish you no harm. We wish to live together with you in peace. Listen carefully to what we can offer you . . . ."

*   *   *

On the far side of the city, by the cypress trees that stood alongside the walls of Jerusalem, Joab issued careful and precise orders to the small platoon of soldiers and artisans that had accompanied him on his daring mission. "Our task is to use one these trees as a catapult to propel one of our men on to the walls of Jerusalem."

The men looked at each in wonderment and Joab added. "I shall be the sling shot in the catapult. With God's help we shall succeed. In the meantime this is what we have to do." Joab pointed to a tree that stood about ten metres from the wall of the city. "I want that tree to have all its branches trimmed off. But not right back to the trunk. Make sure you leave some part of each branch sticking out from the trunk. The tree must be easy to climb. Try to make as little noise as possible."

Joab watched anxiously as his men set to work with saws and axes climbing higher and higher up the tree until all its branches were trimmed back to within a third of a metre from its trunk. He felt certain that the thudding sound of pounding axes and falling timber would signal a horde of Jebusites to flock to the wall of Jerusalem opposite the grove of cypress trees and defend it from attack.

But no Jebusite figure appeared on the top of the wall and the lookout that Joab had posted on top of another tree did not report any human movement at the top of the wall.

Finally the work was finished. The cypress tree stood erect as a flagpole, its clothing of leaves and branches in an untidy heap at its foot.

Joab turned to his men. "One man will climb this tree and fasten one end of a rope to the highest point he can reach. We shall be holding the other end of the rope and when he has descended to the ground, we shall bend the tree into the shape of a bow."

"I volunteer to ascend the tree," said one man, Gideon. "I have a head for heights."

"Good!" said Joab. "But be careful. Don't take any unnecessary risks and make sure the rope is fastened securely."

Gideon took one end of the rope, tied it around his waist and, like a mountain goat, swiftly and surely, climbed the tree till he reached a point slightly higher than the level of the wall of the Jerusalem that stood opposite him. "It's not safe to go higher," he called out to the men craning their necks towards him.

"Then fasten it there," commanded Joab. "And come down."

As soon as Gideon reached the ground, Joab first tested the strength of the rope by tugging it firmly; then ordered fifteen of his men to stand ten metres from the base of the tree and slowly pull the rope down.

The pressure of the rope caused the tree to bend from a point on the trunk about five metres from its top and Joab knew this would not be sufficient to hurl him on to the top of the wall. "If we pull it any harder," he said, "we shall snap the trunk. We must pull the top further down."

"There's only one way," said Gideon. "This is what you have to do . . . ."

*   *   *

"If we could live together in peace," Ittai called out to the Jebusites, "we could both benefit. Both our people would be free of the burden and expense of war with their neighbours. If your city was incorporated into our kingdom it will give added strength to both our nations. You will be better protected and we shall be in a better position to offer that protection. As you can see, we have the equipment and the men to guarantee your safety from your enemies. Let us show you what they can do."

Ittai stepped back and two men in the front row blasted out a note on their trumpets. Immediately, three men stepped forward from the ranks. Two of the men carried dummies made of straw, which they set up in the clearing in front of David's assembled men.

There was a space of about ten metres between the two straw dummies, which were lined up parallel to the rows of the assembled army.

The other man, after taking up a position about fifty metres from the first straw dummy, took off the bow from his back, placed an arrow against the taut, stretched bow string and, in an almost casual manner, shot the arrow towards the straw dummy.

The arrow pierced the centre of the dummy's body, emerged on the other side and embedded itself in the centre of the second dummy.

"We have one thousand archers in our army," the general announced. "Each one can hit his target from a hundred paces. If you make a treaty with us, you too will enjoy the strength of their protection."

"What's in this treaty of yours?" a voice bawled out from the walls. "What do you want from us?"

"We want peace with a God fearing people. With people who fear the God of Israel.

"Show us your God." the voice demanded. "What does he look like? Show us his image."

"Our God has no image. Yet he is all powerful and He can protect you when you worship Him."

"All powerful?" someone laughed. "But he can't defeat the blind and the lame. We don't need your God."

"Where is Joab," David whispered to his general. "What's keeping him? What's he doing now? In the meantime, put on another show for these people.

*   *   *

"The tree is too thick in the middle," said Gideon. "It will never bend as it is. It must be made thinner. I know exactly what to do. Do I have your permission to ask the men to perform some surgery on this tree?"

Joab nodded his assent to Aaron's request and watched impatiently as he waited for his men to complete their sawing and chiselling on the trunk of the cypress tree. "How's it going?" he kept asking, dreading the possibility of his lookout reporting any Jebusite movement on the wall opposite them. "How much longer will you be?"

"Patience," urged Aaron. "These men are working as fast as they can. I'm sure it won't be long now."

Eventually, Joab heard the answer he was waiting for. "We've finished," said one of the men on the tree. "We've reduced the thickness of the trunk by about a half. We're coming down now. This time it should work."

The men swiftly descended the tree and Joab instructed his men to begin pulling on the rope again. To their delight, the tree, under the relentless pressure of their combined strength, slowly began to curve from a point below the middle of the trunk. Eventually, the top of the tree was lowered to a few feet from the ground.

"That should do it," said Joab. "Now hold it firm while we strap this chair we brought to the top of the tree."

With the men on the rope straining against the tension in the arched tree, Joab prepared himself to climb on to the chair but Naphtali stopped him.

"I must make a suggestion before you carry out the next part of your mission," Naphtali said firmly. "You must be aware that in an operation of this sort, correct timing is crucial. If you release your grip too early, you will not have sufficient impetus to reach the wall of Jerusalem. Too late, when the top of the tree is arching towards the ground, you will be hurled headlong into the wall. You must have the presence of mind to release your grip when the tree is nearly upright."

"I understand," said Joab. "So what is your suggestion?"

"I suggest you do not climb on to the tree immediately. Have a test run first. Someone will organise the men to release the rope simultaneously. At that moment of release, you will start counting. Take note of the time taken for the tree to reach the top of its swing and also when the tree reaches the end of its swing.

"Naphtali! I accept your suggestion. Take charge now."

Naphtali positioned himself alongside the men holding the rope and addressed them. "Men! We shall now count back slowly from ten to zero. As we start the word zero each one of you will immediately let go of the rope. Joab! You will start your count at the same time. Are you all ready?"

"We're all ready," the men replied.

"Good! Now count with me. Ten, nine, eight, seven, six, five, four, three, two, one, zero."

Simultaneously, each man released the rope from his hand and like a stone fired from a catapult, the end of the tree shot into the air, arched over slightly towards the wall of Jerusalem and, for a few moments, quivered violently like an arrow that had just struck its target.

"I counted two," said Joab to Naphtali. "That's when it came to the end its flight and began springing back. One will be sufficient for my purpose. Come let's get started."

Naphtali supervised the men, as once more they took hold of the rope and slowly but steadily bent it back until it was only a metre above the ground.

"There's one other thing we must do," said Naphtali. "We must give Joab as much protection as possible. We must cushion him against injury. That's why I have arranged for Ehud to collect a number of thick sheep fleeces."

Naphtali picked up one fleece and ordered one of his men to wrap it around one of Joab's legs. A second fleece was used for the other leg and then more fleeces for the rest of Joab's body.

"Well done, men," said Naphtali eventually. "Now let's get this snowman on to the chair and prepare him for take-off."

Joab, with some assistance from Gideon and his men, climbed on to the chair and held firmly on to its arms. "I'm ready," he said to his men.

"Right men," said Naphtali. "This time it's for real. May God be with Joab and us? We shall now count back slowly from ten to zero. Remember! As we start the word zero each one of you will immediately let go of the rope. Are you all ready?"

"We're ready," the men replied.

Naphtali looked up at Joab. "Are you ready, Sir?"

Joab hesitated. He looked down at the men straining to restrain the rope and suddenly realised the scale of the gamble he was about to undertake. The odds against success were enormous. There was only a remote possibility he would end up a hero, a saviour of Israel. But there was a far stronger possibility; he would end up as a corpse. Or worse still, he could be maimed or crippled for life.

It was too late to back out now. He had cast his die and had to follow it through. There was no turning back. The badge of cowardice would never be worn on Joab's tunic.

"God!" prayed Joab quietly. "Let my mission be successful. Be with me, O' God and guard me from all troubles."

"Are you ready, Sir?" Naphtali asked again.

"I am ready, Naphtali." said Joab, closing his eyes. "Start the countdown."

"Yes, Sir! Now remember. Count with me!" Naphtali looked at the men and began his count. "Ten, nine, eight, seven, six, five, four, three, two, one. Zero!"

Once again, all the men, at the same time, released the rope from their hands and the end of the tree, with Joab on his chair, shot into the air.

At the count of zero, Joab forced himself to ignore the sudden violent thrust on his body as, through gritted teeth, he counted the number 'one'. Then he released his grip on the arms of his chair.

Twenty pairs of anxious eyes followed the figure of Joab as he hurtled towards the wall of Jerusalem, and then disappeared from view. "He's cleared the wall," shouted a jubilant Naphtali. "Pray God, he comes down safely."

*   *   *

"You will soon see the power of our God," the general announced to the Jebusites. "He defeated the Philistines and the Amalekites. He humbled the Egyptians and He split the Red Sea. He will overthrow the blind and the lame. He has many messengers.

"Show us his messengers!" a voice shouted out from the top of the wall.

"We are his messengers. We, the people of Israel are his messengers. We shall show you something of his strength." Ittai raised one of his hands into the air and six men stepped forward from the first row of David's assembled army.

Each of these men carried a sword in one hand and a shield in the other. "These men are but a small part of the army of the God of Israel," Ittai declared. "They will demonstrate the art and skill of attack and defence."

Two of the men stood back to back, their swords and shields poised to defend themselves. The other four men formed a circle around them, at a distance of about three metres.

"Let the battle commence!" commanded Ittai.

Immediately, the four attackers, waiting an opportunity to lunge at their opponents, slowly circled the two defenders.

Suddenly, one of the men in the outer circle roared out a signal and the four men, with outstretched swords, advanced swiftly towards their opponents.

The defenders held their ground. With their swords in their right hands, they skilfully deflected the sword thrusts of two of their opponents. And with their shield in their left hands, they blocked the lunges of their other two opponents.

The two defenders appeared to possess eyes, like a fly, that could see in different directions at the same time. And like a fly, they had the ability and agility to avoid any blow directed at them.

They also had an uncanny ability of unified action. Their movements together were perfectly synchronised. When one turned in one direction, the other matched his movement. It was as though the two men were Siamese twins, joined together at the waist and able to read each other's minds. As they continuously circled to face their attackers, their outstretched swords always appeared to be in a straight line.

Suddenly, the two defenders let out a piercing shriek, stretched out their arms with their shields, jumped forward and whirled violently around.

The whirling shields smashed against two of their opponents, sending them sprawling to the ground, and sending their swords flying into the air.

David's soldiers burst into applause at this spectacular manoeuvre. Shouts of 'bravo' and 'well done' echoed round the plain in front of the walls of Jerusalem. Even some of the Jebusite children joined in the cheering and clapping but their parents and older brothers quickly silenced them.

Ittai stepped forward and held up his hand in a signal for the contest to stop. "What say you Jebusites?" he called out to the enthralled watchers on the wall. "Can you match the strength of our warriors?"

"Can they match the strength of the blind and the lame?" a voice called out.

"Bring them out here!" shouted out one of the soldiers.

"Where is Joab?" muttered David under his breath. "What's keeping him?"

*   *   *

"Can you see him?" Naphtali looked up to the watcher on the top of the other tree. "What's happening?"

"He must have rolled into a ditch," came back the reply. "I've lost sight of him. Hold on! Wait a minute. I can see something moving. It's Joab! He's all right. He's walking back to the wall."

"There he is." The smile on Naphtali's face was as wide as Lake Kinneret. "Blessed be the God of Israel. You're safe. Who shall we send over next?"

"No one," said Joab. "You're all coming over."

"All of us? But who'll hold the tree back?"

"No one," said Joab. "Miracles don't work twice. It was only a miracle I landed here safely. You'll come over the safe way. Attach a rope to an arrow and shoot it across to me. There's a small bush here to which I can tie it. Fasten the other end to the cypress tree. After that you can all swing across. Bring all your weapons with you."

Naphtali nodded his head in a sign of consent and immediately he and his men carried out Joab's orders.

One man shot an arrow with one end of the rope to Joab, another fastened the other end to the top of the tree and the remainder, with all their weapons, climbed to the top of the tree and swung across the rope to the wall of Jerusalem. Within five minutes, they were all in enemy territory standing around Joab and awaiting further instructions.

"Our target," said Joab to his men, "is to seize control of the lake that supplies the water to power the blind and the lame. Once we cut off their water supply, the blind and the lame will be paralysed. The city will be ours. Follow me!"

Joab led his men away from the wall of Jerusalem, across a grassy plain, until they came to a path leading down to the lower level of the city. Joab halted his men and instructed them to remain silent while he sent Aaron to explore the pathway just below and ahead of them.

On Aaron's return, he reported to Joab. "Alongside this path, about ten metres below, is the lake you were talking about. The width of the lake at its far end is about two metres wide. Two men are standing there. They are the guardians of the block of wood that controls the flow of water to the blind and the lame. When the block is raised, the water gushes out and drives the swords of the blind and the lame. When the block is lowered, the blinds and the lame are motionless."

"Well done," said Joab to Aaron. "So! Just two men stand between us and the conquest of Jerusalem. Asher! Zebulun! You are the best two archers in our group. Follow Aaron along that path and make sure your arrows find their target. We don't want the Jebusites to have any hint of our presence here.

Joab and his men did not hear the three men cautiously creep down the path to their target. But they did hear the twang of their bowstrings as they released their arrows. They also heard the dull thud of the impact of the arrowheads on the bodies of the unsuspecting Jebusite guards and the sound of two heavy objects splashing into water.

Minutes later, a jubilant Aaron returned to Joab. "The guards are dead. The lake is ours."

"Well done!" said Joab to Aaron. "Now let's finish the job. Men! Follow me."

Joab and his platoon strode quickly down the pathway to the far end of the lake where the block of wood, like the fin of a shark, protruded above the surface of the water.

"This block of wood controls the blind and the lame," said Aaron to Joab and his men as they stood at the side of lake. "As you can see, even now there is sufficient flow of water to the blind and the lame to make them have some movement. And it's fairly easy to increase the flow. One just has to raise the block of wood and the water will start gushing out. Here you can see the ropes that control it."

"We want to stop the flow completely," Joab said to Aaron. "How do we do it? How can we demonstrate that the blind and the lame are now powerless?"

"First we have to lower this block of wood to the bottom of the lake. Then we have to divert the water pressure towards a different direction. Look over there!" Aaron pointed to another part of the water's surface where the edge of the lake narrowed to a width of just one metre. "Over there is another block. And you can see the ropes and controls to raise and lower it. I imagine that water is used by the Jebusites for their personal use and to irrigate their fields."

"Let's get to work," said Joab to his platoon. "We haven't finished pulling on ropes today. But when the day is done, you will be the heroes of Israel."

After placing their weapons by the side of the lake, Joab's men set themselves to the task of lowering the block of wood that supplied the water to the blind and the lame. Pulling the rope firmly, they watched joyfully as the top edge of the block of wood slowly sank towards the surface of the lake till it blocked the supply of water to the blind and the lame.

After a few moments, Joab was satisfied that only a small trickle was passing under the block, then he and his men raised the other block and sent a flow of water cascading down the other channel.

"Now we shall inform King David that God has blessed us with success," said Joab, taking out his trumpet from the belt of his tunic and placing it to his lips.

* * *

The sound of the trumpet electrified the ranks of David's army by the wall of Jerusalem. Each man recognised the triumphant tone of victory being blasted out by Joab. "He's done it," exclaimed David excitedly. "He's defeated the blind and the lame. Ittai! Tell the Jebusites our God is an All Powerful God. Tell them he has defeated the blind and the lame. Tell them if they throw down their and arms and surrender, we shall spare their lives."

* * *

"Joab! Joab! King Solomon has made his decision."

Joab opened his eyes and looked down from the altar where he was standing. He saw below him the figure of Benaiah accompanied by two judges from the court of King Solomon. "How did King Solomon reply to my request?" Joab asked.

"King Solomon agrees to your request. He will accept his father's curses upon himself and his family. Remove your hands from the horns of the altar. Joab! Accept your punishment."

For a brief moment Joab tightened his grip on the altar and looked up towards the heavens. "Thank you O' God of Israel! I pray my deeds will be remembered for good."

Joab then held up his hands in the air and calmly watched Benaiah, ascending the ramp towards the top of the altar.

Sources: Samuel 2. 5:6
          Chronicles 1.11:6

THE REBELLION

The Gabriel family were sitting together at the dining table. They had just finished supper and were about send their youngest child, Joel, to bed. Joel, however, was a genius at delaying his bedtime. His questions were short and simple. But the answers could take hours.

"Who was David's most dangerous enemy?" Joel asked. "Which person came closest to destroying him?"

Harry looked at his son. "One has to know the book of Samuel pretty well to answer that question. It would also help to look into Midrash and read the stories the sages wrote about David.

"Daddy, you know the books of Samuel and Midrash pretty well. Please give me an answer."

"It's quite late you know Joel. It's time you were in bed. Why do you always wait till the last moment to spring these questions on me?"

"I wanted to ask you all day. But I didn't have a chance. Make it a quick answer. I promise I'll go to bed straight away." Joel knew his father well. Once he got started he would never finish till the end of the story.

"All right. A quick answer. It wasn't Goliath."

"Why not?"

"Of course, Goliath was a tough opponent. He was a giant with tremendous strength. But that's all he had, height, muscles and a very long reach. Goliath could never be considered to be David's most dangerous opponent.

"So if it wasn't Goliath. Who was it then?"

"David had many enemies. But to be really dangerous, you need something more than just big muscles and a long spear."

"Such as?"

"Intelligence for a start. You have to be clever. You also have to have powerful ambitions."

"What does that mean?"

"You have to be fired up with an irresistible urge to do something. You have to be prepared to push aside anything or anybody that gets in the way of those ambitions. And there's another thing that makes someone dangerous.

"What's that?

The desire for revenge. You want to punish someone for a wrong you believe he has done you."

"Like Esau wanting to kill Jacob for taking his blessings."

"Something like that."

"What else makes a person dangerous, daddy?"

"Having respect for your opponent gives him an extra advantage. It weakens a person's confidence. When fighting you cannot afford to hold your opponent in high esteem. In a nutshell, someone's most dangerous enemy has to be intelligent, ambitious, vengeful and, at the same time, highly respected."

"So whom do you have in mind, daddy? Who did become David's enemy? Which one of David's enemies had all these qualities?"

"Only one person had all these qualities, Achitophel!"

"Achitophel? Never heard of him. Who was he? Tell me something about Achitophel, daddy."

"Achitophel was David's teacher. He taught him Torah. He taught him wisdom. And he taught him statesmanship. David had the greatest of respect for him. He actually called him my master, my honoured one, and my superior."

"Wow!"

"So if David was his pupil, you can be certain Achitophel was highly intelligent. He was also ambitious and at the same time he was seeking revenge for a wrong he believed David had committed. Yes, I would say, David's most dangerous enemy was his teacher, Achitophel."

Just then, Joel's mother, Jacqui came in furiously from the kitchen. She looked at her husband sharply. "Harry, it's getting late. It's way past Joel's bedtime."

"Don't worry, Jacqui. I won't be long. Let me tell you a Midrash first. But remember, Joel! A Midrash is a story by the Rabbis that gives us a deeper insight into a person's motives and character. This Midrash will give you some idea of who and what Achitophel was. Afterwards we'll go through the Achitophel stories in the Book of Samuel.

THE MIDRASH OF THE TEMPLE FOUNDATIONS

David had been informed by the prophet Gad that he would not build the Temple. Nevertheless, he was determined to lay the foundations for the magnificent building that would be built by his son Solomon. David knew there could be only one place to build a house for God—the top of a mountain. Israel had to go up to God in order to serve Him.

So, at the top of the highest mountain near the city of David, David himself prepared the foundations for the Temple. He took a pickaxe and began to hew out a gigantic hole in the mountainside. With each swing of his axe, deeper and deeper he went into the mountain, shattering the rocky surface into tiny pieces. He had been denied the honour of building the Temple. But he was determined to lay the foundations for the building that would bring glory to the name of God.

The foundations had to be deep and strong. They had to support the massive stones of the Temple. They also had to contain the drainage system that served the offerings on the altar. The blood of thousands of sacrifices and gallons of wine would flow through them. It was essential for the house of God to be a model of godliness and cleanliness.

After one hour of digging, David paused for breath. He stopped swinging his axe, stood upright and looked around the pit he had dug.

The surface on which he stood was almost completely levelled. Only one small bump spoiled its smoothness. By his feet, a small pot-shaped stone jutted upwards. When that stone was removed the first phase of the digging of the foundations would be complete.

David stepped back two paces and raised his axe to complete his task.

"Stop!" David heard a voice addressing him. "Do not move me."

David looked around. Who was speaking? No one was in sight. The voice could only have come from the stone.

David looked down at the stone. "You dare to tell me to stop. I am building a house for the glory of the God of Israel. No stone is going to prevent me from glorifying God."

"You may not lay the foundations for the House of God. Do not move me."

"No stone will dictate to the king of Israel," said David, preparing to swing his axe.

"Do not move me. I am no ordinary stone. I am the Even Shesiyah. I am the stone of the fountains of the deep. Remove me and you will flood the earth. You will destroy mankind."

"The glory of the Temple will protect me."

"Do not move me. I was placed here at the time of the Creation to hold back the waters of the deep. There is no greater glory than listening to the words of God."

"I will decide how God's name should be glorified." David ignored the stone's objections and swung down his axe.

The jet of water that whooshed out from beneath the stone knocked David backwards on to the ground. By the time he got to his feet, he was soaked from head to toe. He looked in amazement as the water level rose higher and higher up his body.

"Help!" he shouted out to the group of men looking down at his plight in the pit. "Nathan! Gad! Achitophel! Help me. I have sinned. I have moved the Even Shesiyah. Stop this flow of water."

David's request was met with silence. No one was able to offer any advice.

"The whole of mankind is threatened by these waters," said David. "We must save them. In the name of God, I command you, stop!" David shouted out the ineffable name of God to the raging waters and the response was immediate. The waters stopped rising.

But David's relief was short-lived. Within seconds, the waters began to rise as before.

Again, David shouted out the name of God. "Stop! I command you." Again the waters stopped rising.

"There's only one way to stop these waters," David reasoned. "By using the name of God. But I can't stay here forever shouting out the Divine name. Tell me! Nathan, Gad. Will I be permitted to destroy God's name to save mankind and myself? Can I write the name of God on a piece of earthenware and cast them into the waters?"

There was no response from the three men. Again, they were unable to give an answer.

"Achitophel, you are my chief counsellor. You must know the Law. What is your advice?"

Achitophel scratched thoughtfully at his beard while pondering the possibilities that David's plight had created. Were David to drown, he was sure the crown of Israel would fall on his head. He knew that David's solution to quelling the raging waters was permitted. So there was no need to hurry. This was an opportunity to grasp and savour. He could afford to play for time. "Wisdom bows before prophecy," he said with feigned humility. "Let the prophets of Israel speak. Let them consult the oracle of the Urim V'Tumim. The jewels on the breastplate of the High Priest of Israel will give them the answer."

"The Urim V'Tumim is not available on this mountain," said Nathan, at last finding his voice. "By the time we return to Jerusalem it will be too late. We are at a loss to know how to save Israel and ourselves from destruction."

"This is no time for modesty, Achitophel," said Gad. "Advise us what to do."

Achitophel hesitated, calmly watching the water creeping further and further up the body of the helpless David.

"Achitophel!" David transfixed Achitophel with his eyes; eyes that possessed the power of life and death, eyes that could reduce stone into water and creatures into ashes. The eyes of David bored into Achitophel. They pierced his soul penetrating his mind. "I demand you advise me. Who ever can advise me and fails to do so, let that person be strangled."

The supernatural powers of David's eyes terrified Achitophel. He knew his bid for the throne of Israel would have to wait. "Your majesty, there is but one chance. As you say, we must call upon Divine forces to calm the waters. Only God can bring safety and peace to mankind."

"But can one destroy God's name to achieve this? Be quick, Achitophel. There is no time left for hesitation."

"God is showing His displeasure to Israel," said Achitophel. "He believes we have been unfaithful to Him. We are like a wife who has been unfaithful to her husband. The peace of His universe has been disturbed. To restore the peace between husband and wife, one is commanded to write down the name of God and cast it into the bitter waters. Even though the name of God will be destroyed, God forgives the destruction of His name in order to preserve the peace that should exist between husband and wife. If this desecration is permitted to promote peace between husband and wife, how much more so is it permitted to promote peace and security among mankind.

"You are right, O' King of Israel. The name of God must be written down on earthenware. It must be cast into the waters. The name will be destroyed. Then the waters will return to the place from where they came."

David looked at his two prophets. "Does the word of prophecy agree with the words of wisdom?"

The two prophets nodded gravely.

"Very well Achitophel," said David. "Write down the name of God on a piece of earthenware. Cast it into the waters."

Carefully supervised by the two prophets, Achitophel inscribed the ineffable name of God onto a shard of earthenware. Then he drew back his hand and hurled it into the raging waters. It sank like a stone and with unerring accuracy plugged the hole where the stone had stood.

David immediately felt a lessening in the upward surge of the waters around his body. Within minutes they dropped to the bottom of the pit and David once more stood firmly on his feet.

The waters, however, did not stop receding. As though angry at being disturbed, they continued to retreat beneath the earth. Before long the effect of its withdrawal from the earth's surface became evident. The grass turned brown and withered. The leaves of the trees became hard and brittle. Giant cracks disfigured the mud beds of the dry wadis and rivers.

"I have sinned," exclaimed David. "The waters have receded sixteen degrees too far. The land has become parched. Mankind is now in danger of drought. Let them not be destroyed through my folly."

In a state of anguish and despair David composed a psalm of praise to God and the waters responded by rising one degree. David composed a further fourteen psalms and gradually the waters returned until they stood only one stage below its original level. The grass became lush and verdant, the leaves of the trees green and firm; the wadis and streams were replenished with water.

"May these fifteen psalms be sung by the Levites as they ascend the steps to the Temple." prayed David to God. "Let that be my contribution to the Temple.

"As for you, Achitophel, I thank you for your timely advice. You are indeed my lord, master and close friend."

Achitophel reacted differently to David's supernatural deliverance. He did not share David's joy, but prudently hidden his feelings of anger and frustration. He meekly accepted the appreciation offered for his wise intervention. His only consolation was the thought that other opportunities would arise to overthrow David. Then there would be no mistake. The knife would not be withdrawn at the last moment.

*   *   *

Achitophel descended the mountain and headed for Jerusalem. There he would find relief for his troubled feelings. In one of the small houses in the maze of streets that ran alongside David's palace lived his granddaughter with her husband and children. In their company, Achitophel always experienced a sense of soothing tranquillity. There, he would forget the pain of his dashed ambitions.

On a hot and humid summer's afternoon, Achitophel forced himself to blot out the memory of his unsuccessful encounter with David. He looked forward with eagerness to meeting his beautiful granddaughter and her husband, Bath-Sheva and Uriah the Hittite.

"Uriah? Bath-Sheva?" Jacqui exclaimed. "She was his granddaughter?"

"Of course," said Harry. "Now let's continue with the story."

"It's time Joel was in bed," countered Jacqui. "In fact it's time all the children were in bed."

"Mummy," the children protested, "when can we hear the rest of the story."

"Tomorrow's another day," Jacqui said firmly. "Now, all of you! Off to bed."

*   *   *

The following day after supper, the children all looked eagerly towards their father. "What happened next, daddy?" they asked in unison.

"It's getting late," said Harry. "What do you say, Jacqui?"

The children swung round to look at their mother. "Go on, mummy," they urged.

"Children," she said, with a stern voice. "I've just one thing to say to your father."

"But mummy!" the children called out.

"Children!" said Harry. "You must listen to your mother. Well, Jacqui! What do you want to say?"

Jacqui looked sternly, first at the children, then at Harry. She took a deep breath and cleared her throat with a cough. "What happened next, daddy?"

"Thanks, mummy," all the children cried." "Go on daddy. Let's hear the rest of the story."

"There's a lot to tell. I'll have to tell you about events that took place in Jerusalem, in David's palace and in a country called Ammon that's on the other side of the River Jordan to Israel

"Let's start at the beginning. War came to Israel. For three years Israel fought the Ammonites. How did it start? It started through David sending his condolences to the Ammonite king, Chanun, after the death of Chanun's father Nachash."

CHANUN'S PALACE

A servant bows to Chanun. "Your majesty, there are messengers from Israel to see you."

Chanun gives his servant a puzzled look. "Messengers from Israel to see me? What do they want?"

"They say they want to pay you their respects. They've come to sympathise with you on the death of your father, king Nachash."

"My father dies. And the Jews of Israel suddenly wish to visit me. Now they take an interest in me. I wonder what they really want." Chanun's face twisted into a sadistic grin. "We shall soon find out. Bring them to me."

"Yes, your majesty."

"No, wait," commanded Chanun. "Before they come in, inform them of the customs of our household. Tell them. When they come to see the king in the time of his mourning, they must carry no weapons on their persons. They must leave their weapons outside the king's chamber."

"Yes, your majesty."

Without suspecting Chanun's true motives, David's emissaries handed over their weapons to the Ammonite soldiers. Unarmed, they entered the royal chamber to pay their respects to the king. But on hearing the menacing tones of the Ammonite king, they realised they had been deceived.

"So you've come to pay your respects to a bereaved king." Chanun's words sent a shiver of fear through David's men. "You expect me to believe such a story. The son of Jesse is a cunning jackal. He doesn't care a fig for my feelings. He's a man of war, not of compassion."

"No, your majesty," exclaimed David's chief emissary, Menashe. "You do King David an injustice. He wishes to repay the kindness your father, king Nachash did for him."

"My father was indeed a kind man. It grieves me that the son of Jesse is taking advantage of his generous nature. No! You haven't come here to pay condolences. You've come here to spy out the land. The son of Jesse is seeking another kingdom to add to his list of conquests."

"We protest . . ." Menashe began, but was immediately silenced.

"Your protests are noted and dismissed." Chanun beckoned the emissaries to come closer to him. "You are spies! And you shall be treated as spies. Take heed of what I say. You'll not leave here exactly as you came."

"What do you mean?" Menashe said defiantly. "If any of us are harmed, your entire kingdom will be punished. We've come here in peace. Now let us go in peace."

"You're in no position to dictate to the king of Ammon. Have you forgotten the threat made by my grandfather against the citizens of Jabesh Gilead? If they did not immediately surrender to him, he threatened to gouge out the right eye of every man in the city. King Saul denied him that wish. Now I shall avenge my grandfather's humiliation. You will go back to your master, but you will leave something behind. What do you say to this suggestion?"

"We've nothing to say. We've come in peace. Let us go in peace."

"Soldiers!" Chanun suddenly issued a command. "Hold these men tight. See they cannot move. We'll show them a sharp tongue is no match for a sharp blade."

"Your majesty." Chanun's prime minister came over to the king and whispered in his ear. "We don't want to start a full scale war with Israel. We can humiliate these men without disfiguring them . . . ."

Chanun listened intently to the words of his prime Minister. "Yes, I accept your suggestion." He rose from his throne, took a dagger from one his soldiers and advanced slowly towards Menashe. "With this dagger I shall make the first cut."

With one hand, Chanun took hold of Menashe's beard and raised it high in the air. Then he placed his dagger next to Menashe's throat.

"You'll pay for this," cried out Menashe.

"Put your hand over his mouth," Chanun ordered one of his soldiers. "I don't wish to be interrupted with so delicate an operation. I don't want any accidents."

Chanun held up the dagger to Menashe's eyes. "This dagger is going to improve your appearance. My grandfather Nachash would have approved it."

Menashe closed his eyes and braced himself for the thrust. It did not come.

Instead Chanun lowered the dagger to Menashe's cheek and cut off two hairs on the side of Menashe's face. "I've made a start to your new hairstyle," he declared. "Soldiers! Shave off all the hair on one side of their face."

Hopelessly outnumbered and without weapons, David's messengers were forced to submit to the sharp blades of Chanun's soldiers who carried out his instructions with relish.

"Well done, men," gloated Chanun, surveying the embarrassed Menashe and his men. "But something's just not right. Their clothing doesn't fit in with their new appearance. Their tunics and their cloaks. They're too long and too smart. Make a few air holes in their tops. Shorten them from the bottom. Then send them back to the son of Jesse."

*   *   *

David was furious at the public humiliation of his emissaries. First, to spare them further embarrassment, he allocated them living quarters in a secluded place where their beards could return to normal. Then David declared war on Ammon.

For three years David's army besieged Rabbah, Ammon's capital city, with only limited success. The loss of life on both sides was unacceptably high. Then David committed an act that had far reaching repercussions on Israel's future

David married Bath Sheva, the wife of Uriah Hachitti.

At that time, there was a practice among David's soldiers to grant their wives a divorce before going to battle. So, in case they failed to return to their homes and it would not be known if they were alive or dead, at least their wives would be free from the chains of uncertainty and permitted to remarry.

However, a code of honour existed in David's kingdom. No one took advantage of the unmarried status of a soldier's wife during the period of the war. Everyone respected the priority of the claim of the husband over his wife.

David violated that code and Nathan the prophet rebuked him for abusing his royal powers.

David repented for his sin but people began to question his fitness as leader of the nation.

David's popularity was weakened further by another incident involving some of his children; his two sons, Absolom and Amnon; and his daughter, Tamar.

Amnon behaved with Tamar in a disgraceful way; and Absolom, furious at the way Tamar had been treated, arranged for Amnon to be murdered.

David was appalled by Absolom's crime and reacted strongly. As king of Israel, he could have executed Absolom for this murder. Instead he banished him.

For five years David refused to see Absolom till eventually, he was persuaded by Joab, his chief general, to make peace with his son.

A JERUSALEM MARKET PLACE

On a Friday morning, the market was a hive of frenzied bargaining. Everybody wanted to buy—cheaply—fresh fruit and vegetables for the Sabbath table. During the hot summer months, no one prepared for Sabbath too early in the week.

"I've never seen it so crowded." Miriam said to her sister-in-law, Tsiporah. "The whole of Jerusalem seems to be here today."

"It's Friday. It's also the end of the war against Ammon. The soldiers have come home."

"About time, too. What did we get out of this war? I lost an uncle and a cousin. I'm lucky my Jacob came home in one piece. He's been away for so long, his own children didn't recognise him."

Tsiporah picked a grape from one of the stalls and tasted it. "Mm. This is sweet. "You're right Miriam. What did we get out of this war? We've lost relatives, friends and I'm almost afraid to say it. We've also lost our king."

"What do you mean, Tsiporah? We've also lost our king."

"David's no longer the king he used to be. We thought he would be different from the kings of the other nations. But I think we were mistaken."

"I know what you're getting at. You mean Bath-Sheva."

"Yes, Bath-Sheva. Why did David take her for a wife? Her husband's away fighting in Ammon and he's nothing better to do than to marry her."

Miriam picked up an olive from a stall and sucked it. "They're not quite ripe yet. But in this weather, they're better this way." She turned to Tsiporah. "David's the king. He can do what he likes. Besides, you know when the soldiers go to war, they divorce their wives beforehand. Because, if they don't come back and no one knows if they alive or dead then their wives will not know if they're widows or still married. My husband divorced me before he went into battle. And when he came home on leave, we had to get married again."

"Well, that sounds a good arrangement. But tell me, Miriam. Imagine after your divorce from your husband you immediately married someone else. What would your Jacob have said?"

"What would he have said? I know what he would say. I go off to fight a war. And someone marries my wife. What a Chutspah! You know what a temper Jacob has. If he thinks someone's taking advantage of him, he beats the living daylights out of him."

"So how comes David marries Bath-Sheva? It doesn't seem right. By the way, there's something else you should know. People are spreading stories around."

Miriam pricked up her ears. "You know I'm not one for gossip."

"This is more than gossip."

"So what are they saying?"

"They're saying that David arranged for Bath-Sheva's husband Uriah to be sent to the front line, to the most dangerous part of the battlefield."

"I don't believe it. David wouldn't do such a thing."

"I'm not saying he did it. All I'm saying is that people are saying he did it. There's much bad feeling around. I'm afraid someone might take advantage of it."

"Like who?"

"There's one person I know who would have all Israel flocking to his banner. He has everything. Looks, personality, charm. What's more, he has royal blood in his veins.

"You mean . . . ."

"Ladies, ladies." The stall keeper interrupted their conversation. "When you've quite finished munching my fruit. Remember I'm here to make a living. I didn't set up this stall to listen to your views on royalty and politics. Now what do you want for the Sabbath. Grapes, olives, figs, dates, artichokes, cabbage, lettuce, carrots. Hurry up ladies. Remember, I also keep the Sabbath."

THE SANCTUARY

"**D**addy, daddy, I can see them."

"What are they doing?"

"They're running towards us. Lots of men in front of a chariot.

"Can you see who's in the chariot?"

"It's him. It's him. I know it's him."

"How do you know it's him?"

"I can see his hair. It must be him."

Spectators thronged the sides of the road leading to the marble plaza in front of the Sanctuary. Many spilled over into the road itself leaving only a narrow path barely wide enough for a horse and its rider to pass. Samuel, a young boy of five, sat on the shoulders of his father, Naphtali. He looked eagerly towards the riders approaching them.

"You can see his hair? What's special about it?" Naphtali teased Samuel.

"It's so thick and long. I can't see his chest. It's covered in hair."

"Can you see him now?" Hannah asked her husband, Naphtali.

"Just about."

"Is he as handsome as people say?"

"He's not as good looking as Samuel's father."

"You're jealous."

"You want me to take the vows to become a Nazir. You want me to let my hair grow for a year at a time. Hannah, I can grow a head of hair as long as he has. But then you'll have to wash it every day for me."

"You're jealous. Look at him. It's not just his hair. It's everything about him. He's so handsome. He's better looking than anybody I've ever seen. He is a true prince of Israel. A worthy son of his father, David." Hannah trembled with excitement as the horse and its rider came closer and closer to her. Never had she been so close to the man idolised by all Israel for his looks, wealth and splendid physique.

'I must speak to him,' thought Hannah. 'I'll never have another opportunity.' "Absolom! Absolom!" she called out. "Give my son a blessing. Let him become as handsome and as worthy as you."

To Hannah's astonishment, Absolom stopped his chariot and looked directly at her. "Is this your son?" he asked, pointing to Samuel.

Hannah nodded dumbly.

"You have a fine son. May he grow up to be as strong and as worthy as his father. May he not have to fight any wars. Let him grow up in a land that that is blessed with peace and prosperity."

"Amen," said Naphtali. "Those are my feelings too. We've had enough of wars. We want a land where the king mixes with his people in peace. Not leading them into battle."

"Don't blame King David for not visiting his people. My father is forced to spend too much of his time on the battlefield. He is unable to see his people as often as he wishes."

"Will there ever be a change?" asked Naphtali.

"May my father live to a ripe old age. But if I ever become king, I will go out of my palace—to the people. I will listen to their needs and problems. I will banish war from the land."

"May your wish be granted," said Naphtali.

"With men like you and your son behind me, one day it will come true. Here! Give this to your son. What's his name?"

"Samuel."

"Samuel. Take this silver shekel. Use it to pay a teacher to teach you the Torah. Then use your Torah to be a good child to your father and mother."

Absolom handed over the coin to Samuel and rode on through the crowds of people surging around him.

"He's a fine man," said Naphtali. "One day he'll make a good king. Perhaps he shouldn't wait too long. David is going too far with his wars and fighting. The people need a breathing space. What do say Hannah?"

"He spoke to me. He answered my prayer. He's the most wonderful person I've ever seen."

Naphtali playfully shook his head. "Remember, Hannah. I'm still your husband. I must admit though, he's almost as handsome as me. Now, come along. Let's try to get a good view of what's going to happen next."

*   *   *

In the centre of the plaza in front of the Sanctuary, two men set down an ornate chair of wood and copper. Next to it, two other men placed a pair of weighing scales with two giant pans.

Absolom sat on the chair and a group of musicians surrounded him. As the crowd came closer for a better view, they played a gentle lullaby on their flutes, timbrels and harps.

Absolom beckoned to one of the men standing nearby him. He came forward and took out a pair of scissors from his tunic. To the strains of the accompanying music, he cut Absolom's hair.

Another man stepped forward and took each lock of hair as it was cut off Absolom's head. He did not permit any of the hair to fall on the ground.

Instead, he placed it on one of the pans of the scales next to the chair on which Absolom sat.

Before long, the pan overflowed with hair and sagged heavily towards the ground. Another man supported the pan to prevent its falling on to the ground. Another man stepped forward with weights in his hand. He held up one weight to the crowd and announced, "Fifty Shekels!" He placed the weight on the other pan and tested the balance. The hair outweighed the fifty shekel weight.

"Another fifty shekels!" the crowd roared

The man held up another weight to the crowd, "Fifty Shekels!" he announced.

He added the weight to the pan and again tested the balance. The hair still outweighed the weights.

"Another fifty shekels!" the crowd roared

The man held up a third weight. "Fifty Shekels!" he announced again, as he added it to the other weights in the pan.

The balance was tested a third time. The hair was still heavier than the weights.

"Another fifty shekels!" the crowd roared out once more. The man put a fourth weight on the pan and tested the balance. The crowd held its breath as the two pans bobbed up and down before finally settling down exactly opposite each other.

"Two hundred Shekels!" the man announced. Absolom will now donate two hundred silver shekels to the Sanctuary. May its sacrifices bring peace and prosperity to Israel."

"Absolom! Absolom! Long live Absolom. The crowd could contain themselves no longer. They rushed forward, picked up Absolom on their shoulders and carried him towards the Sanctuary. "Long live Absolom. Long live Absolom."

By the time Absolom had concluded the bringing of his sacrifice in the Sanctuary most of the crowd had dispersed. Only a handful of people remained to watch him emerge from behind the curtain that screened the Sanctuary from the public plaza. "Absolom! Absolom!" they shouted excitedly and Absolom acknowledged their presence with a friendly wave.

One man however stepped forward and approached Absolom. "Peace unto you, Absolom," he said with extended hand.

"Peace unto you, Achitophel. What brings you here today." Absolom lowered his voice. "I imagine you must have more serious matters to deal with than attending a haircutting ceremony."

"I have. I must talk to you in private."

"Very well." Absolom gestured with his hands towards his servants and retainers. They immediately retreated from the two men and allowed them to talk without being overheard.

"I couldn't help overhearing some of the comments made by the people at your haircutting ceremony. To a man, they all believe you'll make a good king."

"Thank you, Achitophel. I take that as a compliment. Do you mind if I ask if you agree with them? I value your opinion. You are after all a loyal servant to my father David. What do you think?"

Achitophel side-stepped the question. "David seems to have lost the confidence of the people."

"I agree," said Absolom. He's not as popular as he used to be. Tell me, Achitophel. Should you be making such statements? For a person in your position, your words amount to a betrayal of the king. You would betray David? He has been a good master to you. He has honoured you and rewarded you well for your services to him. Where is your sense of loyalty?"

"I am loyal to the interests of the people. I am loyal to the interests of justice."

"Even to the extent of deserting the king?"

"A king has to champion the needs of the people. A king is the servant of the people. He is appointed to defend their rights. Not to abuse them."

"Uriah?"

"Yes, Uriah!" Achitophel clenched his fists with rage. "Bath-sheva was widowed by command of the king. She was then taken by the king to be his wife. A king should promote harmony in the home. Not shatter it."

"I grieve for Uriah and Bath-sheva. I understand your feelings, Achitophel."

"I share your grief too, Absolom. You punished the person who disgraced your sister. Everyone knows how you were you rewarded? With banishment! The king arranges to kill the man who stands in the way of his marriage to Bath-Sheva. Yet he still sits on his throne. Is that justice?"

"Israel and Judah agree with you, Achitophel. They deserve a ruler who respects their rights. A Jewish king must be just and impartial."

Achitophel seized Absolom by his hand. "You are the man, Absolom. Only you can restore sanity and dignity to Israel. For the sake of the nation, you must become king."

"You would support me?"

"I would support you." Achitophel clasped Absolom firmly by the hand. "You have my word."

"Achitophel! We must prepare ourselves. No word of this revolt must leak out to David. I will seek the support of the South, of the men of Judah. Hebron will be my base. At the moment, I'm not ready to move yet. I dare not leave Jerusalem till everything is in place. You, Achitophel. You seek the support of the North, of the men of Israel. They will follow someone not directly related to the House of David."

"I already have contacts in the Northern Kingdom, Absolom. Some are openly expressing criticism of David. They are also sympathetic towards you. They feel you have been harshly treated."

"How long before you are ready, Achitophel?"

Achitophel looked Absolom squarely in the eye. "Your hair shall be your guide. Have no fear. By the time it reaches your chest, you shall be enthroned as king in Jerusalem."

The two men shook hands fervently. "Peace unto you, Achitophel."

"Peace unto you, Absolom."

*　　*　　*

Absolom alerted his supporters to their new ally, Achitophel and redoubled his efforts to undermine David's authority.

The final move in his campaign was to maximise the element of surprise. He went to see David—to put him off-guard—and allow his seizure of the throne of Israel to take place with as little resistance as possible.

In the privacy of the royal palace, Absolom spoke earnestly to his father, David. "Some time ago, I made a vow. I undertook to bring many sacrifices to God. The time has now come for me to honour my vow."

Absolom, knowing that his part in the murder of his half brother Amnon still rankled David, cunningly played the part of the penitent son filled with remorse over the bad deeds of his youth. He pretended he was no longer the headstrong prince who acted without consultation with others.

"You do not need my permission to bring sacrifices in the Sanctuary," said David. "You know that as well as I. What is the reason for your request?"

"The sacrifices will be brought in the Sanctuary. Have no fear of that, father. I only wish to ensure that the sacrifices I bring are indeed fitting for God. For this reason, I wish to choose them myself."

David idolised his son. He saw no guile or deceit in his words. "So why are you informing me of your intentions. I am sure you are a good judge of a worthy sacrifice."

"I am seeking your permission to leave Jerusalem for a short while. You gave your permission for me to return to Jerusalem. It is only a matter of courtesy for me to seek your permission when I wish to leave."

David smiled approvingly. "To where do you have to go?"

"To Hebron."

"Why Hebron?"

"The rams there have a well deserved reputation for size and quality. I will bring back only the best that Israel can produce."

David was nearing the end of his forty year reign over Israel. He no longer possessed the insight and foresight that had enabled him to rule Israel with such unquestioning authority for so many years. He failed to realise that Absolom's request to leave Jerusalem was merely a ploy; that his visit to Hebron, the capital city of Judah, would ignite the flame of rebellion throughout Israel. "You have my permission, Absolom," he said, embracing his son. "Go in peace."

*   *   *

The two vital factors in a successful coup are speed and surprise. Achitophel and Absolom achieved both.

A chain of trumpet blowers from Dan in the North to Beer Sheba in the South proclaimed the signal for the revolt to begin and the Israelites were left in no doubt as to the significance of their sound. All over Israel, Absolom's followers responded with loud cheers and cries. "Absolom is king! Absolom is king! He reigns in Chevron!"

Many people were confused by the sudden turn of events. They failed to realise that Absolom was rebelling against his father. Believing that David had sanctioned this appointment, they were only too willing to swear allegiance to the new king in Hebron.

Within a short time, Absolom's army grew to a size where he felt he was capable of seizing Jerusalem. He sought advice from Achitophel and the decision was made. "March to Jerusalem."

JERUSALEM

David and his advisors were unaware of the planned rebellion. After almost forty years of uninterrupted power, they never believed that either Absolom, the king's son or Achitophel, the king's trusted counsellor would lead a revolt against David. The news that Absolom had proclaimed himself king and was leading an army to take Jerusalem was a shattering blow to David.

121

Joab, David's chief general, was especially furious at Absolom's treachery. He had persuaded David to be reconciled with Absolom. Never had he expected Absolom to betray his kindness towards him. His immediate reaction was to stay in Jerusalem and fight Absolom and his followers.

David however, thought otherwise. Only a small band of armed men was stationed in the city. They would be no match for the army of Absolom marching towards them. Besides, he saw the hand of God punishing him for his misdeeds. He had no desire to turn the city of peace into a battlefield on his account. This was a time for repentance and reflection. It was not the time for war. David took stock of the situation and decided to retreat.

* * *

The weather reflected David's mood. On a bitter cold winter's day, David and his small band of faithful followers left the royal palace. Weeping loudly at their misfortune, they covered their heads with blankets and strode barefooted through the streets of Jerusalem.

Despite the swiftness of the events and the muted marching, the news of David's retreat spread like wildfire throughout the city. Jerusalem's citizens left their houses to line the streets as in times of victory. This time however, there was no cheering and shouting.

At first there was a stony silence. Everybody looked on in disbelief as the procession wound its way through the narrow streets of Jerusalem. Then the weeping spread from king to subject. Tears ran freely down the faces of men, women and children as they watched their once proud and feared leader humbled by his own son, retreating with his army from Jerusalem.

One little boy, overcome with emotion and unable to restrain himself, broke away from his mother and ran towards David. "Don't leave us," he cried out. "You are our king."

David stopped to pick up the boy and hold him in his arms. "Even a king has to accept the will of God." he whispered tenderly.

"But I want you to be my king. You can't leave us."

"Whatever God decides will come to pass. If He wishes me to return and be your king, then I shall return. If not, then so be it. Now make me a promise."

The boy nodded.

"Always be loyal to your parents. Always be loyal to the king, whoever he may be."

"But I want you to be my king. Come back. Promise me you'll come back."

David patted the boy on his head. "Only God can make promises and keep them. One day you'll understand. In the meantime, I must hurry and leave you." He turned to his general. "Avishai! Return him to his mother."

*   *   *

David, flanked by his two generals, Joab and Avishai, led the retreat from Jerusalem. Behind them was the Kereisi Upleisi, David's special battalion of seasoned troops. The rest of the royal party, David's wives, children, menservants and maidservants and a further detachment of David's personal bodyguard formed the rear of the long winding procession. All walked slowly to the western side of the city, where they ascended the Mount of Olives.

Snow flakes falling from a grey, leaden sky chilled the body and spirit of the once proud occupants of Israel's capital, Jerusalem. The fierce soldiers and warriors who sowed terror and panic in the hearts of their enemies no longer resembled a fighting force. They retreated in shame and humiliation from the Holy City. Believing they would never return to the serenity of its sacred walls, their mood was as dark as the forbidding skies above them.

*   *   *

Two major incidents occurred on this sad journey.

After hearing the news of Absolom's rebellion, Chushai the Archite, one of David's closest friend and advisors, tore his clothing, placed earth on his head and rushed to Jerusalem to offer his assistance and advice. The two men met at the top of the Mount of Olives and tearfully embraced each other.

"I will join you in your exile," said Chushai. "I will serve his majesty wherever he may go."

"No," said David, grasping Chushai's shoulders. "You will serve me better by staying here. Not everyone is leaving Jerusalem. The Fpriets are staying behind to minister in the Sanctuary. You will also stay behind to promote my interests."

Chushai hesitated. "Is that a royal command?"

"Yes, Chushai. That is a royal command. Offer yourself to Absolom. Tell him you wish to be his ambassador, both to the nations abroad and to the people of Israel. You have vast experience in matters of state and the needs of the people. He will require the services of a person such as you. Achitophel cannot act as his only adviser."

123

"Achitophel is the key figure in this revolt," said Chushai. "He is the mastermind behind the rebellion. Your majesty, I fear for Absolom. Achitophel is using him for his own ends."

"I know. Without Achitophel, Absolom would never have revolted against me. He is the rider in the chariot. I also fear for Absolom's safety. May God bring the counsel of Achitophel to nought." Momentarily, David looked back towards Jerusalem, as though expecting an army of warriors to surge through its gates. "We must hurry, Chushai. Absolom's army cannot be far behind. I wish to avoid an immediate confrontation. Go to Jerusalem, Chushai. But first change your clothing. Absolom must not suspect how heartbroken you are at my misfortune."

"Go and return in peace." Chushai once more tearfully embraced David, before taking his leave and preparing to journey to Jerusalem.

The second incident in David's flight from Absolom occurred after ascending the western slope of the mount of Olives and passing the town of Bachurim. As David descended the zigzag path on the hill leading towards the Jordan, he and his men heard a piercing voice ringing out from the pathway immediately above them.

Shimi the son of Garoh, a close relative of Saul, expressed his vengeful feelings towards the man who had replaced Saul as monarch of Israel. He screeched out a string of curses against David. With each curse, he threw a handful of stones at David and his followers.

"Murderer! Villain! Get out! Get out! Murderer of the house of Saul. Saul treated you as a son. And you betrayed his trust. As you sow, so shall you reap. Now your son will take vengeance on you.

"Murderer! Villain! Get off the throne of Israel. Get out of the country. Let the people live in peace. You shall suffer as you made others suffer."

"My sword will cut him down." Avishai was unable to tolerate Shimi's insolence. He withdrew his sword from its scabbard and ran towards one of the pathways leading to the top of the hill. "He has insulted your majesty. He shall be punished with death."

"No," shouted out David. "Sheathe your sword and return to my side. Today, God has taken away my majesty. He has sent a messenger to curse me. The son of Garoh shall not be punished for speaking the words of God. Let him be."

With the words and stones of Shimi falling around him, David continued his journey and as darkness closed his tragic day, he encamped at Bachurim, on the western side of the River Jordan.

JERUSALEM

Absolom was jubilant. He had achieved his goals. He had seized and occupied Jerusalem without a fight. He was king over Israel. But he knew how fickle public opinion could be. He had to consolidate his position. As long as David lived, he was a threat to his kingship.

In the spacious banqueting room in the palace recently vacated by his father, Absolom addressed his advisers and officers at a council of war.

"Gentlemen," he began. "I must first thank you for your loyal support. I could never have achieved this success without your assistance. I realise how difficult it has been for you to choose between a father and his son. Yet I know that we are all acting in the best interests of the people of Israel. They deserve to be treated with justice and respect."

The generals and officers nodded approvingly.

"We have only started our campaign," continued Absolom. "We must finish the work we have started. In the interests of the people there cannot be two rulers over Israel. My father, David must surrender and abdicate. Or be defeated in battle."

"Hear, hear!" roared his assembled followers. "There can only be one king. David must be overthrown."

"Achitophel!" Absolom looked towards his chief advisor. "What is your opinion? How can we ensure peace and security? How do we remove the threat of David from Israel?"

Achitophel rose to his feet and slammed down his fist on the table in front of him. He looked round, commandingly, at Absolom's assembled followers. "David will never surrender. As long as he lives he will be a threat to your rule. He must be defeated. He must be destroyed in battle."

"Is that opinion unanimous?" Absolom asked the assembly. "Does anyone else wish to speak?"

"We agree with Achitophel." A roar of consent echoed throughout the hall. "We agree with Achitophel. David must be destroyed."

"Very well," said Absolom. "We are agreed on that matter. David is to be destroyed. So how do we plan our campaign? Achitophel! Advise us once more."

Achitophel rose to his feet once more. "We must strike David quick and hard. He is demoralised and tired. He has very little support. The element of surprise is still in our favour. We must capitalise on it. Marshal the troops we already have in and around Jerusalem. We have twelve thousand men. I will lead them. I will march tonight.

"If we attack David and his men before they've time to regroup, they will have no stomach for a fight. They know that all Israel is on your side.

At the first sign of battle, they will flee. David will be left alone. We shall smite him at will. Thousands of lives will be saved, if we act quickly and decisively. I will return to you all the men in my charge."

"We agree, we agree." A shout of approval echoed round the hall as Achitophel finished speaking. "Fight David straight away."

"Do you all agree with Achitophel's plan?" asked Absolom.

"No!" Chushai rose from his seat and looked round the hall. "Normally, I have the greatest of respect for Achitophel's opinion. On this occasion, I must disagree. Of course David must be destroyed, but not in the way that Achitophel has proposed.

"I know David. I know his strength and I know his weaknesses. Right now, he is as a bear whose cub has been captured. He will fight to the last breath in his body to get back his kingdom. He is guarded by hand-picked troops who will never desert him. They have all sworn an oath of allegiance to him.

"David is a fighter. Look at the legacy he has left us." Chushai spread out his hands to the trophies of war adorning the walls of the hall; the shield of Goliath, two metres in diameter; his spear, five metres long; a headless statue of Dagon plundered from a Philistine temple; tapestries of silver and gold ransacked from the Edomites and Moabites. A priceless crown adorned with precious stones given as tribute by the Ammonites. "David will fight to the very last breath in his body to recapture his kingdom.

"I can assure you, gentlemen, David will not be caught napping by a surprise attack. David will not camp overnight with the people. He knows they will run away at the first sight of battle. He knows their cowardice will weaken the resolve of his person al bodyguard.

"I know David. He will not be found when you attack. He will be well hidden. Undoubtedly, there will be bloodshed. That cannot be avoided. Men fall in battle and rumours will begin spreading. They will say your forces are inexperienced. They have no knowledge of warfare. They will claim it is your soldiers that have fallen in battle. The nation will be in turmoil. They will regret this rebellion against their king. A premature assault will prove disastrous for you."

"What is the alternative to Achitophel's plan?" asked Absolom. "How can we crush David?"

"There's only one way of crushing David," said Chushai. "You, your majesty must demonstrate to David that the whole of Israel is against him. You must raise an army from Dan to Beer Sheba. You must be at the head of that army. You will show David and his men that their cause is hopeless. Then they will desert him. David will be left alone. He will be at your mercy. The people turned from David to follow you, your majesty. They will now follow you to destroy the king who sacrificed their interests for his own selfish ends."

"We agree, we agree." Another shout of approval echoed round the hall. This time, though, the support was for Chushai. "Mobilise Israel. And destroy David."

Absolom was unsettled by Chushai's surprise proposal. He had not expected any opposition to Achitophel's plan. Yet Chushai's proposals did have merit. They did make military sense. In addition, they reduced his dependence upon Achitophel's counsel.

Absolom reconsidered Achitophel's plan. Why did he suggest he should lead the army? Was he planning to take over the throne himself? Chushai's suggestion had planted the seeds of doubt and suspicion into Absolom's mind. Did Achitophel want the honour of executing David? Would he become the national hero? In that event, would he then turn the army against him, Absolom? On the other hand, what about Chushai? He was a known friend of David. Was he playing a double game? How should he decide?

Absolom weighed up the alternatives. To attack immediately, that night, with Achitophel at the head of the army. Or wait until he could lead all Israel against David and his men. Who was right? Achitophel or Chushai?

The pressure on Absolom was immense. He knew the importance of decisiveness in leading a nation. He forced himself to make a decision. "I have decided. We shall accept the plan of Chushai." He turned to his officers. "Send messengers throughout Israel. We shall raise an army to fight David. I will lead that army into battle."

Achitophel sat stunned in his chair. He could not believe his ears. His plan was the only certain means of victory. As he listened grimly to the sound of cheering and agreement all around him, he knew that he and Absolom were doomed to defeat. God through Chushai had frustrated him. Quietly and unnoticed, Achitophel retreated from the hall.

Chushai however did not share in the jubilation that greeted his words. He knew how short-lived such moods could be. At the same time, he also sensed Absolom's suspicions of his motives. There was always the possibility of a sudden change of plan. He had to warn David. As long as he remained on the western side of the River Jordan, he was in danger.

*   *   *

David had many sympathisers in Jerusalem. Among them were the chief priests, Evyatar and Tzadok. Chushai contacted them.

That night, a short time after Chushai had informed the two priests of his fears, a maidservant carrying a pitcher left Jerusalem. She headed down the lantern-lit path towards the well, Ein Rogal, outside the city. On arriving at Ein Rogal, she lowered the bucket into the well, drew it up and began to fill her pitcher.

The maidservant sang as she worked, every now and then, looking furtively around her. Strangely, in between verses, she started hooting like a night owl, then waited in silence, as if expecting a response.

Before long, her patience was rewarded. The hooting sound of a night owl responded to hers.

The maidservant then spoke aloud. "I hope my master is satisfied. I don't like coming out at night. I'd only do it for him."

A voice sounded behind her. "But would you do it for us?"

The maidservant spun around and faced the two men who appeared to have materialised from thin air. "Who are you? What are your names?"

"We are Jonathan and Achimaats, the sons of Evyatar and Tzadok. What message do you have for King David?"

"He is in danger this side of the Jordan," she said, briefly informing them of the various plans being considered by Absolom. "Chushai advises he flees immediately."

"You've done well," said the two men. "Now return to the city. We shall inform the king."

The maidservant returned safely to Jerusalem. Yehonatan and Achimaats, however, were not so fortunate. Absolom's spies observed them on the road to Bachurim, where David was hiding. In desperation to avoid their pursuers, the two men ran like the wind to the house of another David supporter in Bachurim. They pleaded with the householder for refuge.

Frightened that Absolom's spies might search her premises, the woman in the house hid them in the well of her garden and covered the top with bundles of corn. When asked by Absolom's spies if she had seen two men, she replied, like Rahab, before the battle of Jericho. "Yes, I did see two men, but they fled when they saw me." She pointed towards a barren waste land some miles from her house. "They went in that direction. Over that brook."

The answer satisfied the spies. They followed the women's directions, searched around for a short while, found nothing and returned to Jerusalem.

The woman waited half an hour, then informed Yehonatan and Achimaats it was safe to continue their journey. Immediately, they made their way to David's secret camp and passed on the message from Chushai.

David reacted to the message from Chushai by crossing the River Jordan and encamping in Machanayim.

*   *   *

The following day, Absolom reconsidered his position. He admitted, to himself, he had lost the best opportunity for a swift victory, but still believed he could defeat David.

With more warriors from all over Israel still pouring into Jerusalem to support him, he declared his intention of leading his army into immediate battle. He appointed Amasa as head of his armed forces, gave orders to cross the Jordan and encamped his army in the land of Gilead.

*   *   *

David, a few miles to the south of Absolom, had quickly recovered from the initial shock of the declaration of rebellion. He now planned his counterattack.

Because of the haste in which he left Jerusalem, David was lacking essential supplies. He sent messages to his friends and allies throughout Judah and the neighbouring countries. All stood by him. They responded swiftly and generously to his requests for assistance.

Shovi the son of Nachash from Ammon, Machir the son of Amikel from Lo-debar and Barzilei the Gileadite from Regalim brought beds, basins and earthenware vessels; wheat, barley, flour and parched corn; and honey, butter, sheep and cattle. Within a few hours of his arrival at Machanayim, David and his men were rested, refreshed and ready for battle.

David, now set to one side his feelings as an aggravated father and assumed the role of a military leader. Knowing he would be fighting the most important battle of his life, he prepared his army with painstaking efficiency. First, he counted his soldiers, then set up a chain of command by organising them into groups of thousands and hundreds. Afterwards, he formed these groups into three units under the command of the three most able and experienced generals in the Middle East; Joab, Avishai and Ittai the Gittite.

Before setting off into battle, David put on his military uniform, assembled his army and addressed them. His words winged their way into the hearts and minds of his troops. "My brothers! It is a sad day for Israel when a brother has to take up arms against a brother. But law and order must prevail. God will be on the side of the victor. May God be on our side.

"Loyal soldiers of Israel. I do not know the outcome of this battle. But I do know I owe a debt to your courage and self-sacrifice. It is a debt for which I am deeply grateful and know I can never fully repay.

"I have always tried to be a just king over Israel and today, I will not shirk my duty to you. The place of a king is with his followers. I will go with you into battle . . ."

"No!" said Joab. The sight of David, old and frail, unnerved him. David was well past his prime. He was but a shadow of the man who had thrilled and captivated Israel with his exploits against the Philistines. The last few days especially had taken a heavy toll on David. There were deep rings under his eyes and heavily etched lines in his face. That day, in battle, David would be an expensive liability. His personal guard would be more concerned with defending the king than taking the battle to the enemy. "I speak on behalf of the people. They wish you to remain behind."

David looked at him in astonishment. "My duty is to serve my people."

"You will serve them better, if you remain in the camp."

"Take care, Joab. I am still your king. Explain yourself."

"Your majesty, help us." Joab was determined that David should not go into battle but remain behind. "If you are present at the head of the army, you will become the focal point for attack. Absolom's men will have a target to go for. Anyone who stands in the way of that target will be cut down.

"But if you're not there, Absolom's men have no real grudge against us. They will lack the incentive and direction to kill anyone who stands in their way. Your absence will make it easier for us to win the battle."

As David considered this argument, Joab pressed home a further point. "Besides, your absence will plant confusion in the minds of Absolom and his men. They will assume you are waiting to join battle at a given signal. They will always have at the back of their minds the belief that somewhere we have reinforcements to overwhelm them. The prime rule in military warfare is—bewilder the enemy. Sow the seeds of uncertainty. Your majesty, I beg you. Stay in the camp. With your help we shall achieve victory."

"You have spoken well, Joab." David felt relieved to stand down in this battle against his son. "I shall stay behind. But promise me this." David looked first towards his three generals, Joab, Avishai and Ittai; and then towards his entire army. "Absolom is my son. He is only a lad. Be gentle with him. May God be with you and him. Go and return to peace."

*　　*　　*

The two armies met at the forest of Ephraim on the eastern side of the Jordan.

Despite their advantage in numbers and weaponry, Absolom and his men were no match for David's army. The better discipline, organisation and experience of Joab and his fellow generals proved decisive. They overwhelmed Absolom's army who fled in blind panic through the forest of Ephraim.

The trees of the forest took a heavy toll of the fleeing soldiers. Some tripped heavily over the thick roots bursting out of the ground and were trampled to death by their own comrades. Others were killed by running into the low, overhanging branches that criss-crossed the forest.

One of the victims of the forest was Absolom. As he desperately drove his mule away from David's army, his long hair became suddenly entangled in the low, overhanging branches of an oak tree above his head.

The symbol of Absolom's appeal now became the instrument of his undoing. His fate was sealed by his hair. Unable to abruptly stop the frenzied pace of his mule, Absolom was yanked out of his saddle. Unarmed and exposed, he dangled helplessly above the ground of the forest.

One of David's soldiers espied the unmistakable figure of Absolom swinging from the oak tree. "I must report this," he said to himself and immediately returned to his general, Joab. "I've seen Absolom. He is trapped by his hair in an oak tree."

Joab was incredulous. "You saw Absolom, the enemy of Israel trapped in an oak tree and you allowed him to live? Why didn't you smite him to the ground? I'd have given you ten pieces of silver and a girdle."

The soldier was not intimidated by Joab. "Even for a thousand pieces of silver, I would not take the life of the king's son. All of us were present when the king addressed us. He charged you and Avishai and Ittai with his son's welfare. 'Take care, he said, that no one should harm Absolom.' Had I killed him. I would have been held responsible for defying the king. You, yourself would have held me responsible for disobeying the king."

"Return to your unit," snapped Joab. "I shall deal with Absolom."

Joab dismissed the soldier, then, accompanied by his ten armour bearers, ran swiftly to the oak tree where Absolom was trapped. He looked up, coldly, at the defenceless figure of the man who had betrayed his father and himself.

Without mercy, Joab took three darts from his tunic and thrust them into the heart of the helpless Absolom. Then he stepped back and beckoned to his armour bearers. With outstretched swords, they lunged forward and completed the execution of the man who had plunged Israel into civil war.

"The enemy of Israel is dead," said Joab grimly, as he took his Shofar from his belt and blew out the signal to return to quarters. "The war is over."

*   *   *

"**Y**es, the war was over. And so is the story." Harry Gabriel looked round at his yawning children. The spell of the story had broken. They all looked tired and ready for bed. Except one.

"What happened to Achitophel?" asked Joel. "That can't be the end of the story. You started off with Achitophel, Daddy. You have to finish with him."

"What about David?" asked Jacqui. "How did he feel when he heard that Joab had killed his son, Absolom?"

"David's feelings. Achitophel's feelings," sighed Harry. "What about my feelings? I'm feeling exhausted. It's been a long story. I don't know about you. I'm ready for bed.

"Daddy, daddy." The children suddenly woke up. "What happened next."

"You'll have to wait till tomorrow." Harry gave a long, big yawn. "Tomorrow I'll tell you what happened in David's camp and Achitophel's villa. Good night."

DAVID'S CAMP

David waited anxiously in his camp for news of the outcome of the battle. Again and again, he called out to the watchman for a report. "Is anyone coming?" he kept asking. Each time the answer was "No, your majesty."

Finally his impatience was rewarded. "I can see someone running towards us," shouted the watchman.

"Who is it?" demanded David. "Is it a bearer of good tidings?"

"I cannot see who it is," came the reply. "But wait. There's another runner heading this way."

"Two runners? Two bearers of news? Who are they?"

"They're too far away. I can't recognise them yet. Wait! The second runner is overtaking the first one." The watchman shielded his eyes from the glare of the sun. "Only one man runs like that. It is Achimaats the son of Tzadok."

"Achimaats the son of Tzadok." David felt relieved. "He is a bearer of good tidings. But why the second runner. The news is mixed. There is good and bad news."

Achimaats ran straight to David and bowed before him. "Your majesty. May God be blessed. The men who rose up against you have been defeated."

"What of the boy Absolom? What news is there of him?"

"I have no news of Absolom."

"No news," cried David. "Stand aside. Let the other runner give his message. Come here," he ordered the Kushi, the black man, sent by Joab. "What news do you have?"

"Good news, your majesty. Your enemies have perished."

"The boy Absolom? What news is there of him?"

The Kushi answered without any thought for David's feeling. "May the enemies of the king and all who rise against him become like the lad."

David's blood ran cold at the Kushi's words. With the colour drained from his face, he made his way to the room by the gateway to the camp, weeping as he went. "My son, Absolom, my son, my son Absolom. Would that I had died instead of you, Absolom, my son, my son."

The news of the depth of David's anguish distressed Israel. When a brother fights a brother and a father fights a son, there are no victors. All are losers. Despite their triumph in battle, David's soldiers returned home dejected and depressed.

ACHITOPHEL'S VILLA

Achitophel left the hall in a furious mood. He knew Chushai's plan could never succeed. Had they attacked immediately, David would have been annihilated. His men were dispirited, tired and few in number.

Achitophel understood, only too well, Chushai's motives. Chushai was no friend of Absolom. He was a loyal servant of David. Time was an ally of David not Absolom. The greater the delay before the final battle, the stronger and more confident became David and his followers.

Achitophel knew his gamble to become king had failed. Only one course of action was left.

Achitophel went to his villa on the outskirts of Jerusalem and summoned two of his servants. "I am going to my summer house," he informed them. "Be there in five minutes. Bring with you a long, strong rope."

The cedar-wood summer house stood at the rear end of the garden on the southern side of the villa. For Achitophel, it was a haven of coolness and solitude in the hot dry Israeli summers. To increase its ventilation, it had two entrances, with doors, facing each other.

Precisely at the end of five minutes, the two servants entered the summer house. Achitophel, a person of rigid self-discipline, demanded high standards from his servants.

Achitophel took the rope from the two men, inspected it carefully, then tested its strength by tugging sharply at various points along its length. "The rope is sound. Now, listen carefully. Both of you, go outside the summer house and wait outside the doors. Close the doors slightly. Do not attempt to peer inside the house. Yaphet, you go to the southern side. Bugal, you go to the northern side. Wait there, till I give you further instructions."

The two servants took up their positions and Achitophel, now hidden from them behind the partially closed doors, took hold of the middle of the rope. Without hesitation, he coiled it once round his neck.

"Yaphet," Achitophel called out, raising his hands to the level of his shoulders. "Pull the rope slightly. Make sure there's no slack in the rope. Good. That's enough."

"Bugal," Achitophel called out in the other direction. "Do the same. Pull your end of the rope slightly. Make sure there's no slack in the rope. Good. That's enough.

"Now both of you listen carefully. When I command you to pull, do so with all your strength. Do not stop till I command you to do so."

With his legs spread out wide, Achitophel stood in the centre of the room grasping the rope tightly in his hands; he felt its rough edge against the back of his neck and his throat.

Achitophel knew he had little time. Joab would seek him out. He would be tried and executed for treason. His estate would be seized by David. Even now, Joab might be thundering towards him, determined to snatch the final fruits of victory. He must not lose this opportunity of thwarting David. "David shall not possess my property," said Achitophel through clenched teeth.

As Achitophel uttered the name David, an image entered his mind. His thoughts turned towards the dramatic events at the peak of Mount Itum. He saw himself, once more, calmly watching the water creeping further and further up the body of the helpless David.

"Achitophel!" David transfixed Achitophel with his eyes. Eyes that possessed the power of life and death, eyes that could reduce stone into water and creatures into ashes. The eyes of David bored into Achitophel.

They pierced his soul, penetrating his mind. "I demand you advise me. Who ever can advise me and fails to do so, let that person be strangled." Achitophel had advised David. He had carried out David's request. But the words of David, God's anointed one, had become a Divine decree. They had to be fulfilled.

Achitophel braced himself, then issued his last command. "Pull!"

*   *   *

Jacqui was so moved by the last part of the story that she was unable to speak for a few minutes. Finally, she found her voice. "Tell me, Harry. What did the Talmud have to say about Achitophel? He seems a most unpleasant character. First, he nearly got David killed by his own son. Then he takes his own life. What can you say about such a person?"

"Our Rabbis say," said Harry, "that Achitophel was one of four people, who were not kings, who did not merit a portion in the world to come."

Sources:
Samuel 11

One of the prayers in the Synagogue liturgy is called Tachanun, the supplication prayer. It is a prayer of immense solemnity and when reciting it, the supplicant sits down, leans forward and rests his forehead on his arm in a gesture of total submission to the will of God. Benny's Dream traces the origin and significance of this prayer.

BENNY'S DREAM

Like a bullet from a gun, Benny Gabriel sprang from his chair at the first ring of the bell. "Grandma and Grandpa are coming to tea," he thought as he dashed to the door, "I wonder what present they'll bring me today."

He was not disappointed. The neat brown parcel in Grandpa's hand winked directly at him. "Come on in," he said somewhat breathlessly. "I hope I haven't kept you waiting."

"Each time we come here you seem to open the door faster," smiled Grandma. "I don't know where you get the energy from." She bent down and gave him a hug and a kiss. "Mmm," she said on straightening up. "I'm sure I had to bend down further last time. You youngsters seem to grow so quickly."

"Your Grandma is right," said Grandpa. "You are growing fast. But I'm sure you're growing in learning as well. By the way, we have something for you."

"Oh yes," said Benny casually. "What is it?"

"Open the parcel and you'll find out."

Just then Benny's parents arrived in the hall to welcome their visitors and immediately the house rang with the sound of warm greetings and pleasant exchanges. In all the flurry and fuss, Benny slipped away to examine his present.

Benny sat on the carpet in the morning room and quickly removed the brown paper wrapper. His eyes shone with excitement at the words on the colourful cover of a story book—'King David: Fighter of Philistines and Sweet Singer in Israel.'

"Thank you, Grandma, Thank you, Grandpa," shouted Benny, running from his room and into the lounge where they were sitting and talking to his parents. "Thank you for such a lovely present. It seems such an interesting book. Do you mind if I go upstairs to my room and read a bit of it straight away?"

"I don't mind," said Grandpa.

"In that case," chorused the others, "nor do we."

"See you soon." Benny clutched his new book and rushed up to his room.

"Benny! Come down and have your tea," his mother called up some time later.

There was no response and she called out again. "Benny, Benny, come down and have your tea."

"I'm not hungry," came the reply.

"There are cream cakes on the table," cooed his father teasingly.

"I'm still not hungry."

"He must have got involved in the book we bought him," said Grandpa. "I must confess I read a few stories myself and found them fascinating. Anyway, it's better he gets wiser with reading than fatter with eating." Everybody nodded their heads wisely in agreement.

"On the other hand, it's a pity to waste the cakes. Do you mind if I have just one more?"

"Next time," said Grandma to Grandpa, "I'll send you upstairs with the book."

"Go ahead. Enjoy yourselves," laughed Benny's mother. "There's plenty for everyone."

*   *   *

The adults soon forgot about Benny who remained in his room totally absorbed by the dramatic and moving stories of King David of Israel. Even long after his bedtime, he continued to read word after word and page after page.

Eventually his father came up to his room. "Benny, I'm sorry we forgot all about you. Come downstairs, have your supper and then—straight up to bed and get some sleep."

"Yes, daddy," said Benny meekly. But although he went to bed, he didn't go to sleep. He carried on reading.

Not surprisingly the following morning when his father called out "Wake up! It's time to go the Synagogue," Benny had to make a supreme effort to get out of bed. It seemed as if he had only just fallen asleep. He had. He had spent almost the whole night reading.

In the Synagogue all through morning Service, Benny kept yawning and rubbing his eyes. Try as he might, he found it impossible to concentrate on what he was saying. For the first time in his life he actually looked forward to saying the Tachanun prayer. Then he could lean forward, rest his head on his arm and snatch a few moments of much needed rest without attracting too much attention. With his head falling closer and closer to his prayer book, he waited for the reader to finish his prayers, then tapped his hand on his chest and fell forward.

'And David said to Gad (the prophet), I am so very upset . . .' The familiar opening words of Tachanun swam hazily before him. Where had he seen them before? In an effort to remember he tightly closed his eyes and immediately fell into a deep sleep.

*   *   *

Benny looked round and saw that he was now inside a large palatial building. He stared in wonder at marble pillars supporting high ceilings; at richly coloured tapestries decorating the walls; at soldiers with swords guarding the entrance to the hall in which he stood.

At one end of the hall, a king sat on a throne surrounded by a small group of people. An attendant came forward and addressed him.

"Your majesty, the Chief of your armies, Joab, has returned from his mission. He wishes to present you with his report."

"Let him enter," said King David.

The attendant bowed low before the king, and then walked backwards to the entrance of the hall in order to admit Joab who approached the throne and waited for permission to speak.

"You still look upset Joab. I can see my mission did not agree with you. Tell me! Did you carry out my instructions?"

"Yes, your Majesty. But I must confess I wish I had been less successful."

David frowned. "I ordered you to count the people of Israel. That was a royal command and you have the insolence to hope that your mission would be a failure. Explain yourself."

"Our Torah says they should not be counted unless it is absolutely necessary. I had hoped the people themselves would refuse to take part in your census."

"Did they?" David asked sternly. "What about the tribe of Dan? They're very outspoken. Did they object?"

"No, your Majesty. In fact, I went to them first. I was hoping they'd start a riot and prevent me continuing."

"Obviously they did not. So you see your fears were unjustified. I was acting correctly."

"I still have my doubts, your Majesty. I just cannot understand why all of Israel consented to be counted. Some mysterious and dangerous power appears to be at work."

"Nonsense, Joab. You're letting your imagination run away with you. Let me have all the facts and figures."

At the royal command, Joab stepped forward and handed over a sheaf of papers which David began to study.

All this time, Benny had been watching the king closely. Now he saw an amazing transformation take place. David's gentle expression first hardened into a frightening grimace. It then turned into a look of intense despair. His strong shoulders sagged and his body appeared to crumble and wilt away. He still looked down at the papers in his hands—but with unseeing eyes. Suddenly his body shook and a torrent of tears fell unchecked down his cheeks. He staggered to his feet and stood, a broken old man, as he cried out in a voice filled with pain and torment. "I have sinned! I have sinned!"

Benny could not believe his eyes. Could this be the same man who had fearlessly killed a lion and a bear when they had attacked his flock of sheep?

Could this be the hero of Israel who had courageously volunteered to fight the giant Goliath and then slew him with a single shot from his sling? Was this the man who had united all Israel under the banner of his leadership?

David came forward and placed his hand helplessly on Joab's shoulder. "Help me! Help me! I have endangered the whole nation."

As Joab supported his grief-stricken king, a man entered the hall and strode swiftly toward them.

"Your majesty," said Joab. "It is the Prophet Gad."

David raised his head slightly to look at the Prophet. "What must I do to atone for my sin? I have violated a Torah command. I commanded, without good reason, that the people should be counted."

The reply came immediately. "Counting people inevitably leads to disaster. The nation cannot avoid punishment. But God has given you three choices."

"What are they?" David asked cautiously.

"War, famine or disease," Gad said coldly. "Three months of war; seven years of famine; or three days of pestilence."

With bated breath, Benny waited for David's reply. Each option required careful consideration he reasoned. As a king in times of war his armies would protect him from attack. In famine, his vast treasures and resources would enable him to obtain adequate supplies for himself and his household. At least with these two options, people would be able to exercise some degree of control over their fortunes; but the rich would survive and the poor perish. Disease was different. Prince and pauper would be equally helpless in its deadly grip. This would be a punishment entirely in the hand of God.

Benny's thoughts were interrupted by a further striking change in David's appearance. The words of the Prophet had had an extraordinary effect upon the king. His bowed and broken body resumed its upright stance; his face once more radiated the splendour of majesty and nobility. Here indeed was the hero about whom the maidens of Israel had sung 'Saul has slain in his thousands but David has slain in his tens of thousands.'

The Divine decree had been made. Uncertainty was over. Now a decision had to be made on behalf of the nation. With honourable selflessness, the king selected the punishment of disease. And David said to Gad: "I am very distressed. Let us fall, I pray you, into the hand of God for his mercies are many. But let me not fall into the hand of man."

"That's Tachanun, that's Tachanun," shouted Benny excitedly. "That's where it comes from."

He felt a hand on his shoulder and heard his father's voice speaking gently in his ear. "Wake up Benny. You can't fall asleep during prayers."

Benny seemed embarrassed, "I was saying Tachanun, daddy and I must have fallen off."

"There is no Tachanun today Benny. One of the Synagogue members is making a circumcision this morning. His celebration is ours as well. Today we do not say the Tachanun prayer."

"Oh," said Benny said. "Anyway it doesn't matter. I had a lovely dream. I'll tell you all about it on the way home."

*   *   *

As they walked slowly away from the Synagogue, Benny related his vivid dream to his father. "Now I understand what David was saying to Gad," he concluded. "It's no wonder that Tachanun is such a mournful prayer."

"I'm not quite sure if you have all the facts correct," said Mr Gabriel, "but your account doesn't appear to be too far from the truth."

Benny looked up at him. "There's one thing I still don't understand daddy. Why did God cause David to count the people, and why should all the people have to be punished if one man commits a sin?"

His father scratched his chin thoughtfully. "That's a hard question Benny. Let me look up some books on the subject and I'll try to give you an answer."

*   *   *

A few days later on Friday night, Benny and his family were sitting around the Sabbath table and Mr Gabriel was expressing his appreciation for the first course of the meal. "Mmm. This really is an excellent hors d'oeuvres. Jacqui dear, you've done it again."

Mrs Gabriel's responsive beam had just the right balance of shyness and pride. "It's my pleasure," she murmured demurely.

"Ours too," was the gracious reply. "But now it's time for a few words of Torah. Benny, what have you been learning this week?"

"I'd hoped you would answer my questions tonight, daddy. About David and the counting of the people."

"Very well then. I knew you wouldn't let me off the hook. Let's go back a few years before the time of David. Let's go back to the last few days in the life of Eli the High Priest. Do you know about the terrible calamity that happened to the Children of Israel?"

"What was that?" asked Benny's younger sister, Elishevah.

"In those days, they were always involved in fights with the Philistines. One day a really big battle took place between them."

"Things weren't going too well for the Children of Israel. So they fetched the Ark of God from the Sanctuary in Shilo and took it with them onto the battlefield."

"Why should they do that?" asked Elishevah.

"They thought God would help them. And what do you think happened?"

"They started winning of course."

"No, unfortunately the very opposite. They began to lose heavily. Thousands were killed and the Ark was captured by the Philistines. When Eli the High Priest heard the news he was overcome with grief. He just collapsed in his chair and fell backwards. He died from a broken neck. I think, from a broken heart too. So the whole of Israel was plunged into mourning and despair."

"The Ark, daddy?" Elishevah seemed really worried. "What happened to the Ark? What happened to the two tablets of stones inside it?"

"Well, it seems as if the Philistines had the audacity to open up the Ark and look inside. They found the two stone tablets and started to examine them. The Children of Israel were so shocked by their defeat that they just stood watching helplessly from a distance. Especially, as the person holding the stone tablets was the giant Goliath."

"Wow," said Elishevah.

"Fortunately, there was one brave man among the Israelites. He ran forward and snatched the tablets from the hands of Goliath and ran quickly away."

"Did they catch him?" all the Gabriels asked.

"No, he ran like the wind. By the way, do you know his name?"

"Tell us. Tell us, daddy," pleaded Elishevah.

"All right," laughed her father. "It was Saul and later he became the first king of Israel. He certainly deserved it for being so brave."

"But what happened to the Ark?"

"That was taken by the Philistines to one of their capital cities. Believe me. It brought them nothing but disaster. First, their favourite idol Dagon mysteriously fell to pieces. Then a terrible plague broke out. They had a miserable time."

"So what did they do?"

"They sent the Ark back to Israel."

"I bet the people were pleased to see it again. Did they make a big fuss over it? Did they build a new house in which to keep and honour it?"

"No, they didn't. It's strange that all this time no one bothered to build a permanent home for the Ark. They still used the same temporary Sanctuary that had been built in the desert. Everybody was too busy with their own affairs to start thinking about a better building to house the Ark."

"That's disgraceful."

"Yes, even after it came back from the Philistines, it had no permanent home for another twenty years."

"And then?"

"Eventually David took it back to Jerusalem and put it into a tent."

"Again in a tent?"

"Yes, but this time God spoke to a different Prophet, to Nathan, to complain about the temporary accommodation for the Ark and the tablets."

"Did this help?"

"Not immediately. In the meantime there was the terrible incident with the counting of the people. When God gave David three choices of punishment, famine, war or plague. As you know, David chose the plague. He didn't want his position as king to give him any special protection against God's anger."

"Tell Mummy and Elishevah how it finished," urged Benny.

"As soon as the plague started, thousands of Children of Israel collapsed and died. Do you know David actually saw the angel responsible for the plague? He was hovering over Jerusalem with a sword in his hand.

"As David looked up, the angel stopped his slaughter of the Children of Israel; yet he still remained suspended over Jerusalem. He seemed to be pointing to a certain spot; to the threshing floor of a man called Araunah.

"What was the significance of that?"

"One of the reasons for the delay in building a Temple was a technical matter. No one knew the exact spot for its construction."

Mrs Gabriel appeared surprised. "I always thought it was built on Mount Moriah, the place where Abraham took up Isaac to become a sacrifice to God."

"Yes, it was, but people had forgotten the exact location and now the angel was pointing it out." Mr Gabriel took a glass of water to clear his throat. "I believe that David suddenly realised the reason for the plague; the people were being punished for their failure to build a Temple. They weren't being punished simply because he had counted them."

Elishevah wrinkled her eyebrows in puzzlement.

"You see, counting weakens the unity of a nation. So people are judged as individuals and at that time they were all guilty of neglecting the Sanctuary and the Ark."

"I see," said Benny. "You're saying that God decided to bring the plague through the counting of the people."

"Yes, in fact it says in the book of Samuel that God enticed David to count the people."

"So how did the plague stop?" asked Mrs Gabriel.

"Through the advice of the Prophet, Gad. He told David to build an altar on the place where the sword of the angel was pointing."

"The threshing floor of Araunah" added Benny.

"That's right."

Elishevah was still not satisfied. "But it didn't belong to him. How could he do that?"

"David arranged for the tribes to contribute an equal amount of money, and buy the site from Araunah. By the way, Araunah wasn't even Jewish. He was a Jebusite."

"So why did David buy it. He could have seized the land. He was the king."

"David didn't want the Temple to be a symbol of robbery and violence. He wanted it to be a symbol of peace."

"I see," said Mrs. Gabriel. "That's why God let Solomon have the honour of building it."

"Yes. Unfortunately, David wasn't destined to build the Temple but at least he'd helped to lay its foundations."

Benny looked at his father appreciatively. "That's quite a story. Next time I say Tachanun I'll have plenty to think about."

"You certainly will," laughed Mr Gabriel. "But first make sure you're not the only one saying it."

Sources:
Book of Samuel 2 ch.24.

DANGER BELOW

In the dead of the night, eleven men stood on a small, natural plateau more than half way up a mountain. The leader, wearing a long black cloak, his face and head closely shaven, carried a small earthenware lamp in one hand and a wooden staff in the other. "This'll do." He pointed to the mountain surface. "We shall start digging here."

"Digging? Excavating is more like it," said one of the men. "That's solid rock."

"It's not as bad as it seems. There's earth just below the surface. Besides, you won't have to go too deep." Now listen carefully. I want an area dug out, one meter wide, four meters long and half a meter deep. That'll be the tunnel. After he's inside, we'll use the planks to cover him. Then we use the stones to hide the wood.

"In the meantime—he pointed to the men—while you four are building the tunnel, the others will be building the stone altar.

"Now remember the instructions I gave you about that altar! You must allow for ample air space between each brick and you must also allow for the wooden rods to freely stand upright within the stones of the altar. Remember they will be coated with olive oil and carry the fire from below to the surface of the altar. They will ignite the layer of wood at the top of the altar.

The men, who had brought up with them a huge pile of stones, wooden rods, planks of wood and an assortment of digging tools, immediately commenced their tasks. Four of the men took their pickaxes and attacked the surface of the mountain while the others carefully built up a meter high altar.

*　　*　　*

The leader looked up at the sky. "There's another hour to sunrise. We must make sure we're at the foot of the mountain when the crowd begins to gather. I don't want any accusations of trickery."

"They won't notice anything," said one of the men. "All they'll see is smoke and fire coming from thin air. They'll think it's the genuine thing."

"And we know what's going to happen next," came a raucous laugh. "I wouldn't like to be in his shoes, when the crowd turns on him."

The leader smiled. "Well said. Let's hope that Chiel will be out in time to see it. In the meantime, let's get started. Chiel! Are you ready?"

Chiel stepped forward.

"You have everything Chiel? Blanket, water, taper, oil? And the lamp of course."

Chiel nodded.

"Good. Wrap yourself up well. Hide in the tunnel besides the altar until you hear the signal. Then light the fire. Good luck."

"Before you go," said Chiel, "there's just one thing. Have we thought of everything?"

"What do you mean?"

"This man's no normal person. He's a magician. He makes decrees and they come true. He'll find a way to protect himself. He'll undermine all our plans to ensnare him."

"No, Chiel. He is no god. He is a man like anyone else. He has no supernatural powers. Rest assured. I have placed our men all around the foot of the mountain. No one can get near you. There's nothing he can do. Now lie down and we'll cover you up." He turned to the other men. "Careful when you cover him. Make sure he has enough room to light the taper and kindle the wooden rods."

Under the pile of stones and bricks by the altar, Chiel waited for dawn to break. He knew it would not be too long. He smiled savagely as the crowing of a rooster signaled the beginning of the end of his vigil. Soon, he would light the fire and rid his people of a madman and troublemaker.

*   *   *

During those final moments, Chiel thought sadly of the events that had led to this day of destiny. He recalled his six children playing happily in front of his large, comfortable villa in one of the smart suburbs of Samaria in the Northern Kingdom of Israel. Then his eyes filled with tears as he recalled their untimely end. In a space of a few short years all had become victims of a mysterious and fatal disease.

His thoughts then turned to the time he had sat Shiva—when mourning—for his youngest son and been visited by Elijah the prophet and Ahab, King of Israel. The scene of that dramatic encounter flashed through his mind. Every word, every gesture was vividly relived.

*   *   *

"You Chiel!" said Elijah, "you committed the sin of rebuilding the city of Jericho. You knew what Joshua declared after he destroyed the city. He placed a curse on anyone who rebuilt it. It is for this reason your sons died."

"Nonsense!" replied Ahab. "That cannot be, I'll never believe that Chiel was punished for rebuilding the city of Jericho. The curse of Joshua was never intended to be fulfilled."

"How can you be so certain of this, your majesty?" asked Chiel.

"Because," said Ahab, "Moses also decreed a curse that has never been fulfilled."

"What curse was that?"

"Moses used these words in the Torah. 'Be very careful, and do not serve idols. Because if you do, then no rain will fall. I ask you Chiel. Has that curse been fulfilled?

"Just look around at the countryside. It is awash with water. The grass is lush and verdant. The cattle are strong and meaty. Yet my people and I have been serving idols for as long as I can remember.

"If Moses' curses were not fulfilled, do you expect Joshua's curse to be carried out? Can Joshua the servant be stronger than his master Moses?

Ahab roared with laughter and Chiel, despite his recent tragedies, joined in with him. But they had forgotten the presence of the Prophet of Israel.

"You, Chiel! You have been punished for your sin," he thundered. "And as for you, Ahab, listen to me. There will be no more rain in Israel until I command it. That I swear."

With this dire prophecy Elijah stormed from the house and strode quickly away; the sound of laughter still ringing in his ears.

"That man is no laughing matter. He's a troublemaker," were Ahab's final words to Chiel. "He has caused all your tragedies. He is responsible for the death of your children. One day, I swear to you, we shall get even with him."

*　　*　　*

From that day on, Ahab had scoured the countryside for Elijah, the arch enemy of Israel. He had put a price on his head and warned his people that no one should assist or shelter him.

Despite Ahab's efforts, Elijah could not be located and Chiel had to wait many years for his day of revenge.

During that time no rain fell in Israel and the fertile soil crumbled to powdery dust. Throughout the land, people and cattle grew weak and lay dying.

No one escaped the ravages of drought. Both king and commoner thirsted for water. Even Ahab himself searched desperately, in far off fountains and brooks, for water for his household and cattle. On one of these expeditions he met Elijah

"The time has come to settle this matter," said Elijah to Ahab. "Assemble all Israel at Mount Carmel, together with the prophets of Baal who eat at the table of Jezebel."

*   *   *

Chiel aroused himself from his daydreams. "The day of reckoning has now come," he said to himself. "As soon as they give the signal, I will be avenged for my sons' death."

Just then, a change in the mood of the crowd caught his attention and he listened attentively to the sounds from above. He clearly heard the voice of the Prophet Elijah addressing the people.

"People of Israel! Today we shall see who the true God is." Elijah looked around the vast gathering spread out over the mountain and beckoned them closer. "The prophets of the idol Baal are soon to make a sacrifice to their god. But they shall not place fire on the altar. Instead, they will pray to their god. If he is the true god, he will answer them with fire from heaven."

"And if he does not?" someone shouted out.

"Then he is a false god."

"That will not prove that your God is the true God."

"Agreed. Then it will be my turn. And I shall pray to God and He will answer me."

Chiel heard these words and smiled grimly. "Elijah doesn't realise I'm hidden under the altar of Baal. When the sacrifice is placed on it, I'll light the wood from beneath. When the crowd sees the offering burning, they'll stone him to death."

Just then, Elijah turned to the priests of Baal. "Here are the two bullocks for the offering. Choose your sacrifice. And I will choose mine."

Chiel heard the sound of footsteps as one of the priests went to take one of the bullocks to the altar. Then he heard a babble of frenzied shouting.

"The animal has knocked over the priest of Baal."

"It's running into the crowd."

"Careful it doesn't trample you."

"Bring it back here," bawled out one of the priests.

Eventually the animal was led back to the priests of Baal. But, when one of them attempted to place his hand on the unwilling sacrifice, it bolted once more.

"Wait!" Elijah commanded the bullock. "Come here!"

The young bullock walked docilely to the Prophet and stood in front of him.

"I understand why you're running away. You don't wish to be a sacrifice to a false god."

The animal looked up at the Prophet with tearstained eyes.

"Go quietly with these men. I promise you, your sacrifice today will be a sanctification of God's name." Elijah personally handed over the bullock to the priests of Baal and it tamely allowed itself to be prepared for the sacrifice.

The crowd watched in awed silence. Even Chiel felt a sense of wonder at the powers of the Prophet. Could I have been mistaken, he thought. Can there have been any truth in the curse of Joshua?

Almost immediately though, the bitterness of grief overcame his doubts. "Oh Baal!" he said feverishly. "Let your priests give the signal. Let this lighted torch show the people who the true god is."

*　　*　　*

Inside the altar, as shafts of sunlight struggled to penetrate the maze of cracks at its top, an unexpected sound thrust all thoughts of revenge from Chiel's mind. Coming from the top of the altar and slowly descending along one of the wooden rods, Chiel heard a sinister, slithering sound.

Chiel fought back the surge of fear threatening to overwhelm him. "No, no, it can't be," he panicked. "He's not a god." Despite the early morning chill, beads of sweat covered his forehead.

Lying prone on the ground, with very limited movement, Chiel knew he had few means of defence. 'Fire will destroy him. Fire will protect me,' he thought, as he desperately clenched his fist around the long taper and fumbled to set it alight from the lamp.

The slithering sound continued.

'Why don't they give the signal? Why are they waiting? Why has the animal not been slaughtered? Why is the taper not burning? 'Oh Baal,' he prayed desperately. 'Command them to give the signal! Command this taper to catch alight'

At the base of altar, Chiel sensed a movement. He strained to focus his eyes in the gloom and saw, to his horror, the jagged patterned head of a viper at the foot of the wooden rod.

Suddenly, the taper caught alight and Chiel slowly inched it towards the base of the altar. But the viper, ignoring the small flame in the hand of the enemy of Elijah, snaked steadily towards his uncovered face.

'That man does have magical powers. He has sent a serpent to destroy me,' were the last words of Chiel before the viper struck, plunging its poisonous fangs deep into his cheek.

"Fire! Send fire O,' Baal! Fire! Send fire O,' Baal!"

The signal was repeated again and again by the desperate men on the mountainside. They shouted and ranted as they wildly slashed and mutilated their bodies. But to no avail. Neither Chiel nor any other agent responded to their pleas. No smoke arose from the mound of stones. No fire kindled the wood and the dead bullock lying on top of the altar.

"Fire! Send fire O,' Baal! Fire! Send fire O,' Baal!"

The prostrate Chiel faintly heard the priests' signal seemingly coming from a vast distance. But his soul, like the yellow flame of the taper, was struggling to survive. Soon both were extinguished in the powdery soil of the underground chamber.

*　　*　　*

On that historic day, as the priests of Baal exhausted themselves with their frenzied prayers to a god that did not exist, Elijah mocked them mercilessly.

"Shout out louder for he is a god," he called out. "Perhaps he's engaged in conversation or discussion. He might even be on a journey. Perhaps he is sleeping and should be woken up."

His words goaded the priests to a renewed outburst. "Fire! Send fire O,' Baal!" they screamed hysterically. "Fire! Send fire O,' Baal!"

Eventually the crowd became restive. The priests of Baal were compelled to retire and Elijah was given the chance to make his prayer and sacrifice.

In front of the people, Elijah rebuilt the ancient altar of King Saul that stood on top of the mountain. To add to the miracle, he commanded that water from the sea should be poured over the sacrifice, the wood and the trench around the altar. Then, at the time of the afternoon sacrifice in Jerusalem, he offered up a simple and dignified prayer to God. "Answer me, O 'God. Answer me. Let the people know that You, God are the Lord . . ."

The response was electric. Lightning flashed from a cloudless sky, kindling and consuming the wood, the offering, the stones and the dust; it also evaporated the water in the trench around the altar.

The people were overcome with awe and dread at this dazzling display of Divine power. They fell on their faces and shouted out. "God is the Lord! God is the Lord!" Then they rose up and executed the evil priests of the false god Baal.

Without delay, Elijah went to the top of the mountain and, after offering a short prayer for rain, repeatedly asked his servant. "Can you see anything on the horizon over the sea?"

Each time the lad answered. "No!" But on the seventh occasion he reported: "There is a small cloud the size of a man's fist rising out of the water."

Within minutes, the sky was overcast with dense black clouds, a strong wind blew and, like stones from the sky, huge drops of rain crashed to the ground to be greedily swallowed by the thirsty soil.

*   *   *

At the top of Baal's abandoned altar, the rain swiftly found gaps in the unburnt wood and penetrated the underground chamber. It cascaded on to the still, silent figure and slid to the surface below. Before long, the chamber was completely filled with water.

Sources:
Kings I Chapters 16,18

THE VINEYARD

The Vineyard is a story about the conflict between Ahab and Naboth as recorded in Kings 1 ch. 21.

After the death of King Solomon, Jereboam successfully led the ten northern tribes in a rebellion against the House of David. He established a new monarchy and a different 'religious' order in the northern part of Israel. He stationed armed guards on his southern border to prevent worship in Solomon's Temple; set up idols in Beth-el and Dan; and transferred the festival of Tabernacles from the seventh to the eighth month in the Jewish year.

Ahab became king over Israel about fifty years after the death of Jereboam. In his reign, the physical and religious barriers between the two kingdoms remained. Yet, many Jews from the North persisted in defying Jereboam's original decrees and remained loyal to the religious codes of the Southern Kingdom of Judah.

The sun was setting in the Jezreel Valley.

In his lantern-lit garden, Naboth, the man with the finest voice in Israel, was entertaining a privileged circle of family and friends. To a backdrop of palm trees, orchids and verdant lawns, he sang with breathtaking sweetness; of the tragedies and triumphs of Jewish history. The 'horse and rider' thrown into the sea; the defeat of Sisera at the brook of Kishon; and the blind Samson chained to a threshing mill in the darkness of Gaza.

He sang of his hopes for the future; of a united Israel where the barriers dividing the kingdoms would be lifted; where once more, he and all Israel would be free to worship in the Temple in Jerusalem.

At the end of the recital, as the last notes of an accompanying harp faded into the warm, still air, there was a momentary silence. Then the cries of congratulations rang out. "Excellent Naboth! I've never heard you sing better! Well done! May we all merit spending the next year in Jerusalem. May we all merit hearing you sing with such sweetness, next year in Jerusalem."

"Next year in Jerusalem!" Naboth repeated the words as if in a dream. Then a forest of arms overwhelmed him; shaking his hands, slapping his back and ruffling his hair. All he could hear were shouts of "Well done! Well done! Again and again, he heard the cry "Next year in Jerusalem!"

As the applause for Naboth continued unabated, three men appeared at the edge of the garden and pushed their way through the crowd. Their leader Jonah, a short man who appeared to have tree trunks for thighs and a wine-barrel for a chest, spoke brusquely to Naboth. "Yes Naboth! Next year in Jerusalem. Can we discuss this? Now!"

Naboth eyed the men cautiously. He had no doubts about the reason for their visit and had carefully prepared his defence in advance. Yet he still felt a sense of guilt—and foreboding. "Peace unto you," he said as casually as possible. "I missed you at the concert. Is there anything wrong?"

"There is nothing wrong with us Naboth." An air of menace clouded Jonah's words. "Whilst you were singing to your friends of your hopes for the future, we were planning this year's journey to the Temple.

"What about you though? What are your plans Naboth? Are you coming with us to Jerusalem this year? Or are you too frightened to test the strength of the guards at the border? I assume you don't mind me discussing the matter in front of all these people. There are no spies among us. Let me explain to you what we plan to do."

"Save your breath" interrupted Naboth, "and your strength. You'll certainly need it this year."

Jonah looked at Naboth with disbelief. "Why is this year any different?"

"Because of one person, Jonah. One person who is more determined than ever to stop us going up to Jerusalem; Jezebel, that pagan wife of Ahab. You must have heard. She's increased the number of border guards."

"We're not afraid of Jezebel—or her patrols," said Jonah fiercely. "We've got through in the past, and we'll get through again. She is determined, but we're even more determined. Nothing will stop us going to Jerusalem this year."

"Jonah, Jonah," Naboth spoke gently, as though reasoning with a child. "Of course you'll get to Jerusalem this year. You're strong and experienced. But why don't you ever think about others for a change?"

"What do you mean others?"

"Others who are weak and inexperienced. You know what happens when people hear I'm going to Jerusalem. They try to follow me. Young people, foolish people. They come without money to bribe the guards and without knowledge of the safe paths across the border. I ask you, Jonah. How many will be killed? by the guards, by wild animals. How many will be murdered by gangs of robbers?—No! I will not have the lives of those innocent people on my conscience."

"So you're thinking about others," Jonah's voice dripped with sarcasm. "I'm sorry I misjudged you, Naboth. I'm pleased that the rumours I heard about you are untrue."

"Rumours?" A hint of uncertainty crept in Naboth's voice but he quickly controlled it. "What rumours?"

"People are saying you're worried about your vineyard, Naboth. It's common knowledge that Ahab wants to buy it and you've refused to sell it to him. They're saying you're afraid to go to Jerusalem so Ahab cannot find an excuse to kill you."

"That is not true."

"Good. I'm pleased you remembered the law about war and vineyards."

"What law?"

"The law that releases a man from military service if he has not properly established his vineyard. Your vineyard is, thank God, well established. Don't you realise we're fighting a war against Jezebel and her gods. In time of war you go to battle."

"Jonah, you misunderstand me. I'm not afraid to fight and die for a righteous cause. But don't you realise that Ahab will gain nothing by murdering me. My vineyard would not go to Ahab. It would pass on to my family."

"Yes, and what would they do under pressure from Ahab and Jezebel. After they've seen what's happened to you. How will they resist? You're no fool Naboth. You know you're not dealing with Ahab. You're dealing with Jezebel. A thwarted woman will stop at nothing to get her revenge. Your family will not have the stomach to stand up to that devil of a woman."

Naboth breathed heavily. "I repeat. I do not believe my life is in danger from Ahab. He would not be a party to such a crime. He might be an idolater. But he is not a murderer."

"But she is. She will murder to get what she wants. Don't be so stubborn, Naboth. Sell Ahab your vineyard and come with us to Jerusalem this year."

"I appreciate your concern, Jonah. But in all honesty, I do not share your fears."

"Listen to me, Naboth, for the last time." Jonah's aggression faded away, as he put forward a different argument. "No voice in Israel and Judah compares with yours. People come from all over the country to listen to you singing in the Temple. Your singing enhances the holiness of the Holy Festivals. It adds beauty and dignity to the Temple Service. Forget this obsession with your vineyard and come with us to Jerusalem. You want to fight Jezebel. Well, choose the right issue. Not your vineyard. But the Temple. That is where your responsibilities lie. In singing to God."

"Don't lecture me about responsibilities," said Naboth impatiently. "There is a time to sing—and a time to be silent. I don't want my voice to become an instrument of death. I know what to do. Now, if you'll excuse me. I have urgent business to attend to." He pushed his way through the crowd of people milling around him, feeling all the time Jonah's eyes boring into his back. Whilst through his mind rang the accusing refrain—Next year in Jerusalem.

*   *   *

On the fifteenth day of the seventh month, in defiance of Jereboam's original decree, Naboth celebrated the Feast of Tabernacles in traditional manner. He abandoned the comfort and luxury of his villa to dwell, by day and by night, in a cedar-wood hut covered with pine leaves and palm branches.

Naboth instinctively felt that Ahab would investigate his 'revolutionary' behaviour. He was not surprised, therefore, at the sudden appearance of four soldiers at the doorway of his tabernacle.

"Come on in," he said to the soldiers, "I have nothing to hide. Make yourself at home."

"We're here to enforce law and order." The officer-in-command, a retired soldier who had lost an arm in the recent Syrian campaign, marched imperiously into the tabernacle. He stood rigidly to attention in front of his soldiers and immediately stated the purpose of his visit. "You know it's forbidden to keep the Feast of Tabernacles before the official date. In the Northern Kingdom of Israel, the Festival is celebrated in the eighth month of the year."

"I can assure you, officer," said Naboth, "I am committing no crime that will bring about the fall of the Northern Kingdom. What harm am I doing by sitting in an open hut at this time of the year? Join me in enjoying God's bounty. Look at the exquisite carvings and paintings on the walls. Breathe in the aroma of the citron and the myrtle. Savour the view of the grapes and pomegranates above your head."

As Naboth spoke, he began to sing and the richness of his voice softened the angry glare of the soldiers. "You must know the grapes are now at their best. Here! Have some." He gestured to a bowl of fruit on his table.

The officer, who had two cousins and a brother-in-law in Judah, secretly had more sympathy with Naboth than Jezebel. He hesitated, then looked uncomfortably towards his soldiers.

Again Naboth urged them to partake of his hospitality. "This wine is ten years old. I guarantee it's the best I've ever made. Try some for yourself.

155

Take back a bottle for King Ahab himself." Naboth could not resist snapping his fingers at Ahab's repeated attempts to force him to sell his vineyard.

He recalled that only two days earlier, Ahab had met him at his vineyard and begged him to reconsider his decision. He had emphatically refused. He had suspected Ahab of wishing to convert the vineyard into an idolatrous shrine. Indeed, he had openly accused Ahab of desecrating God's holiness. His words had sparked off a furious argument between them.

With the memory of this encounter still fresh in his mind, Naboth held up his glass to the soldiers. "Come now. Let's drink a toast to God and to King Ahab."

The succulent grapes, aromatic wine and golden timbre of Naboth's voice melted the resolution of the soldiers. Forgetting the purpose of their visit, they sat down at the tabernacle table—to wine and dine under an exotic canopy of fruit and foliage.

*   *   *

In Samaria, Ahab, from the time of his heated encounter with Naboth, had refused to eat. Now even two days later, he still could not bring himself to break his fast. He just sat and sulked in the dining room of his palace.

Naboth's gift of a flagon of wine had only added to his misery. It had opened up old wounds and sores. It had revived his feeling of humiliation in the eyes of his people. How could he Ahab, son of the mighty Omri, conqueror of Moab and scourge of Syria, submit to the will of a commoner? Without pause, Ahab strummed his fingers nervously on the table in front of him. "How much longer would Naboth refuse to sell him his vineyard," he kept asking himself. "How could he be persuaded to change his mind?"

Opposite Ahab, his wife, Jezebel, a glass of wine at her lips, reclined on a sofa. "Ahab!" she called out contemptuously. "How much longer do you intend to fast? When will you assert your authority as king over your people?"

Ahab ignored the question. "Why does Naboth not accept the other vineyard I've offered him? He knows it's a better vineyard. Why is he so stubborn?"

"You're as stubborn as he is." Jezebel picked up a grape from the table and crushed it between her bejewelled fingers. "You can crush him as easily as I crush this grape. You are the king of Israel. Force him to hand over his vineyard to you. In my country, no one would dare to defy the king."

"This is Israel not Sidon. The king has to obey the law."

"The law? All you ever speak about is the law. The king is the law."

"No! The law is the king. My subjects would not tolerate any interference with the law. I cannot force him to act against his will."

"His will? Since when does a king have to consider the will of his subjects? In a kingdom, there is only one will. The will of the king."

"No, Jezebel! Not in the kingdom of Israel. A king has to bend his will to the wishes of his subjects."

"That is not kingship. That is servitude."

"Then I was chosen to serve."

"I was chosen to rule." Jezebel looked angrily at her husband. "Force him to obey you." She waved her hand towards the diamond-studded tapestries adorning the walls of the chamber. "Wealth without power is a Samson without hair. Show me and show your people that these riches are not empty symbols. Make an example of this Naboth. Compel him to sell you his vineyard. Or make him suffer the consequences."

"I will not break the law."

"My dear Ahab, as I told you before, the king cannot break the law. He is the law. You are upholding the law."

"I will not sacrifice Torah law for the sake of his vineyard," said Ahab, regretting his wife's interference. "I am prepared to forget it."

"Forget the vineyard? You go two days without food or water. Now you want to forget it." Suddenly the shrewd Jezebel realised that Naboth's vineyard was not the only reason for her husband's depression. "Tell me Ahab. What did Naboth say to you when he refused to sell?"

"Nothing of consequence."

"In that case, you can share those words with your wife. What did he say to you?"

Ahab finally unburdened his troubled mind. "He said, 'God has forbidden me to give away unto you the inheritance of my fathers.' But he meant much more than that. He used the word God. He accused me of deserting God for idols. He refuses to sell me his vineyard in case it becomes a shrine for one of our gods."

"He dared to insult you," raged Jezebel. "He dared to insult our gods. Naboth is a traitor to Israel. Uphold the law Ahab. Put him to death."

"No Jezebel! I cannot execute a person because of my interpretation of his words. My people will not allow it."

"Your people will not allow it," mocked Jezebel. "What are you? a king or a peasant? Well, let me tell you this, Ahab. Naboth will be executed for his crime against you and your gods. Your people will not only allow it, they will demand it; that I assure you. Now rise up from your chair, Ahab. Eat and drink. I will give you Naboth's vineyard."

*   *   *

Five years earlier, two men, Netanyahu the son of Emori and Ishmael the son of Chiti, had sunk all their capital into a flourishing olive grove in the Jezreel Valley. They enjoyed two successful harvests, but failed to reinvest their profits. Instead, they lost them in the gambling houses and race courses of Samaria.

In the third year of their venture, the entire olive crop was destroyed by locusts. The two men borrowed heavily from Jezebel at an extortionate rate of interest.

During the next two years, Jezebel took increasing advantage of their misfortunes. Instead of payment of some of her interest, she persuaded them, to wreak arson, theft and other criminal damage on anyone who questioned her decrees or belittled her beliefs. Inexorably, she manoeuvred the two men into a position of total compliance with all her evil wishes.

Now, on a wind-swept night in Tishri, one hour after nightfall, the two men stealthily entered an unguarded entrance at the rear of Ahab's palace. They walked up a flight of stone steps and tapped on the door of a room on the first floor.

"Come in," commanded a voice. "And lock the door behind you."

Netanyahu and Ishmael, still deeply in debt and desperate to release themselves from a lifetime of financial bondage, entered the room and closed the door behind them. They stared uneasily at the painted face of their pitiless creditor, Jezebel.

"Sit down." A bright-red fingernail glowed in the lamplight as Jezebel waved towards two chairs by a table in the centre of the room.

The two men walked warily towards the table and sat down; Netanyahu, short and stocky, with a face reddened by excessive drinking at the taverns of Samaria; and Ishmael, tall and slim, who had acquired a particular habit at the gaming tables he so unsuccessfully frequented. His eyes constantly flashed from one side of the room to the other.

"I've invited you here to give you a golden opportunity."

With barely disguised cynicism, Netanyahu wrinkled his nose. Ishmael however, knowing the danger of enraging Jezebel, kept his emotions to himself.

"An opportunity from Jezebel." The same thought shot through their minds "One can only imagine the price to be paid."

Jezebel ignored the sceptical looks. "I'm giving you an opportunity to pay off your debts and enjoy wealth, real wealth for a change."

"What do we have to do?" asked Netanyahu.

Jezebel came straight to the point. "You will ensure a criminal and his crime are exposed and punished. You will testify you heard a crime being committed."

"Heard a crime? In Israel, speech is no crime."

Jezebel's eyes blazed with righteous indignation. "Blasphemy is. Ahab, king of Israel and his gods were blasphemed."

"By whom?"

"By Naboth the Jezreelite." Jezebel spat out the name.

"You want us to commit perjury." Netanyahu drew in his breath sharply. "You know the penalty if we're found out. I'm not prepared to risk my neck by testifying against Naboth."

"Your neck at this moment Netanyahu is not worth a bronze shekel. You don't have much choice. You're both in debt. If I call in the loans, you'll both be finished."

"The risk is too high. Naboth is too popular. The people will rebel. Even the judges will throw out the case. You can't take your private vendettas into the public court room."

"This is no private vendetta. This is a matter of public concern." Jezebel pointed to a document lying on the table in front of the men. "Look at that document. It's signed and sealed by Ahab himself. It testifies to Naboth's blasphemy. Read it."

Jezebel leaned forward to emphasise her point. "Copies of this document, all signed and sealed with the royal seal, have been sent to the most prominent nobles and judges in Israel. All agree that Naboth has committed an unsavoury crime. All agree he must be executed."

"Judges and nobles can be persuaded to act in the best interests of the king and his queen," argued Ishmael, "but what about the people? You can't send a copy of this document to every man, woman and child in the country. Naboth's execution will fuel a rebellion."

"The people?" smiled Jezebel. "I haven't forgotten the people. The people will be more than satisfied with the death of Naboth."

Netanyahu and Ishmael looked at Jezebel in puzzlement.

"The people are complaining. There's been a series of disasters in Israel recently. I've no doubt there will be more in the next few weeks. They want to know who is responsible for these disasters. They want action. They want the priests to pray to the gods for forgiveness. I can assure you the priests will do their job. They will pray to the gods. And the gods will reply. They will ask the people to expose the sinner who is poisoning Israel.

"Naboth," whispered the men.

"Naboth is poisoning Israel," said Jezebel, with total conviction. "In three weeks time, the priests of Israel will proclaim a public fast. On the fifteenth of the month, everybody will assemble to pray, repent and confess; to confess their sins—and the sins of others. The chairman at this assembly will be Naboth.

"Now listen carefully. You will also be there—as the saviours of Israel. You must prepare yourselves well. You must know every detail of his crime. You must know every word he said. You must know the place of his crime. You must know the time of his crime; the hour, the day, the month, the year. You must even know the type of clothes he wore when he uttered his blasphemy. Remember, you are genuine witnesses who saw and heard a crime being committed.

"Rehearse your evidence carefully together. This hearing will be conducted strictly according to the Laws of the Land of Israel. I don't want your evidence dismissed because you can't agree with each other."

"What do we get out of it?" the two men asked.

Jezebel rose to her feet. "Naboth has a large estate. After his execution, it will become the property of the king. It is only right that you as the saviours of Israel be rewarded. You will each receive one talent of silver."

"One talent of silver?" exclaimed Netanyahu. "By the time we pay off our debts, there'll be nothing left. You want us to risk our lives for one talent of silver. Who knows we might have to leave Israel for a little while. That could also be expensive."

"Your debts to me will be cancelled. And I will arrange to provide you with another talent of silver—to be shared between you."

The two men, believing they could force a better deal from Jezebel, looked guardedly at each other. But Jezebel was in no mood for haggling. "I have many other debtors prepared to make sacrifices for the sake of Israel. If my offer is not to your liking, then leave quickly and quietly."

The men remained silent.

"Good. I take it you agree to my terms. We shall meet again next week. I intend to monitor your progress. In the meantime," she said, handing over two bags of coins, "this will give you a foretaste of the good life you can expect in the future.

"Good night, gentlemen. Make sure you leave as carefully as you came."

*   *   *

Israel assembled for a day of prayer and confession. Peasants and landlords, artisans and merchants, ministers and judges; all thronged into the large amphitheatre in the centre of Samaria. On the semicircular rows of stone steps rising from the floor of the amphitheatre, they waited noisily for the proceedings to begin.

On the stage in the front of the theatre sat two rows of dignitaries. Nobles, princes and High Priests from the cults of the sun god, moon god, Ishtar and Baal; in the front row, in the centre, sat the chairman, Naboth.

At a discreet signal from Naboth, three men with Trumpets stepped forward to stand in front of the marble steps. In unison, they raised their instruments to their lips, and boomed out a long, loud blast that silenced the crowd.

A second blast quickly followed and Naboth rose to address the vast audience.

"Men of Israel!" Naboth's rich voice resounded round the amphitheatre. "We have come here today to uproot the evil from our midst. We have come to do penitence for the sins that have brought tragedy and disaster throughout Israel.

"In the Bekaa Valley, a young child was travelling with his parents. He suddenly fell out of his carriage. No one knows how and why. He was crushed to death by the wagon behind him.

"The family was respected by their neighbours. They performed good deeds on behalf of others. They were diligent in prayer, service and charity.

"God has snatched a priceless soul from our people. God has brought grief and bereavement to an innocent family." With heartfelt passion he sang out. "There is an evildoer among us."

The refrain was taken up by one section of the crowd, then quickly spread throughout the assembly. "There is an evildoer among us."

"In Shechem, a father of seven children was working at the foot of a hill. For no reason, a boulder fell down the hillside and crushed him to death. He was a man without sin, without an evil thought in his mind, without an enemy in the world. Again God has brought grief and bereavement to an innocent family. There is an evildoer among us," he sang out and again the assembly joined in the refrain.

"In Beth-el, a bride of twelve years old was seized by bandits from under the marriage canopy. She has never been seen again. There is an evildoer among us."

Using his voice skilfully to convey the full effect of these tragedies, Naboth evoked a series of impassioned outbursts from the mesmerised crowd. Tears flowed freely down their faces.

"These are not natural happenings. God is showing his anger to the people of Israel. There is an evildoer in our midst. 'And you shall remove the evil from amongst you,'" he sang out.

"Men of Israel! Step forward. Step forward and confess. Step forward and testify against the sinner who has brought tragedy to Israel."

Throughout the vast crowd, men spontaneously pulled back their heads to look up towards the heavens, beat their chests with clenched fists and loudly shout out, "I confess! I have sinned. O' God. Punish me for the evil I have done."

The men pushed their way through the milling crowd and ran to the front of the amphitheatre. They threw their arms around wooden stakes that had been set into the ground and cried out. "Beat me! Punish me!"

Immediately, priests of Baal, with leather thongs in their hands, stepped forwards from the side of the theatre and lashed the repenting sinners on their back.

"Confess and testify." The voice of Naboth, accompanied by the priests, rose above the noise of the crowd and the cries of the beaten men. "Confess and testify."

More and more people responded to the challenge until the theatre was turned into a frenzy of wailing and weeping, at the evil destroying Israel.

To the rear of the theatre, a man, his florid face aglow with effort and excitement, pushed and elbowed his way through the clamouring crowd. "Let me through! I wish to testify. Let me through!" He reached the front of the theatre and spoke, somewhat breathlessly, to the high priest of Baal. "I have come to testify. I have important evidence to give for Israel."

"I have also come to testify." A second man from the crowd came to the front of the theatre. Panting slightly from nervous tension and exertion, his eyes rapidly darting from side to side, he echoed the other's cry. "I too have important evidence to give."

The High Priest, tall and upright, his face lined like a crinkled citron, looked down haughtily at the two men. "What are your names?"

"Netanyahu the son of Emori."

"Ishmael the son of Chitti."

"From what town are you?"

"From Samaria," they both answered.

"What crime did you witness?"

"We are witnesses to the crime of blasphemy."

"Blasphemy! Against whom?"

"Against God. And against the King of Israel, Ahab."

"Blasphemy is a serious crime. It could well explain the disasters that have befallen Israel. You have evidence of this crime. Take care! You know the penalty for making a false charge."

The men nodded gravely.

"Very well, whom do you accuse of this crime?"

The two men looked towards the centre of the front row of dignitaries. Simultaneously, they raised their hands and pointed their fingers at Naboth. "There is the destroyer of Israel. There is the man who has brought disaster to the nation. That man, Naboth cursed God and Ahab, king of Israel."

Naboth rose angrily to his feet. "Remove these men from here. They are troublemakers."

"Take care, Naboth," the High Priest cautioned. "No one is immune from just accusation."

"This is not just accusation. These men are liars. I've never seen them before. How can they testify against me? They've been paid by Jezebel to tell lies against me."

"We shall decide that. We shall question these men and consider their evidence." The High Priest beckoned to the captain of the guard standing by his company of soldiers. "Seize Naboth and keep him under close custody. See he does not escape."

*　　*　　*

At these special assemblies of public prayer and confession, it was the custom for evidence of wrongdoing to be quickly heard and assessed. The rights of the individual were pushed aside by the interests of the nation.

*　　*　　*

After a hurried and one-sided discussion among Jezebel's puppet judges and priests, the High Priest gave a signal to the trumpeters to step forward to silence the confused crowd.

"Men and women of Israel!" Like thunder, the voice of the High Priest, deep and strident, reverberated in the ears of the people in the theatre. "Two men, Netanyahu the son of Emori and Ishmael the son of Chiti, both of Samaria, have testified that Naboth is guilty of an inexcusable crime. They claim that four weeks ago, on the thirteenth day of the seventh month, two hours after sunrise, Naboth in his vineyard at Jezreel cursed the names of God and of Ahab, King of Israel. We have heard their evidence and have found Naboth guilty of this crime.

"Men of Israel! Listen carefully. Before we carry out the sentence of stoning, who can testify for Naboth. Who can testify against the two witnesses, Netanyahu the son of Emori and Ishmael the son of Chiti?"

Initially a wall of silence greeted the words of the high priest, then shouting broke out from all over the crowd.

"He has bereaved me!"

"He has stolen my daughter!"

"Death to the traitor!"

"Stone the hypocrite!"

"Execute the destroyer of Israel!"

"You are condemned by all Israel," the High Priest said to Naboth. "You have betrayed them."

"No one will stand up to Ahab and Jezebel," said Naboth bitterly. "They have terrified the people. Her secret police are everywhere. No crime is too loathsome for them."

"Take care Naboth. Do not belittle the people of Israel. See how they repent for their sins. See the blows they suffer for the sake of repentance. They know right from wrong."

The High Priest turned back to the crowd. "We are duty bound to act according to the law of Israel. The execution will take place immediately."

* * *

An ashen faced Naboth, his arms bound behind his back, escorted by the throng from the theatre and an ever increasing crowd of spectators was rudely pushed through the streets of Samaria. Then, with two soldiers grasping firmly at his arms, he was dragged up the ramp to the ten-foot high execution platform standing outside the walls of the city. Closely behind came the High Priest of Baal and the two witnesses, Netanyahu and Ishmael. Below them, with hate in their eyes, stood the seething, vengeful crowd of Israelites, in the hand of each one, a stone picked up from the floor of the valley.

The High Priest held up his hand and the crowd fell silent. "People of Israel, when Joshua son of Nun conquered Jericho, one man, Achan, committed a sin. For that sin, all Israel was punished. We too have been punished for the sin of one man.

"But Joshua was merciful. Before the execution, he asked Achan to confess. He wanted Achan to have atonement for his soul.

"We are also a merciful people, said the High Priest, turning towards Naboth. "I ask you now to confess to your sin."

Naboth was outraged. "How can I confess to a crime I did not commit? Your witnesses are liars. They have been paid by Jezebel. I never said such words."

"Confess to your crime," the High Priest insisted. "You were found guilty by a court of law. You would not be executed and punished by God unless you were guilty of a crime."

'Unless you were guilty of a crime.' The words of the High Priest struck a responsive chord in the mind of Naboth. Unnerved by the hostile shouts of the crowd and bewildered by the sudden turn of events, he heard the words as if in a trance. Round and round his mind they spun. 'You would not be executed and punished by God unless you were guilty of a crime.'

Naboth turned away from the High Priest and, as if in a dream, gazed round the vast crowd awaiting his execution. Closing his eyes he recalled another crowd that used to gather around him. He saw again the majestic walls of the Temple towering above him; the priests carrying out their holy duties; the upturned ecstatic faces of the festival pilgrims as they listened in awe to the sweet splendour of his extraordinary voice rising from the steps of the Temple courtyard and ascending to the very heart of heaven.

'Next year in Jerusalem' People come from all over the country to listen to you singing in the Temple. That is where your responsibilities lie. Not in fighting Jezebel. But in singing to God.' The words of his friend Jonah filled his mind.

The High Priest broke into Naboth's thoughts. "You are given the choice of confession. Confess to your crime before you die. This will grant you pardon in the next world for your evil deed."

For a moment, Naboth looked into the implacable eyes of the high priest, then he turned away, sobbing quietly. "O,' God," he said to himself. "I confess. I have sinned against You with my voice, by not using my voice for your glory."

"But," he shouted out, "against Ahab I committed no sin. He and Jezebel are the destroyers of Israel. O,' God, let my murder be avenged."

The High Priest ignored the outburst. In a loud, steady voice, he instructed the soldiers. "Blindfold his eyes. Hold him fast at the edge of the platform. Face him towards me." He beckoned to the two witnesses. "Netanyahu the son of Emori. Ishmael the son of Chiti. Come forward. Place your hand on Naboth's chest. Remove the evil from the midst of Israel."

The High Priest nodded gravely towards the two men and two pairs of willing arms thrust the condemned man into Eternity.

"O' God, let my murder be aveng . . . ." The brief cry echoed and re-echoed throughout the valley. Then a hail of stones rained down on the twisted, crumpled body at the foot of the platform, until its limbs were still, its voice silent.

THE ARROW OF JUSTICE

"Hallo, Daniel," said Mr Gabriel as his youngest son walked into the house after school. "Did you have a good day?"

"Yes," said Daniel with some hesitation.

"What's the matter? You don't seem your usual cheerful self."

"I'm not. We had a very upsetting Bible story today."

"Oh yes. What was it about?"

"About King Ahab and Naboth's vineyard."

"What part of the story upset you, Daniel?"

"The whole story daddy. It didn't seem right that Naboth should've been stoned to death for something he never did. Why did God not stop Ahab from taking the life of an innocent person?"

"That's a good question Daniel and you're in very good company. A lot of people have asked that very same question."

"So what did they answer?"

"Don't be so impatient, Daniel. You first have to know who asked the question."

"Why?"

"To show it is an important question and it deserves a proper answer."

"So who asked the question?"

"Daniel for one."

"I know that already daddy. My memory's not that bad."

"Of course I know that. And you have a good head as well."

"Thank you daddy. Now stop playing games."

"I'm not playing games. One of the first people to ask your question in such an open manner was Daniel, the prophet, after the destruction of the Temple."

"One of the first. Who was the first, then?"

"Jeremiah"

"The prophet?"

"Yes, Jeremiah the prophet."

"Wow! I'm in good company. What was his actual question?"

"I'm sure you remember your Bible. Nebuchadnezzar destroyed the Temple in the time of Jeremiah. Naturally, Jeremiah was very distressed at what he saw. He saw the Temple desecrated, the Babylonians dancing in the Holy of Holies, the place where only the High Priest was allowed to go once a year. And he saw the Jewish nation taken in chains to Babylon.

166

Jeremiah poured out his heart to God. How can You allow such a thing? How can You allow such desecration? Where is Your awesomeness? Where is Your power?"

"These questions would not go away. And Jeremiah could not find an answer to them. They played on his mind so much that it affected the way he prayed to God."

"In which way, Daddy?"

"When Jeremiah prayed, he could no longer bring himself to use the word 'awesomeness' when speaking about God. He left out that word from his prayers."

"Only Jeremiah left out that word? What about the other people at the time?"

"Well Jeremiah was the leader of his generation. And if he left out the word awesomeness, others followed his example. But it didn't stop there."

"Why what happened?"

"Daniel the prophet went one stage further. After the destruction of the Temple, the people of Israel were exiled to Babylon and became slaves to the Babylonians. This time Daniel was distressed. So he complained to God. 'How can you allow your children to be enslaved by the Babylonians? Where is your might?"

"So what did he do?"

"He took out the word 'might 'from his prayers"

"So how did those two words get back into the prayers? Everybody says them today."

"They were put back by Ezra and his Rabbinical Court. And from that time Ezra and his Rabbinical Court were known as the Men of the Great Synagogue, the Men who restored the greatness to God."

"Before the Temple was rebuilt, daddy?"

"Yes."

"So why did they put those words back? How did God show his greatness before the Temple was rebuilt?"

"Because they argued as follows. Greatness is not measured by showing off your strength and stopping evil people from doing bad things. Of course God could have stopped the Babylonians from destroying the Temple. But God, when He created the world, decided not to interfere with people. Nature has to take its course. No matter how badly people behaved, God does not openly intervene. Of course God was distressed at the destruction of the Temple but He restrained Himself from interfering—and that Daniel is true greatness."

167

"But if God allows people to do what they want, they could destroy the Jewish people. How can we survive?"

"What you say, is true, Daniel. I've often wondered myself, how do we survive? But the answer to that question was also given by the Men of the Great Synagogue. They said that the Jewish nation among the seventy nations of the world is like one little sheep in the midst of seventy wolves. Yet somehow they manage to survive. That demonstrates that God is still there and looking after us. But not with the same open miracles as in the time of Moses. The nature of God's awesomeness has changed. But it is still there. And we have to mention this in our daily prayers."

"Your explanation does make things a little bit clearer, daddy. But with Naboth and Ahab, how did God show that He was in charge?"

"Good question, Daniel. So, let's continue the story from where you left off."

Naboth's Vineyard

The day after Naboth was stoned to death and his properties transferred to the king, Ahab, escorted by a troop of his soldiers, came to the vineyard in Jezreel—to plan its demolition and rebuilding as a shrine and vegetable garden for the pagan gods of his wife, Jezebel.

Ahab ordered his soldiers to wait by the gate of the vineyard as he walked slowly and triumphantly towards the rows of vines glimmering in the morning sun. "Now, at last, I can build a worthy shrine to Baal. Jezebel will be proud of me," he said to himself. "These vines will be a fitting sacrifice to so powerful a god."

"Is that the only sacrifice you have made to your worthless idol?" The voice of Elijah thundered in the ears of Ahab. "An innocent man has been killed so you can pretend to be a man of god in the eyes of your pagan wife, Jezebel. And who is your god? What does he stand for? He is nothing but a god of deceit, of vanity, and of destruction.

"Ahab! Listen very carefully. In this vineyard you have unjustly acquired, the warm blood of Naboth is shrieking out from its ground for vengeance and justice. Your god is a murderer and a liar. The God of Israel will never let such an injustice go unpunished."

"How did he get into this vineyard past my soldiers?" thought Ahab. "Where did he come from? What sort of man is he?" With fear in his heart, Ahab looked at Elijah, as he strode purposefully towards him. He wanted to shout out a command to his soldiers to seize and execute him. But he was unable to do so. Deep down in his heart, he accepted the truth of Elijah's rebuke. He knew his soldiers would never raise their hands against a prophet of the God of Israel. He listened meekly as Elijah roared out the fate that would befall him, his wife, Jezebel and their descendants.

"The God of Israel holds you guilty for the death of Naboth," declared Elijah. "Jezebel's crime is your crime. The blood of Naboth will be avenged. In the place that the dogs licked up the blood of Naboth, the dogs will lick up your blood as well."

"You cannot hold me responsible for Jezebel's crime," Ahab pleaded.

"A king of Israel is held responsible for the crimes of his subjects," countered Elijah. "A husband is held responsible for the crimes of his wife. "Not only will you perish but your entire household will be destroyed. And as for Jezebel, She did not live as a queen of Israel and she will neither die nor be buried as a queen of Israel. The dogs will also lick up her blood in the valley of Jezreel."

Like thrusts from a dagger, Elijah's dire words penetrated the mind and soul of Ahab. He knew his fate had been sealed. He knew he was powerless to escape the justice of the God of Israel.

The passion of Elijah's words transfixed not only Ahab, but his soldiers as well. They felt they were in the presence of God's personal messenger. One soldier, especially, felt the full majesty and power of the God of Israel and His servant, Elijah. A Divine decree had been made. It had to be fulfilled.

The wheels of God's retribution were beginning to whirr. At the appropriate time and signal, that soldier would fulfil his Divine mission.

*   *   *

Ahab, on his return to Samaria, his capital city, immediately put on sackcloth and ashes. He refused all offers of food and drink and passed his time by wandering aimlessly in his palace from one corridor to another. "I have sinned against the God of Israel," he kept repeating to himself. "How can I get atonement for my sin?"

Initially, Jezebel permitted Ahab to express his feelings of remorse and repentance but eventually she began to reassert her authority over her husband. "You have no allegiance to the God of Israel," she declaimed to him. "Baal is your god! Worship Baal and your sins will be forgotten and forgiven"

"Leave me be," Ahab whispered to her. "It is your god Baal that has brought this evil upon me. I must make my peace with the God of Israel."

"Do not belittle my god," snapped Jezebel. "Belittle him and you belittle me. Do not be ungrateful to Baal. Through him you have become one of the most powerful kings in the region. Ever since you married me you have gone from strength to strength. Now forget about this Elijah. He and his God can never harm you."

Ahab knew he could never get the better of his wife, Jezebel. And for him to stay moping in the palace would only allow her to wield more power over him. He had to get away from her suffocating presence.

"You are right," he said to her. "I have been successful in my battles. Now is the time to extend my empire. My first campaign will be to get back Ramot Gilead from the Syrians."

"Well spoken!" smiled Jezebel. "Come, Ahab. Let us bring an offering to Baal."

*　　*　　*

Fortunately for Ahab, he was soon presented with the opportunity of recapturing Ramot Gilead. His daughter's father-in-law, Jehosophat, king of Judah, visited him in his capital city Samaria and immediately accepted Ahab's invitation to join him in battle against the Syrians.

"We are brothers," said Jehosophat to Ahab. "My army is at your disposal. My men and my cavalry will fight side by side with your forces. The Syrians will soon learn that Israel's property is not theirs for the taking. But I have one request to make before we prepare for battle."

"Of course," said Ahab. "What do you require?"

"I must have an assurance from God that we have a good chance of victory. Do you have any prophets who can predict the outcome of this battle?"

"I have. I shall immediately summon them to inform us of the words of God."

*　　*　　*

Four hundred prophets, led by Zedekiah the son of Knaanoh assembled in the gateway of Samaria to pass on the word of God to Ahab and Jehosophat. "We have come in response to your royal request," announced Zedekiah to the two kings seated on their royal thrones surrounded by an impressive brigade of fully armed soldiers. "We shall pass on to you the true word of God. What is your request of God?"

"We are considering waging a campaign against the Syrians to regain possession of the city of Ramot Gilead, which belongs to Israel. Will we be successful in battle?"

Zedekiah turned to his four hundred prophets. He closed his eyes and, with an expression of deep passion, began chanting to them in a low melodious voice. "Prophets of God!" he suddenly called out. "Concentrate on your holy task. Concentrate on the request of Kings Ahab and Jehosophat. Bring down the word of God to these mighty kings"

The prophets, all dressed alike in pure white robes, started swaying rhythmically in unison from to side and began chanting in the same melodious way as Zedekiah.

"What do you see?" called out Zedekiah. "What do you hear? What do you see? What do you hear?"

In one voice the prophets responded. "We see a mighty battle taking place. We see victory for the king of Israel."

Zedekiah reacted immediately to the favourable prophecy. He took hold of the pair of ox horns he wore around his neck as an ornament and held them high in the air for everyone to see. "As the ox gores and defeats anyone foolish enough to challenge it, so shall King Ahab defeat and overthrow his enemies."

Ahab was delighted with Zedekiah's unequivocal prophecy in the name of God. Undoubtedly, Elijah's prophecy had been overturned. Indeed his survival over the last three years since the murder of Naboth had already weakened his belief in the powers of Elijah. "Our victory is assured," he said to Jehosophat. "Come! Let us make plans for the battle."

Ahab, however, had made a fatal error of judgement. He had only been granted a three year stay of execution because of his courage in standing up to his wife, Jezebel and by repenting for his sins. He had never been protected by the idol Baal. And the God of Israel would still bring him to justice for his unforgivable crime against Naboth.

*   *   *

Jehosophat, however, was not convinced of the genuineness of the Zedekiah and his prophets. "Four hundred prophets should all prophesy, word for word, the same message?" he said incredulously. "There is trickery here."

"There is no trickery here," retorted Ahab. "I know these men to be genuine."

"I have my doubts," said Jehosophat. "These men all belong to the same school. Surely there must be someone from another school of prophets who speaks in the name of God. Summon him here! Let us hear his opinion."

Ahab, seeing the resolute look in Jehosophat's eyes, reluctantly agreed to his request. "There is another prophet. But we can never expect any good news from him about me. He is my sworn enemy."

"Nevertheless, bring him here!" commanded Jehosophat.

"As you wish," replied Ahab and instructed one of his generals to immediately find and bring before him the prophet Michyohu.

* * *

Ahab's general, on locating Michyohu, gave him a word of warning. "The king is very happy with the words of Zedekiah and his army of prophets. They all prophesy his success. For your own sake! Do not displease him by bringing news he does not want to hear."

"I can only speak the truth," said Michyohu. "Whatever God instructs me I will say."

* * *

Ahab looked at Michyohu with undisguised displeasure. "Shall we go to war against Ramot Gilead—or not?" he asked bluntly."

"Go up and be successful," replied Michyohu. "May God deliver the city into your hand."

"I did not summon you here for a personal opinion," Ahab was visibly irritated by Michyohu's casual tone. "You claim to be a prophet of God. Speak in the name of God! What will be the outcome of the battle?"

Michyohu, despite his intense dislike of Ahab's idolatorous regime, still retained his respect for the king of Israel. He avoided any clear mention of the dire fate awaiting Ahab and carefully composed himself before answering. "I see the men of Israel roaming the hillsides—like sheep without a shepherd. I see and hear God saying, "the men of Israel have no leaders, let them return safely to their homes."

Ahab had no doubts as to the meaning of Michyohu's prophecy. Michyohu had only mentioned his kingdom, Israel. Jehosophat, the King of Judah would survive. And the armies of both kingdoms would survive. But he was destined not to return from this ill fated battle. He alone would perish in battle.

Ahab was overcome with rage at the words of Michyohu. "I told you," he said to Jehosophat. "I told you he hates me. His prophecy is tainted by his dislike of me."

Ahab turned Michyohu. "I told you to speak in the name of God. You have allowed your feelings towards me to cloud your judgement. Now! I command you. Speak in the name of God."

Michyohu could no longer conceal the full words of God from Ahab. "Very well. Now hear the word of God!"

MICHYOHU'S PROHECY

"I see God in all his splendour sitting on His throne. To God's right and to His left are assembled the entire hosts of the heavens. I see and hear the words of God as He addresses them.

'Who will persuade Ahab to go up and fall in the battle for Ramot Gilead?'

There was an immediate response. Hundreds of spirits volunteered for the task. Each one had a grievance against Ahab and wished to exact vengeance for the wrong they believed he had done them. But God rejected them all. None of their grievances qualified them for the task God had in mind

Then one spirit stepped forward and offered his services to God. 'I will go, I will persuade him.'

God recognised the spirit. He also acknowledged the justness of the spirit's grievance "How do you propose to persuade Ahab?" asked God.

"I will become a false spirit in the mouths of Ahab's prophets."

'A false spirit!? What right do you have to act falsely? The Kingdom of Heaven is a Kingdom of Truth and Justice. I can only permit you to act in a principled manner.'

'Your majesty! One of Your principles of justice is an eye for an eye; a tooth for a tooth. In the manner that one sins—is one to be punished. My human life was taken away from me by a falsehood. With your permission, O' Holy God. Allow me to punish my murderer through the same means. I beg you! Allow me to act as a false spirit to the prophets of Ahab.'

'Your request is granted. And I guarantee you will succeed. Go and do as you suggest.'

"That is the prophecy I have seen," said Michyohu to Ahab. "God intends to repay you for the evil you have done. "Your prophets have been enticed by a false spirit to give you a message of comfort and hope."

"How dare you slander me and my prophets?" an enraged Zedekiah struck Michyohu on his cheek. "You claim to speak in the name of truth. Is it truth to use falsehood to entice a person to go to his death? God spoke to me first. You heard God's words through me. But you have distorted God's words for your own evil purposes. The truth is—Ahab will win a glorious victory at Ramot Gilead."

"On the day of the battle you shall see the truth," said Michyohu to Zedekiah. "But that truth will be unbelievably harsh. It will compel you to flee and hide from the subjects of Ahab. Take care! son of Kenaanoh. They will avenge their king with your life."

*   *   *

Throughout the entire account of his vision to Ahab, Michyohu had never once openly claimed that the spirit was the soul of Naboth. Only Ahab was aware of the true identity of the spirit.

Normally, Ahab would have punished Michyohu with an immediate sentence of death but a sense of doubt and guilt restrained him.

"Take this man!" Ahab ordered his guards. "Place him in the custody of the city governor and my son Joash. Tell them! He is to be placed in jail. Only give him bread and water. He is to stay there till I return safely."

"If you return safely, then God has not spoken to me." Michyohu said to Ahab. "Take heed of my words, O people of Israel."

Unfortunately, the people of Israel failed to take heed of Michyohu's warning of impending disaster. They were overwhelmed by the mesmerising display of prophecy by Zedekiah and his four hundred disciples. Ahab prepared himself for the forthcoming battle at Ramot Gilead.

*   *   *

Three years had passed since Ahab's dramatic encounter with Elijah in the vineyard of Naboth. During that time, no descendant of Ahab had come to an untimely end nor passed away naturally. Unsurprisingly, Ahab had begun to doubt Elijah's dire prophecies and had virtually accepted Jezebel's assurances to place his trust in her god Baal. But the vivid imagery of Michyohu's prophecy was unsettling him. It brought back memories of Elijah's powerful rebuke in the vineyard of Naboth. Ahab now believed that his survival depended upon thwarting the intentions of the God of Israel.

"What did Michyohu say," Ahab thought desperately. "Their leader has been taken away from them. What would happen if the battle started without a leader? If there is no leader in the first place, then he cannot be removed."

Desperate to avoid the outcome of Michyohu's prophecy, Ahab urged Jehosophat to go into battle without him acting as their military leader. "My soldiers are the best in the region," he explained to Jehosophat. "They do not need a leader. Their generals have already planned the tactics they will use to defeat these Syrians. Of course, I will take part in the battle. Not as a leader but as an ordinary soldier. I will not wear my royal garments. I will wear the outfit of an ordinary soldier."

Jehosophat, however, was not too keen to accept Ahab's proposal. "The Syrians will take me for the leader of the army of Israel. I will become their prime target. You will be putting my life into danger."

"Have no fear. The Syrians have no quarrel with the king of Judah. Their quarrel is with me, the king of Israel. You can wear your royal robes with impunity."

"Very well," said Jehosophat. "Let the campaign begin."

*   *   *

Unfortunately for Jehosophat, his worst fears were soon realised. The Syrians did mistake him for Ahab and began to close in on him. Arrow after arrow whizzed through the air towards Jehosophat's chariot and the Syrian infantry made every effort to break through to him. However on coming closer, the Syrians realised their mistake. "We have no quarrel with Judah," they cried out. "Ahab is our enemy. "Find Ahab! Find the traitor."

Like wildfire the cry reverberated around the Syrian soldiers. "Find the traitor! Find Ahab!"

*   *   *

Ahab had changed his appearance. But he had not changed his chariot. He had neglected to realise that the crude paintings adorning the sides of his chariot were visual evidence of his presence. With dismay, he heard the Syrian generals shouting out instructions to their soldiers. "Look for the painted chariot! Find the chariot and you find Ahab!"

"There he is. There's Ahab!" The cry rolled over the battlefield like a clap of thunder as the Syrians raced towards their target.

Ahab's soldiers responded immediately to the danger to their leader. They raced towards Ahab and encircled him in a ring of iron chariots. Again and again, they resolutely repelled the wave after wave of Syrian soldiers attempting to break through the Israelite defences.

As Ahab saw the Syrian casualties steadily mounting and no Israelite soldier falling in the skirmish around his chariot, his confidence began to rise. He believed his strategy of disguise was triumphing over the words of the prophet of God.

But his complacency was fatally premature. At a distance of 300 metres from Ahab, a Syrian general stood up in his chariot and placed an arrow in his bow. He pulled back the bowstring with all his strength and, without aiming at any particular target, released his arrow randomly towards the Israelite soldiers surrounding Ahab.

* * *

The arrow descended from the clear blue sky above the fields outside Ramot Gilead, penetrated a chink in Ahab's armour and embedded itself deep in his flesh. The arrow of God had found its first target.

Ahab looked down disbelievingly at the arrow protruding from his side but still stood obstinately upright. He would not allow his men to become disheartened at the sight of their mortally wounded king. "Sound the signal for withdrawal," Ahab commanded his driver. "I cannot continue the battle. But do not allow the men to see how badly I am wounded."

Immediately, his driver grasped the trumpet hanging by his side and blasted out the signal for retreat. It was quickly re-echoed throughout the ranks of the Israelite soldiers.

* * *

For the Israelite soldiers, since the act of retreat was always preceded by a frenzied attack on their enemy, they redoubled their efforts to finish off their Syrian foe. Wave after wave of Israelites chariots raced towards the Syrian ranks causing them to flee in terror. But the Israelites did not pursue them. Instead, they withdrew from the battle with the Syrians who were only too pleased to allow the Israelites to retreat from the battlefield.

Although the Israelite soldiers could see Ahab standing erect in his chariot as long as he was visible to the Syrian forces, they sensed their king had been grievously wounded. The hour was not late and their superiority in numbers was having a devastating effect on the Syrians. Evidently, the order for withdrawal indicated the king was no longer able to continue the battle. Confused and baffled, they wandered aimlessly from the battlefield before heading back towards Samaria.

* * *

On the way back to Samaria, the royal surgeons worked ceaselessly to save the life of Ahab. But their efforts were in vain. The Syrian arrow had not killed Ahab outright but his jarring flight from the battlefield had aggravated the wound and caused him to bleed profusely. The floor of the chariot was awash with blood. Ahab died on his homeward journey.

Only the body of Ahab was buried in Samaria. His chariot was cleaned in the pool of Samaria and the dogs lapped up his blood. The fulfilment of Elijah's prophecy had begun.

*   *   *

Ahab's death did not bring about the end of his dynasty. Fourteen years later, one of his sons Jehoram ruled the Northern Kingdom of Israel and his nephew, Achazia ruled Judah. But these two kings would not escape the dire words of Elijah.

*   *   *

At that time, Elisha was the leading prophet in Israel. Seventeen years earlier, when Elijah had been taken up in a fiery chariot to heaven, Elisha had seized the prophet's mantle and committed himself to purging the stain of Ahab and his dynasty from the people of Israel. Elisha now believed the time was ripe for Elijah's prophecy to be fulfilled. All he had to do was to persuade two men that the future of Israel lay in their hands.

One of these men would be ruthless, ambitious, intelligent and cunning. He would be driven by a psychopathic zeal that would enable him to butcher hundreds of defenceless people without regret or remorse yet still possess a self-discipline that would restore justice and morality to Israel.

He was the man who been present at Naboth's vineyard when Elijah had stood up fearlessly to Ahab and thundered out his prophecy of justice and vengeance.

This man had never forgotten that moment. His name was Jehu the son of Nimshi.

Elisha also required someone who could persuade Jehu that he had been selected by God to successfully purge Israel of the stain of Ahab and his wife Jezebel. Someone who could convince Jehu that he should have no fear of the established monarchs in Israel and Judah; and that the army and people of the Northern Kingdom would welcome him as their saviour.

Such a mission would require courage and resourcefulness. Courage to propose to a loyal servant of the house of Ahab, that he should bring about its downfall and destruction. And resourcefulness—to escape with his life if his proposals were rejected.

177

The man for this mission would be Jonah the son of Amitai.

*   *   *

In a large makeshift tent outside Ramot Gilead, the Israelite generals were planning their next campaign against the Syrians who occupied the city. Their first campaign had been a disaster. After the Syrians had targeted King Jehoram and severely wounded him, he had withdrawn from the battle and convalesced in the nearby city of Jezreel where he was visited by his nephew Ahazyohu, King of Judah. Significantly, their presence together would hasten the tightening of the web of fate being spun around the House of Ahab.

The generals were only too glad of a break from the fierce battle with the Syrians. Sheltered from the blazing heat of the midday sun, they drank thirstily as they analysed their defeat and planned their strategy for the next encounter with the Syrians.

"Tell us Jehu! Why do these accursed Syrians always seem to get the better of us?" General Baasha looked expectantly at Jehu. "Every time, we fight over Ramot Gilead, there's a disaster. How do you explain it?"

"There is a curse on the house of Ahab," Jehu said bluntly.

"A curse? Do you really believe in curses?"

"Normally, no. But I do in this one."

"Are you suggesting we get rid of the house of Ahab?"

"Don't put words in my mouth, Baasha! It is not up to us to pre-empt God's wishes. If He commands us then we obey."

"Noble words, Jehu. But why are you so convinced?"

"Because of two incidents. Two incidents that will always be in my memory. Seventeen years ago, I was privileged to be one of the personal bodyguards to King Ahab. I was present at the vineyard of Naboth the day after he was unjustly stoned to death . . . . ."

As Baasha listened enthralled, other generals gathered around the two men as Jehu related the dramatic encounter between Elijah and Ahab.

". . .Elijah was fearless and courageous. He was every inch a man of God. He knew Jezebel had put a price on his head and he was outnumbered by Ahab and his soldiers. But he didn't flinch from his task. His prophecy is now being fulfilled."

"You said two incidents," urged Baasha. "What was the second one?"

"Three years after that encounter between Elijah and Ahab, I was beginning to doubt the powers of Elijah. Then I witnessed the second incident. Yes! Again the Syrians; again Ramot Gilead." Jehu looked up at the people around him. "Many of you were there that day. I was in the chariot next to Ahab. We formed a ring of steel around him. No Syrian could break through our defences. We were prepared to protect Ahab to the last man. Then for some reason I looked up from the battle and saw a Syrian arrow silhouetted against a clear blue sky. As a peregrine attacking its prey it swooped towards Ahab. I shouted to him to take care. But it was too late.

His armour should have protected him. But that arrow had the cunning to find a weak link."

"Are you saying that arrow had Ahab's name on it?"

"Yes. That arrow did have Ahab's name on it?"

"And who wrote his name on that arrow?" Baasha asked. "Elijah? Three years after he died?"

"No, it was not Elijah who killed Ahab. Ahab was the bravest king Israel ever had. Even with that arrow in his body, he refused to sit down and discourage his men. The pain must have been excruciating. But he stood tall and firm. He was an unselfish leader to the end.

"Who put Ahab's name on that accursed arrow? Not Elijah! Ahab was a man of honour and integrity but he had one weakness. He could not stand up to that woman Jezebel. She bullied him into betraying Naboth. She put Ahab's name on that accursed arrow. She killed him."

"Take care, Jehu. There may be spies here today."

"There are no spies amongst us today. I know these men. They are all loyal to the memory of a great king."

"Jehu," Baasha whispered cautiously. "There's a stranger here. Who's that coming towards us?"

A man was threading his way, apparently aimlessly, through the weary soldiers lying and sitting on the floor. Every now and then, he stopped and looked around in bewilderment. His facial expressions indicated he was unaware of where he was, what he was doing and where he was going. He seemed totally lost.

The man finally stopped opposite Jehu. "I must speak to someone urgently."

"To whom?" asked Jehu.

"To anyone. The matter cannot wait."

The man's tone of voice and the expression in his eyes intrigued Jehu. This man was not lost. He was a man who knew exactly what he was doing. He was a man with a mission and Jehu felt compelled to discover the nature of that mission.

"If the matter's so urgent, you may as well speak to me," Jehu said casually.

"Very well. But it must be in private." The ring of authority in the man's voice was unmistakeable.

Jehu stood up and spoke to the people around him. "Gentleman," he said with a hint of light-heartedness. "This man has something of importance to tell me. Please excuse us while we converse in my private chamber."

*　　*　　*

In Jehu's private chamber, Jonah swiftly introduced himself. "My name is Jonah the son of Amitai. Elisha, the prophet, my master sent me here to anoint you as king over Israel."

Jonah drew out a small bottle from under his tunic and poured its olive oil over the head of Jehu. "Thus says God, the God of Israel." Jonah declared. "I have anointed you as a king over the people of God, over Israel.

"You shall smite the house of Ahab and I will be avenged of the blood of my prophets and of the blood of the servants of God who were slain by Jezebel.

"The entire dynasty of Ahab must be destroyed. No one must survive . . .

"And as for Jezebel, the dogs shall lap up her blood in the portion of Jezreel. She will be denied a proper burial."

Jonah did not wait for any response from the startled Jehu. Elisha had given him explicit instructions. Without a further word, he swiftly exited the door of Jehu's chamber and fled.

A bemused Jehu, his head in a whirl at the dramatic events in his chamber, returned to his companions. 'How should he react to the words of Jonah?' he thought. 'Was Jonah a man of God? Was his message genuine? Could he just declare himself as king over Israel? What should his next step be?'

His indecision was resolved by the blunt comments of his companion, Baasha. "Well Jehu! What did that weirdo have to say to you?"

Jehu was taken aback by Baasha's derisive tone. 'Was Jonah a weirdo?' he thought. 'Would a weirdo risk his life to deliver such a message? The anointing oil and the message seemed authentic. And the morality of Jonah's words was undeniable. The scheming, murderous Jezebel had to be brought to justice.'

Jehu had to buy time to collect his thoughts. "He didn't say much," he said nonchalantly. "It's hardly worth repeating."

Baasha was unconvinced. "Come along Jehu! It's not like you to tolerate fools. That man said something of importance. What did he say?"

"Baasha! You're wrong and you're right. You're wrong! That man was no weirdo. What he did coming here was an act of sheer bravery and courage. And you're right! He did have something of importance to say to me."

Baasha looked at Jehu incredulously. "What did he say?"

"He said a number of general things. And he also said to me. Thus says God. I anoint you as king over Israel."

Jehu's words 'Thus says God. I anoint you as king over Israel' were picked up by everyone in the room. Spontaneously, everyone took off one of their garments and placed it on the steps of the stairs leading to a sundial standing at the side of the room. Then they seated Jehu on this improvised throne and shouted out. "Long live King Jehu. Long live the king of Israel."

*   *   *

News travelled fast in ancient Israel. Jehu had to travel faster. He had to reach Jezreel—some fifty kilometres away—before the two kings resting there had any inkling of the rebellion against them.

At Jezreel, one of the watching sentries spotted a small band of men riding furiously towards the city. Immediately, he reported this information to King Jehoram who commanded him to investigate the matter. "Convey this message to the master of the royal cavalry," he said to the sentry. "Send out a rider immediately. He must find out who these men are; what their intentions are? Are they for us or against us? If he suspects any danger, he is to return immediately. We shall be watching his every step. Go now! May God be with you.

"Yes, you majesty." The sentry bowed low to the king and exited the royal chamber. He passed on the message to the master of the cavalry who ordered his best rider to carry out the king's command and race towards the fast approaching dust cloud billowing in the wake of Jehu and his men.

The rider, wary of approaching an unknown group of men too fast, slowed to a trot till he recognised Jehu and his men, then with a look of relief on his face, cantered towards them.

Jehu did not slacken his furious drive towards the city and the king's rider had to wheel round his horse to keep up with him. "I have a message from the King. Is everything all right?"

"What do you know about rights and wrongs?" retorted Jehu. "Follow me!"

The watcher in Jezreel, uncertain of what to make of the situation, reported his observations to Jehoram. "Our man has contacted these men and he appears to be unharmed. He is now riding back with them to Jezreel."

Jehoram responded angrily. "Why does he ignore my instruction? Send out another rider. Order him to return immediately with information about these men."

The second rider, assured of a friendly reception, rode directly towards Jehu and his men. "King Jehoram demands I return immediately. Tell me! Is everything all right?"

Once again, Jehu ignored the rider's request. "What do you know about rights and wrongs? Follow me!"

The tone of command and menace in Jehu's voice persuaded the rider to meekly comply with his demand and join the band of men speeding towards the city.

In Jezreel, the watcher reported to the kings what was happening. "Our second rider is also unharmed. He is now returning with the group of soldiers. I now recognise the leader of the group. Only one man in Israel drives in such a lunatic way. It is Jehu the son of Nimshi. He must have an urgent message for your majesties."

"If the matter is urgent," said Yehoram. "The quicker we found out the better. Come Ahazyohu! Get the chariots ready."

*   *   *

Seventeen years after Elijah prophesied the destruction of the House of Ahab, Jehoram, King of Israel and Achazyohu, King of Judah took their chariots and drove out from Jezreel to fulfil the prophet's decree. It was no coincidence that they encountered Jehu in the portion of land belonging to Naboth, the Jezreelite.

*   *   *

"What's going on, Jehu!?" shouted out Jehoram, when only a short distance from the approaching men. "Is everything all right?"

"How can everything be all right?" snarled Jehu. "Israel is being run by your mother, Jezebel, a harlot and a witch."

Jehoram wasted no time in arguing with Jehu. Pulling hard on one side of the reins of his horses, he forced them to veer away from Jehu.

"Treachery, treachery! Take care, Achazyohu!" he shouted out, as he desperately attempted to flee to safety. But he was too close to Jehu to escape his fate.

Jehu took his bow, placed an arrow against the bowstring and drew it back with all his strength. Then, after taking careful aim along the shaft of the arrow, he released the bowstring.

The arrow penetrated Yehoram's back with such force that it emerged through his heart, killing him instantly and sending him sprawling to the floor of his chariot.

Momentarily, Jehu glanced dispassionately at the crumpled body of Jehoram, then, turning to his captain, Bidkar who was riding beside him, gave him instructions. "Bidkar! Take that body and throw it into the field of Naboth the Jezreelite. You must remember the time when we escorted Ahab, his father and heard the words of Elijah Prophet. It was the day after Naboth had been unjustly executed for a crime he did not commit. I still remember Elijah's words to Ahab. 'Yesterday, says God, did I not see the spilling of the blood of Naboth and his sons? I will therefore bring retribution to you in this very place.'

"We heard those words. We are responsible for carrying out God's wishes. Bidkar! Take that body and throw it into the field of Naboth the Jezreelite, according to God wishes.

"Bidkar!" added Jehu. "I cannot stay here. I must pursue Ahazyohu. We shall meet in Jezreel."

*   *   *

Ahazyohu survived only slightly longer than Jehoram. Hotly pursued by Jehu's men, he fled southwards towards Samaria. But although no single arrow struck him a mortal blow, he was so severely wounded that he died in Samaria and taken back to Jerusalem for burial.

*   *   *

The news of Jehu's successful rebellion stunned the inhabitants of Jezreel. However, they welcomed the overthrow of a monarchy that was idolatrous, immoral and corrupt. When Jehu arrived in the city, he was immediately accepted as the new King of Israel.

Jehu had total military control over the entire city. All Jehoram's men had accepted his leadership. Only one source of danger challenged his authority. Jehu tackled this threat with his usual decisiveness.

*   *   *

Jehu, astride a magnificent white stallion and accompanied by a small troop of his cavalry, rode to a large palatial building in the most desirable area of the city. He entered the paved courtyard and called out loudly. "Who is with me? And who is with her?"

Within minutes, a figure appeared at one of the windows in an upper chamber of the building.

Jezebel had had plenty of time to prepare for her confrontation with Jehu. She was dressed in her most regal clothing and adorned with a dazzling array of cosmetics and jewellery. "I see the upstart has finally arrived," she said coolly, looking at Jehu and his men. "Is this the man you want for your king?"

Jehu ignored her remarks. He beckoned to the servant standing behind her, "Throw her down!"

The servant did not hesitate. Without ceremony, he picked up Jezebel and cast her to the ground at the feet of Jehu and his men.

The sudden movement and wild screams unsettled the horse. They reared up and down over the prone body of Jezebel; their hard hoofs repeatedly slamming into the soft flesh of the former queen of Israel until Jehu called out. "Enough, enough! The hour is getting late. We shall eat and rest, then return and decide what to with what is left of this body."

When Jehu returned, only the skull and the hands of feet of Jezebel remained. No body was left for burial. The dogs had picked up the body and taken it away to eat in a quiet, safe place. They consumed it in the portion of land that belonged to Naboth, the Jezreelite.

*   *   *

"Well, Daniel," Harry said to his son. "Does that answer your question? Can you can see how God treats people who act unjustly?"

. "Yes Daddy!"

"What else can you see from this story?"

"God's justice doesn't take place immediately. It can take a long time."

"Yes, it sure can. But be assured Daniel. God does not forget.

THE BETRAYAL

The Gabriel family, after finishing the second course of their Sabbath afternoon meal, would always spend a few moments inviting one of their children to talk about their Torah studies during the week. This week it was Akiva's turn.

"Well, Akiva," said Mr Gabriel, "tell us something your teacher taught you this week."

"We've got a new teacher for Bible studies, daddy. She expects us to teach ourselves."

"That's not such a bad thing. It's good for a teacher to make you work hard, Akiva."

"I agree with you, daddy. But not too hard."

"Too hard? In what way?"

"She asks difficult questions."

"Such as?"

"Such as finding out the meaning of hard words."

"That's not hard. You look up a dictionary. Or you can always ask us."

"It's not as easy as that, daddy."

"Okay, Akiva. What's bothering you?"

"This week's homework. She asked us to find out the meaning of the word betray. Then to find examples in The Bible."

"You could have found the answer to the first part of the question."

"I did. I think I know what betray means. It's the other question, where in the Bible? I don't know where to look."

"Go on Harry, help him." Jacqui, Mr Gabriel's wife felt uncomfortable at seeing Akiva look so upset. "Tell us about betraying."

"Betraying means a number of things," said Harry. "It can mean helping the other side. A spy for example betrays his country when he sells secrets to an enemy. It can also mean acting in a way that hurts your friend. In other words you betray your friendship. You betray the trust your friend has in you. Let me tell you a story."

"From The Bible?" asked Akiva.

"Of course from The Bible," said Harry. "There are plenty of stories in the Bible about betrayal. But I want to tell you about someone who betrayed his master simply because of greed and love of money. This story is about a man called Gechazi, a pupil of Elisha the prophet. We first hear about him in the story of the Shunemite woman."

"I know that story, daddy. The woman kindly offered Elisha and Gechazi a place in her house to eat and sleep when they stayed in the town of Shunem in the north of Israel."

"That's right, Akiva. And how did Elisha reward her for her kindness?"

"The woman and her husband did not have any children and Elisha gave her a blessing to have a son and, lo and behold, the blessing came true."

"Excellent," said Harry. "Now let me continue that story and perhaps it will answer your question about the meaning of the word betrayal."

ELISHA AND GECHAZI

"Elisha and Gechazi stayed in Shunem for a few years and by the time they eventually continued their journey throughout Israel, the son of that woman was old enough to help his father in harvesting the crops of their field."

*   *   *

After leaving the village of Shunem, Elisha and Gechazi, slowly ascended the gentle slopes of Mount Carmel. They left behind the criss-cross of green fields and vineyards in the valley below and headed towards the altar used by Elijah at the time of his victory over the priests of Baal. In the sweltering heat of the afternoon sun, both men welcomed the sea breeze fanning their long robes and cooling their feet.

Gechazi looked down at the people working in the fields below. "Those people will have to stop soon and drink some water," he hinted to his master. "It's a hot day for such work."

Elisha did not answer. He seemed deep in thought. Suddenly he turned round and looked down the slope of the mountain. "There's someone following us," he said to Gechazi. "It's the Shunemite woman; the one who kindly provided us with food and lodging. She is trying to catch us up."

About a hundred metres from the two men, a man was leading an ass directly towards them. The woman was sitting on the back of the ass, and even from that distance, Elisha detected their sense of determination and urgency from the man's hurried pace and the woman's anguished looks. "Something is wrong," he said quietly, "and God has not informed me. We must see what she wants. Run to her," he commanded Gechazi. "Ask her, if she is well, if her husband is well, if her child is well."

Gechazi carried out his master's bidding. But the woman's reply was cold and without conviction. "All is well," she said curtly without stopping.

Then she hastened past Gechazi and, on reaching Elisha, alighted from the ass and threw herself at his feet.

Gechazi strode up to her and roughly attempted to push her away.

Elisha, however, rebuked him. "Leave her alone! She is upset. God has hidden it from me and not told me. Let her speak."

The woman's word poured out bitterly. "Did I request from you a son? Did I not say, do not deceive me?"

Elisha immediately understood the reason for her bitterness and why she did not express herself more openly. He understood why she could not utter the words that would make her tragedy irreversible. She had to desperately cling on to the hope that Elisha could miraculously assist her.

Prudently, Elisha refrained from asking for more details of what had happened. He turned to Gechazi. "Hasten! Here, take my staff in your hand and go. Do not greet anyone. Do not respond to anyone's greeting. Go straight to the house and place the stick on the boy's chest."

*   *   *

This was the first time Gechazi had carried his master's stick. The symbol of Elisha's power and authority was now in his hand. He should have been exhilarated. Instead he was bemused. 'How can a stick, a plain shepherd's stick made from a branch of a tree, be an instrument of God? No special words or carvings are on it. How could it perform miracles?'

But was the stick a symbol? Or was it a tool? Perhaps its powers lay in the cleverness of its construction. Perhaps it acted as a magnet that used natural forces to perform extraordinary acts. Or the written name of God might have been inserted into the stick and given it the power to instil an inanimate object with some of the attributes of life, with speech and movement.

He, Gechazi, had once observed the extraordinary behaviour of the metal calves that Jereboam had set up as idols in Beth El; the powers of movement and speech.

Subsequently, he discovered the secret of these powers.

One of Jereboam's priests informed him—in confidence—that magnets were used to make these idols perform simple movements with their heads and tails. And, the name of God, when inscribed on a piece of parchment and inserted it into their mouths had enabled them to utter simple words.

Miracles, Gechazi believed, could be performed by anyone. Natural forces could always be harnessed to achieve a supernatural effect. And knowledge of God's ineffable name could be used to achieve extraordinary feats of magic. Was this the secret of his master's powers?

Gechazi's respect for Elisha was slowly eroding. He no longer felt compelled to obey his every wish and command. His master had given him definite instructions. "Do not stop. Do not greet anyone. Do not respond to anyone's greeting. Go straight to the house and place the stick on the boy's chest."

But Gechazi had other ideas.

At first he obeyed his master's instructions. He strode across the fields away from his master and the Shunemite woman, heading for the house where they had been sheltered for the last few years. Then when no longer visible to his master, he cast off the bonds of his loyalty.

He pointed the stick towards a passing donkey. "Speak! I command you to speak. Pretend you are the ass of Bilaam and shout out a few words."

There was no response, not even a bray. The donkey did not even glance in his direction.

"It must be deaf," said Gechazi. "Let's try something else." He pointed the stick towards a metal spade in the hand of a passing farm hand. "Come to me!" he urged the spade. Again there was no response. The farm hand seemed oblivious of Gechazi presence.

With a feeling of frustration, at his inability to unlock the secrets of his master's stick, Gechazi finally arrived at the outskirts of Shunem and shouted out to the first person he met. "Hi! Do you know where I'm going?"

The stranger looked at him blankly.

"I'm going to bring a boy back to life. I'm going to put this stick on his dead body and he's going to get up and walk around. Do you believe me?"

The stranger looked at the stick in Gechazi muscular hand. But, not wanting to get involved in an argument with a lunatic, especially one holding a stick, he merely muttered. "Yes, I believe you."

"Do you believe me?" Gechazi asked another passer-by.

"You're mad," was the reply.

"Perhaps you're right," said Gechazi, but continued walking towards the house where the boy lay on his bed, dead.

Gechazi reached the house and went immediately to the bedroom where the boy was lying. He placed his master's stick on the boy's chest and waited expectantly.

* * *

Elisha and the Shunemite woman walked slowly towards the house. Although anxious about the welfare of her son, the woman retained her confidence in Elisha. Never had she met a person like Elisha who radiated such an aura of piety and sanctity.

* * *

Gechazi looked coldly at the boy on the bed. He was not surprised by what he saw. Nothing was happening. There was no chest movement. The boy lay still, a deathly white face on a clean white sheet.

"I thought as much," said Gechazi. "How can a stick revive a dead person? This time he's gone too far."

Immediately, Gechazi left the house and went to meet his master. "There's no response to your stick. I came as quickly as possible."

Elisha looked coldly at Gechazi, then quickened his pace and within minutes arrived at the house where the boy was lying. "Wait outside!" he ordered the woman and Gechazi. "I shall enter the house alone."

Elisha entered the bedroom and went over to the bed. He lay down on the body of the boy and stretched himself to cover it completely. He placed his hands upon its hands, his feet upon its feet and his face upon its face. For several minutes Elisha lay motionlessly, then got up and looked down at the body of the boy.

The body was moving. The chest rose and the nose twitched. Finally, the boy sneezed, and then opened his eyes.

Elisha offered a short prayer of thanksgiving to God, and then called out to the woman. "Here is your child," he said to her. "Enjoy the fruit of your womb. He lives—and he will live."

* * *

"That story tells you something about Gechazi," said Harry. "It's a strange thing. He was the pupil of a prophet, of Elisha, and yet he had such little respect for him."

"Why is that daddy?" asked Akiva.

"I don't know how to answer such a question. Gechazi is a bit of a riddle."

"He's more than a bit of a riddle," said Jacqui. "He just doesn't make any sense."

189

"You may be right, Jacqui," said Harry, "but we still haven't fully answered Akiva's question. Who, in The Bible, was guilty of betraying someone? So let's continue with the story. This time we're going to one of Israel's neighbours and worst enemies, Syria."

SYRIA

"**R**evah! Come here."

"I can't come now. I'm washing and peeling the radishes. You asked me to get them ready straight away."

"Forget the radishes. I need you here in the house."

"I'm coming," sighed Revah. She put down the bowl of radishes on the ground, straightened her tunic and walked briskly towards her mistress's villa.

The sun beat down on her mercilessly. Flying insects were everywhere. Giant wasps buzzed incessantly around her body. Revah constantly flicked them away from her arms and legs.

Revah welcomed the thought of a few moments in the company of her mistress, Karishima. Thick, white bricks would shade her from the afternoon heat and muscular Negro slaves would cool the warm air with fans made from the fronds of palm trees.

Such relief, however, would only ease her physical discomforts. Nothing could ease the pain of being taken from her home and birthplace.

Would she ever see her father and mother again?

Would she ever again see the Land of Israel? Six months had passed since she had been captured by a band of Syrian soldiers and taken to Damascus. Now she was a maid in the house of a high-ranking Syrian officer. They treated her well. But she wanted desperately to get home.

Revah entered her mistress's apartment and waited for further instructions.

"My husband's coming home earlier than expected," said her mistress, Karishima. "He's feeling very tired. He wants to rest."

"It is very hot today."

"And dusty. The wind last night carried a lot of sand. It gets into the folds of the skin. You know how much it irritates him. Make sure his room is ready. Fetch fresh water from the well and bring in a bunch of grapes from the vineyard, the red ones."

Revah resented her captivity, yet still had sympathy for her master's condition. "Is there nothing you can do?" she ventured.

"We've tried everything."

"Perhaps we can help." Revah blurted out the words without thinking.

"We? You? You're just a child." Karishima's mild tone indicated she did not dismiss the offer out of hand. She frantically wanted to help her husband. She was prepared to go to any lengths for his sake. She knew it did not pay to underestimate the Israelites. Their cunning had taken a heavy toll of the Syrian forces. Who knows? Perhaps the Israelites had placed a curse on her husband for slaying their king in battle. If the curse was lifted, her husband might be cured. "How can you help?"

"We have a prophet, a man of God."

"We too have priests, men of god. We have visited every shrine in Syria. We have prayed and offered sacrifices to every god in Syria. None has answered us. Why is your man of God different?"

"Our God is a living God. He took us out of Egypt and across the Red Sea. One day, he will redeem me."

"Cure my husband and you will be redeemed. That I promise you."

Revah remained silent. She felt she had spoken enough already.

"Come here child," said Karishima. "Sit next to me. It will be cooler for you. Tell me more about your man of God. What is his name?"

"Our man of God is called Elisha. Like our teacher Moses, he speaks with God and he speaks with people. He knows that nature is God's tool and God, if He wishes, can make nature do as He wishes. Elisha knows how to talk to nature. He can make nature obey God's laws."

"Give me an example of the power of this man, Elisha."

"When Elisha first became a prophet, his teacher Elijah was taken up to heaven in a fiery chariot. Elijah left behind his mantle in the hands of Elisha and from that time on, Elisha inherited the powers of Elijah.

"The first miracle Elisha performed was at the River Jordan. Nature decrees that water runs downhill. Elisha decreed otherwise. He struck the Jordan with Elijah's mantle and the waters to his right stopped flowing downstream. The other waters flowed away and Elisha walked across the dry bed of the river.

"Then there was another miracle. Nature decrees that iron sinks in water. Elisha decreed it should float. When one of Elisha's pupils lost his axe in a river, Elisha made it rise from the bottom of the river and his pupil recovered it."

"Tell me child. These miracles were performed in front of people."

"Many people witnessed these miracles. The whole of Israel believe in the powers of Elisha"

"Has he ever cured anybody from illness?"

"Illness is from God. So is its cure. Elisha can change a decree. He can curse and he can bless."

"Can he cure my husband?"

"Of course," said Revah simply, "if he wishes."

"My husband is an enemy of Israel. Will he still help him?"

Revah hesitated. How could she speak for the prophet? "Your husband is a good man. Elisha will help the righteous who seek his assistance."

Karishima took hold of Revah's hand. "He is a good man. If only he could be whole again."

"I see you have become attached to our maid from Israel." The voice came from outside the room in which the two women were sitting. Karishima's husband had returned. Wearing the military uniform of the head of the armed forces of Syria, he strode up to the two women and looked down at them. "I shall only be here one night. I must return to the king immediately. There is much to do." Revah looked up at her master. In a mixture of awe and fear, she stared at his powerful body; at the hardened muscles of a veteran soldier; and the ugly red and white blotches that discoloured his skin. Unmistakably, her master Naaman was a leper.

The King Of Israel's Palace

The king of Israel looked at the letter in despair. "The man is impossible. He is seeking an excuse for war. He knows I cannot answer his request."

"Your majesty!" the prime minister tried to calm the king's feeling. "It could be the request is genuine."

"Genuine? How can it be genuine? Does he take me for a god? Can I perform miracles?"

"No, your majesty, but there are people who can."

"You've taken leave of your senses. This request from the king of Syria can never be fulfilled. Cure my best general from leprosy, he demands. He knows it can't be done. He's seeking an excuse for revenge. They murdered my father. Now they intend to murder me. How can I cure his general, or anyone else from leprosy? What possessed him to think of such an idea?"

"People talk without thinking, your majesty. Someone must have mentioned it to him. Perhaps it was one of the captives he took. They might be looking for an opportunity to return home."

"Who cares?" the king ranted. "It doesn't concern me who informed the king of Syria. I'm only concerned about one thing right now. What's he going to say when I answer, I cannot help him. I've had enough of war. Why can't he leave us in peace? Who's that?"

A loud rapping on the door of the room where the two men were talking interrupted their conversation. "Who is it?" called out the prime minister.

"Someone wishes to pass on an urgent message to the king," called out a voice from behind the door.

"Tell him, the king cannot take messages at this moment. He is busy with important matters of State."

"The man is insistent and the message is short."

The prime minister looked towards the king. "Shall we take the message, your majesty?"

"Yes, take the message," snapped the king. "Only, make sure it is short."

"It is short," the voice called out. "The message has only five words. 'He says, I can answer his request.'"

In the small, private chamber of the royal palace, the words of the messenger stunned the king and his prime minister. As if a thunderbolt had sizzled through the air between them, they both looked at each with open jaws. The king was first to recover his composure. "Quick! Let him in," he bawled.

THE HOME OF ELISHA

Somewhat sheepishly, Naaman stood outside the open door of the house of Elisha, the prophet of Israel. First, he looked uncertainly inside the house, then towards the two men who stood on either side of him. "Call out to the man of God," he said to one of them. "Announce that we're here."

"We have come to see the prophet," said Naaman's servant. "May we come in?"

There was no answer. The only response was the sound of footsteps approaching the three men. Suddenly, as if materialising out of thin air, a young man emerged from the shadows in the house and went over to them.

"You are the prophet?" asked Naaman disbelievingly.

"No. I am his servant. He asked me to give you a message."

"We have come all the way from Syria to see the prophet of Israel," said Naaman. "Surely, he can spare a moment so we may speak to him face to face."

"My master is unable to see you. His message to you is to go and bathe seven times in the River Jordan. Your flesh will return to you and you will become clean."

"Is that all he has to say?" Naaman asked incredulously.

The servant did not reply. He turned on his heels and vanished in the gloom of the house.

Naaman was furious. "I didn't come all the way to Israel to bathe in the Jordan. He calls himself a man of God. Doesn't he know there are rivers in Syria. Bigger rivers, purer rivers. I could have stayed at home and bathed in Syrian rivers, in Avanah and Farfar."

"You've come all this way," Naaman's servant, Brachmin tried to reassure his master, "the least you can do is to bathe in their river. Who knows? It might have special properties."

"Water is water," raged Naaman. "Syrian water, Israeli water. It's all the same."

"Tell me, my master. What did you expect him to do?"

"I expected him to come out and see me. To hold a holy scroll in his hand. To pray to his God and ask Him to cure me. I expected him to show compassion and kindness towards me. I expected him to place his hands on my skin and to miraculously restore my skin to purity."

"That is what the holy men in Syria do, my master. How many times have they prayed for you? How many times have they touched you? How many times have they shown compassion and kindness to you? Yet you have still not been cured. This is Israel, not Syria. Their ways are different from ours. Their holy men are different from ours. My master, I beg you. Listen to this man of God. Do what he says. You have nothing to lose."

For a moment, Naaman looked at his servant in stunned silence, then he found his voice. "You are right, Brachmin. I have nothing to lose—except my leprosy. Come let us find this Jordan River. Let us test the word of the man of God."

The Home Of Elisha

Gechazi had to force himself to walk away from Naaman and his two servants. He had only caught a brief glimpse of the three men at the door and the tribute they had brought from Syria. But he had taken in every detail.

From the robes Naaman wore, Gechazi knew he must be a person of extraordinary means. In addition, since the king of Israel allowed them free access to any part of the country, he must be a person of considerable importance. His mind seethed with the frustration of being a servant to the servant of the Almighty. His master might be content with the simple life, with dry bread and sips of water. But he, Gechazi, wished for something of greater substance. Why should he not have part of the wealth of this heathen, a small part of the gold and silver he would give to anyone who cured him from his leprosy?

Now, thought Gechazi, he would never see Naaman again. He appeared to be far too arrogant a person to follow the cold, impersonal advice of a prophet of Israel. Why had not Elisha acted in a more personal way towards Naaman? Why had he deliberately avoided speaking directly to Naaman before offering his advice of bathing in the River Jordan? Elisha should have treated him face to face in the same way as he treated the son of the Shunemite woman.

*   *   *

Naaman lowered himself into the Jordan and slowly waded towards the centre of the river. After only five strides, with the water already up to his chest, he stopped and prepared to dip.

"Seven times, master," his servant, Brachmin shouted out from the bank of the river. "Only seven dips and you will be cured."

'Brachmin is more confident than I am,' thought Naaman. 'But will it work.' He looked round to see if anyone else was watching and suddenly felt foolish. A shiver ran through his body as the cold water bit into his bare skin. 'What I am doing in the middle of an Israeli River? I'm acting like a child. How can dipping into water help? I'm coming out.'

Brachmin, sensing the sudden change of mood of his master, called out urgently to Naaman. "Dip, master! Dip. We shall count with you. Dip! One! Two! Three!"

As if in a trance, Naaman followed the directions of his servant. Again and again, he dipped in the waters of the Jordan. He no longer thought about the rivers of Syria, about the abrupt behaviour of Elisha and his servant.

"Four! Five! Six!" Brachmin's voice rose to a crescendo as he came to the last number. With a triumphant roar, he called out "seven!" then jumped into the water to wade towards Naaman. "Master, master," he said, holding out his hands to Naaman as he emerged from the final dip. "Master, your skin. It is whole again."

Naaman looked down at his body and his face broke into a smile. "I am whole again," he said, taking hold of the outstretched hands of Brachmin. "I am whole again."

*   *   *

Naaman, overjoyed at his miraculous cure, returned to Elisha's house and poured out his heartfelt gratitude to the man of God. "Now I know there is no God in the land, except in Israel. I beg you; take a small gift from your servant."

"As the Lord, before whom I stand, lives," said Elisha. "I will take nothing."

"I insist. I must express my gratitude to you. I insist I give you something as a token of my appreciation."

"I also insist. I will take nothing from you. I have everything I need. Keep your presents."

Naaman tried again and again to persuade Elisha to accept his gifts. But Elisha was adamant. He would not take even a shekel for the miracle that had transformed Naaman's life.

"Very well," said Naaman. "If you will not take from me, let me take from you. I beg you. Let there be given to me some soil from the Holy Land of Israel. With it I shall build an altar. Your servant shall no longer offer sacrifices to the gods of others. But only to the God of Israel."

Elisha said nothing. He waited for Naaman to apologise for having to break faith, at times, with the ways of the God of Israel.

"Let the Lord pardon your servant when I accompany my master in the house of the god Rimmon and support him by the hand." Naaman's words came as no surprise to Elisha. "When I have to bow down, let the Lord pardon your servant for this matter."

With an inner feeling of contempt, Elisha looked coldly at Naaman. "Go in peace," he said.

*   *   *

Gechazi waited until Naaman and his party were out of sight of Elisha's house. Then he ran after Naaman.

Naaman hearing the sound of running footsteps from the direction of Elisha's house, stopped his chariot, alighted and waited for Gechazi to reach him. "Is all well?" he asked.

"All is well," panted Gechazi. "My master sent me. See." He turned and pointed to two figures coming towards them. "There are two young men, disciples of the prophets, who are coming from Mount Ephraim. Give them, I pray you, a talent of silver and two changes of garments."

Naaman was delighted to be given the opportunity to reward Elisha. "One talent of silver? After what your master did for me. Is that all you ask for. No. You must take at least two talents."

Gechazi was overwhelmed at the generosity of Naaman, but, although tempted, disciplined himself to say no.

Naaman however was insistent. "You will take two talents. Your master deserves it."

Again Gechazi refused. But Naaman wore down his resistance and gave him two bags of silver with two changes of garment. They were handed over to the two young men who carried them to Gechazi's house.

*   *   *

On returning home, Gechazi took the bags and garments from the two men and hid them in his house, then went to see Elisha.

"Where have you been, Gechazi?"

Elisha's words were as a knife thrust into Gechazi ribs. For a moment, Gechazi stood in front of his master not knowing what to say. His mouth went dry, his heart beat furiously and one of his hands shook uncontrollably. "How does he know?" he thought desperately. "How can he know?" He tried to be as casual as possible. "I didn't go anywhere," he said in a voice so soft he could hardly himself speak.

Elisha looked at Gechazi coldly. "Did not my heart go with you, when the man turned from his chariot to meet you?

"Is this the time to take silver? Is this the time to take garments? Is this the time to take olives and vineyards; and sheep and cattle; and menservants and maidservants?"

The guilt of Gechazi's betrayal showed clearly as the blood drained from his horrified face. Despite the warmth of the afternoon sun, he felt an icy coldness enveloping his body. As though in a dream, he listened to Elisha's final words of condemnation and punishment.

"The leprosy of Naaman shall cleave to you and your seed forever."

Gechazi, with a gasp of pain and disbelief, looked down at his body. Then he staggered away from his master, a leper as white as snow.

*   *   *

Akiva looked at his father. "That was quite a story, daddy. I see what you mean now when you say that Gechazi betrayed his master. He deserved to be punished in that way."

"Becoming a leper was not the only way he was punished," said Harry. "He was punished not only in this world, but also the next. Our Rabbis say, that Gechazi was one of only four laymen, who did not merit a place in the World to Come."

THE BARBARIAN

'The Barbarian' is a story about Zedekiah, the last king of Judah. Seven years before the fall of Jerusalem, he came to Babylon at the summons of the ruler of the ancient world, Nebuchadnezzar.

Deep in thought, his bowed head in turmoil, Zedekiah knew there could be only one motive behind Nebuchadnezzar's invitation to his palace in Babylon; a further levy and tribute on his impoverished subjects.

"O,' God! What shall I do?" Zedekiah repeated to himself. "Where shall I go? What choices do I have? To rebel or to obey? Either way would impose fresh burdens on the Jewish nation."

Zedekiah walked aimlessly through the corridors of Nebuchadnezzar's palace. Desperate for relief from the images of idolatry encircling him, he seethed with anger and frustration.

Anger from the knowledge that the source of Nebuchadnezzar's wealth was the unjust burden of taxes Judah was compelled to pay to Babylon.

Frustration from his inability, in this heathen environment, to pursue the study of those teachings that were the very essence of his life—the words of God's Torah.

Zedekiah felt surrounded. Marble pillars soared up to ceilings of soft lavender blue. Gold threads shimmered in tapestries on walls. Mosaics of sapphire sparkled from marble floors. Gemstones of diamonds, topaz and jade gleamed from the eye sockets of ivory images. Nebuchadnezzar's palace was a monument to extravagance.

"O God! What shall I do?" Zedekiah said once more. "Where shall I go?"

This time, as though in answer to his prayer, he noticed a door behind one of the pillars in the corridor.

He stepped aside, opened the unlocked door and entered a small candlelit room. Unwittingly, he plunged into a nightmare that would haunt him the rest of his life.

*   *   *

Zedekiah was unprepared for the gruesome scene that assaulted his senses; the piercing shriek of a wounded animal and the primitive savagery of a fellow human being.

In the centre of the room, by a small marble table, sat Nebuchadnezzar. In front of him lay the warm, twitching carcass of a large hare. Like a lion devouring its prey immediately after the kill, Nebuchadnezzar was about to stuff another furry limb into his mouth, when he noticed Zedekiah standing by the door.

"Close the door quickly," he commanded icily and Zedekiah instantly obeyed. "It's a pity the king of Judah is devoid of manners. Bursting into a room without knocking is not fitting behaviour for a royal member of the chosen people."

The chilling nasal tone of Nebuchadnezzar unnerved Zedekiah. He stood uneasily near the door waiting for Nebuchadnezzar to speak.

"Your face betrays your feelings Zedekiah. Your eyes and ears are far too sensitive for such an unexpected sight. Now it's too late. You are a witness. But make sure your mouth never reveals what your eyes have seen. Swear that to me! Swear you will never inform anyone what you have just seen."

Zedekiah hesitated. He felt tempted to expose Nebuchadnezzar as nothing but a barbarian. He wanted to undermine his authority and standing in the eyes of the world. He wanted to shout out to the nations of the world that Nebuchadnezzar's display of civilisation was nothing but a sham. Would he be given the opportunity, though? The naked aggression in Nebuchadnezzar's eyes cowed him.

"You hesitate? You've already forgotten the promise you made me when I gave you the throne of Judah? Remember! Your name is no longer Matanyah. I gave you a new name, Zedekiah. May God bring judgement on you, if you rebel against me."

Zedekiah finally recovered his senses. "That promise was made to a fellow human being. How can I be loyal to someone who acts like an animal?"

"Don't preach to me Zedekiah. Your promise still stands. Now swear to me you will never reveal this secret."

Like a fly helpless in a spider's web, Zedekiah realised he had no choice in the matter. Still fresh in his memory was the brutal way in which Nebuchadnezzar had crushed the revolt of his brother Jehoachin and looted the treasures of the Temple and Jerusalem. He turned away from Nebuchadnezzar and cupped his face in his hands. Never had he felt so weak and humiliated. He, a descendant of David and Solomon, had to yield to a barbarian. To his people, he was a king. To Nebuchadnezzar, he was a pawn, a pawn that could be sacrificed at the slightest whim, simply to ensure his secret remained untold.

"Well, Zedekiah!" Nebuchadnezzar relentlessly pressed his demand. "The king of Babylon awaits the assurance of the King of Judah. Swear to me!"

"I swear." Zedekiah forced himself to utter the words of the oath. "I swear never to reveal your secret."

"You're a wise man," Nebuchadnezzar said. "Now I think it's time for you to leave this room and forget what you've just seen. Our scheduled meeting will take place in an hour's time. Good day, Zedekiah."

*   *   *

Zedekiah staggered from the room, a crosscurrent of thoughts plaguing his mind. "The man is an animal. How can Jeremiah suggest he's a threat to Jerusalem? There's more holiness in one small Jerusalem back-street than throughout the whole of Babylon. God would never use such a barbarian to punish Israel. Perhaps the warmongers are right. Now is the time to throw off the yoke of Nebuchadnezzar. If they knew his secret, even his own people will reject him.

"But who will tell them? I am sworn to secrecy. No, matter how difficult it may be, I am forced to honour my oath."

*   *   *

As Zedekiah had anticipated, at a meeting held later in the palace, Nebuchadnezzar cruelly tightened the screw of taxes that he levied on his vassal Sates. Zedekiah desperately attempted to wring some concessions from Nebuchadnezzar, but the ruthless monarch refused to concede on any of his demands.

Zedekiah returned home dejected and depressed, bowed down under the two heavy burdens he now carried—the burden of extra taxes on his people Israel; and the burden of silence upon himself.

*   *   *

Zedekiah soon discovered he had underestimated the difficulty of his undertaking to Nebuchadnezzar. Even after returning to Judah, he could not erase the memory of the scene he had witnessed in Babylon. His life became a nightmare. At mealtimes, the sight of a morsel of flesh sent the deed of Nebuchadnezzar flashing through his mind. At night, on closing his eyelids, he saw once more the limb of the hare in Nebuchadnezzar's mouth. During the day, sometimes the most innocent of events would unexpectedly set off a chain reaction leading back to Nebuchadnezzar's secret dining room.

Unable to eat or sleep, Zedekiah sought relief in the healing words of the Torah. Inevitably, here too the image of the hare intruded.

Zedekiah tolerated every discomfort except the loss of his Torah studies. Ten days after returning from Babylon, while learning with his rabbinical teacher in a Torah academy, he cried out in agony. "O' God! Help me! Rid me of this burden."

The Rabbi, a short thickset man with shoulders hunched from years of Torah study, was one of the few survivors of Nebuchadnezzar's purge of Torah scholars. Zedekiah, on his appointment as king, had persuaded Nebuchadnezzar to allow him to remain behind as his personal teacher. The Rabbi now looked at Zedekiah with astonishment. "Your majesty, what is the matter?"

"I cannot learn," Zedekiah shouted out, "every time I concentrate on Torah, I see . . ." He broke off his sentence and looked at his teacher with despair. "I see—that image again."

"What image, your majesty?" The Rabbi looked at Zedekiah with concern. He could not help noticing the telltale signs of fatigue and hunger, the right eyelid twitching uncontrollably from tiredness, the deep black circles around the eyes, the morose expression and the clothes hanging loosely on a shrunken figure. "You are bottling up something and the pressure is killing you. If you have a burden on your mind, I beg you share it with someone. As King Solomon told us, 'two are better than one.'"

"I cannot tell anyone. I must bear this burden alone." The words came slowly and hauntingly from Zedekiah's lips. "Only God can help me."

"God has many messengers. Someone must be able to help you."

For the first time since his return from Babylon, Zedekiah spoke openly about his troubles. "I have an image in my mind. It is always there. No matter what I do. Eating, sleeping, learning Torah. It won't go away. Until I forget that incident, I will be unable to learn Torah. How can one remove a memory from the mind?"

"What memory?"

"I cannot say. I am sworn to secrecy."

"Your majesty, please listen to me." The Rabbi leaned across the table and put his hand on Zedekiah's arm. "It is not the memory that is haunting you. It is the promise you made. You must feel free to speak out about what you have seen. You must feel free to share your thoughts with someone.

"I cannot. I made an oath. I cannot break my word."

"There is no need for you to break your word. Even if your oath is annulled, you do not have to reveal your secret to anyone. Your knowledge alone of the oath being removed will give you immediate relief from your burden."

"Can you annul my oath?"

"I cannot annul your oath. But other authorities can. Consult the head of the Supreme Court. He will advise what to do."

Almost immediately, Zedekiah felt a lightening of the burden he had carried so long. "My ancestor Solomon was a wise king. If only I had a fraction of his wisdom, Judah would not be subject to Nebuchadnezzar. Two are better than one and your advice is greatly appreciated. I will arrange to see the head of the Supreme Court."

*   *   *

The basic laws of vows are clear and concise. An undertaking, expressed in the form of a vow or an oath, is as binding as a Torah command. Thus the breaking of a vow can lead to the penalty of either corporal punishment or the bringing of a sacrifice.

Vows however, can be repealed. Any Jewish Court of Law, even one made up of three 'ordinary' people, has the power to perform repeal a vow.

One method of annulment operates by the Court determining the state of mind of the person at the time he made the vow. If they can establish that there was never a moment when he was happy with the oath, and, at the outset, made it by mistake, then they can annul the vow or oath.

Another method is by examining the change in the person's circumstances. Typically they could ask him one of the following questions. 'Do you sincerely regret having made the vow in the first place?' Or, 'had you known these new circumstances would arise later, would you have made the vow?' If the answer in either case is "no," then the vow can possibly be repealed.

For example, many generations later, the wealthy philanthropist, Kalba Savua vowed to disinherit his daughter because she married an ignorant shepherd. The act of annulment was performed by the Court asking him—'Had you known this ignorant shepherd would become a renowned Torah scholar; that he would become the great Rabbi Akiva, would you have still made your vow?' Kalba Savua's emphatic 'no,' earned him an immediate annulment.

Annulment of Zedekiah's vow seemed a formality. However, in his case there was a complication.

*   *   *

On the following day, desperate to obtain annulment for his vow, Zedekiah accompanied by two senior courtiers, went to the Temple. He first offered a peace offering on the altar, then entered the courtroom of the Supreme Court in Israel that stood in the Temple courtyard opposite the altar. There he requested an audience with the senior judge of the Court.

His request was immediately granted and in the small stone chamber next to the main courtroom Zedekiah explained the reason for his unexpected visit.

"So your majesty," said the judge after listening carefully to Zedekiah's statement, "in essence you are saying that you made a promise to someone that you are no longer able to keep. In other words, if, at the time of your promise to Nebuchadnezzar, you would have realised the anxiety and depression it would cause—you would never have made that promise?"

"Correct," answered Zedekiah. "I would never have made such a promise. It was a mistake. I would have accepted any penalty from Nebuchadnezzar rather than live with the nightmare that is now my life. What is more, I never wished at the outset to make this vow. It was forced upon me against my will."

"So, on that basis you want the Court to grant you annulment."

Zedekiah nodded his head.

"Your case has some unusual features, your majesty. I do not wish to accept responsibility by myself. I must consult my colleagues."

"What's unusual about this particular vow?"

"It involves someone else. A promise to someone else cannot be easily repealed."

"Even if that someone else is a non-Jew, a barbarian," said Zedekiah with passion.

"Your majesty, at this stage let us not get carried away with emotion. Let me consult with my colleagues. I am sure we can find a way of helping you."

"Can find a way? You must find a way. I cannot live with this vow. Consult your colleagues. I'll wait here until you return with an answer."

"It might take time your majesty."

"I'll wait."

"As his majesty wishes. We shall return as quickly as possible."

*   *   *

One hour later the judge, together with two of his colleagues, returned to the impatient Zedekiah who once more repeated his request and responded to their questions with the same answers as previously.

This time however there was neither debate nor hesitation. The three judges, without wasting words, delivered their verdict. "Your majesty," they said, "we can grant your request."

In unison, they recited the threefold traditional formula for the annulment of Vows. "You are released from your promise. You are released from your promise. You are released from your promise. Your majesty, go in peace."

"Thank God," beamed Zedekiah, warmly embracing the senior judge and his colleagues.

He left the courtroom, his mind clear. The evil spell of Nebuchadnezzar's secret was now broken. His regular Torah sessions would be resumed. Life could return to normal."

*　　*　　*

Nebuchadnezzar was a demanding emperor, exacting heavy tributes to fund expensive enterprises. At home, he lavished astronomical sums on building, beautifying and fortifying Babylon, making it the showpiece of the ancient world. Abroad, he was constantly engaged in defending or expanding his empire. Nebuchadnezzar was always seeking extra revenue.

Nebuchadnezzar's empire included Judah and its neighbours, Edom, Moab, Ammon, Tzor and Tzidon. He had appointed Zedekiah to govern this region.

*　　*　　*

One week after the annulment of his vow, at a specially convened meeting in his palace, Zedekiah informed the five kings of his visit to Nebuchadnezzar and the impact Babylon had made on him. In graphic terms, he described the impregnable eighty-foot thick wall around the city, the spectacular marble frescoes adorning the walls of public buildings, the giant ziggurats lining the streets and the network of canals from the River Euphrates that irrigated its gardens and parks. Then he spoke, at length, of Babylon's strength, power and iron determination to dominate the kingdoms it had conquered. "God has decreed," he concluded, "that we shall be subject to Nebuchadnezzar. That is His will. We must accept His decision. Now let me tell you of Nebuchadnezzar's latest requests."

"Wait!" interrupted the Edomite king, a powerfully built giant of a man with thick locks of ginger hair spilling over his forehead on to his eyebrows. "We can guess what you have to tell us. You didn't bring us here to give us a lecture on the sights of Babylon. Nebuchadnezzar wants only one thing from us. Money! Well, I've had enough. I say we stand up and fight. The man is a monster, a barbarian."

"I know," said Zedekiah in a barely audible whisper, the word barbarian conjuring up the harrowing image he had witnessed in the palace, "I know only too well."

Stimulated by Zedekiah's tone of voice and his guarded mannerisms, the five kings leaned forward eagerly, awaiting further revelations of Nebuchadnezzar's barbarity.

Zedekiah refused to be drawn. Despite the annulment of his vow by the Court, he did not wish to divulge Nebuchadnezzar's secret behaviour. "We have other matters to discuss," he said quickly.

"We are aware of the other matters. Let Nebuchadnezzar wait for his taxes. What do you know about that monster?"

"It's of no consequence," was the lame reply.

"Let us be the judge of that," said the king of Moab, a small, slender man whose lack of physical strength was more than compensated by an abundance of cunning and ambition. It was openly rumoured he had gained the Moabite throne by poisoning his father and two older brothers. He added to the pressure on Zedekiah. "Let's be blunt. We must at all times be united to defeat our common enemy, Nebuchadnezzar. Any weakness in his armoury must be exploited. If you know a secret about him, it's your duty to share it with us, your friends."

"I've already told you. It's of no consequence," said Zedekiah angrily.

"Why must you kow-tow to him?" said the king of Moab. "Who is he? He is nothing but an upstart. Of course he claims he has royal ancestry. He goes round boasting he's descended from King Solomon and the Queen of Sheba. Rubbish! Solomon would never marry someone like the Queen of Sheba. What person in their right mind would believe such nonsense? You, Zedekiah, you are a true king of Judah. You are an honourable descendant of the House of David."

Someone else added more fuel to the flames about to engulf Zedekiah. "He is no descendant of King Solomon. Who knows who his father was? Why should the royal kingdom of Judah support a barbarian? Why should you fund his orgies and idols?"

"Well, Zedekiah," demanded the Moabite. "Are we your friends or enemies? What is this secret you know about Nebuchadnezzar."

The pressure on Zedekiah was unbearable. For a moment he considered walking out of the meeting. But he had to conclude his business on behalf of Nebuchadnezzar. He had to persuade the five kings to accept the new terms imposed on them. Hastily reviewing his various options, he recalled the act of annulment granted by the Supreme Court. He was no longer bound by Jewish Law to withhold Nebuchadnezzar's secret.

In his innocence, Zedekiah did not realise he was being led into a trap; the kings disliked him even more than they disliked Nebuchadnezzar. Their feeling of concern was only a ruse. They waited, expectantly, for Zedekiah to rise to the bait.

They were not disappointed. Zedekiah, justifiably proud of his royal ancestors, resented the slur cast on Solomon's character by associating him with Nebuchadnezzar. Without thinking of the consequences, he suddenly shouted out with passion. "Nebuchadnezzar is not fit to be included in Solomon's descendants. No royal blood flows in his veins. Somewhere along the line of his ancestors, there's been an intruder—a barbarian, an animal."

The kings looked at each other incredulously. Never before had they heard Zedekiah speak so frankly. With looks of feigned innocence, they encouraged Zedekiah to expound on his unexpected outburst.

"A barbarian, an animal?" they said with surprise. "How is that possible? How can you say such a thing?"

Zedekiah poured out the whole story. "I had been sworn to secrecy but the Supreme Court annulled my oath. On my recent visit to Babylon, I was a guest in Nebuchadnezzar's palace. One day when I entered his room I saw him sitting and eating . . . ."

*   *   *

The five kings, knowing the futility of rebellion against Nebuchadnezzar and Babylon, found a different way of releasing their frustration. They informed Nebuchadnezzar of Zedekiah's betrayal of confidence, and then waited eagerly for the wrath of Babylon to fall upon Judah and its king.

It was not long in coming.

Reacting swiftly to their disclosures, Nebuchadnezzar, without explanation, summoned Zedekiah and the judges of the Supreme Court to his palace in Babylon.

*　　*　　*

At that time, many leading Torah scholars were living in exile, in Babylon. From them Nebuchadnezzar learnt of the role of the Torah in Jewish life, the rights and privileges of a King of Israel, the manner in which a Jewish court conducts its duties and—more importantly—the laws concerning annulment for vows and oaths.

Using this information, a room was prepared in Nebuchadnezzar's palace to resemble the courtroom by in the Temple courtyard; the seats being arranged in semicircular rows. At the front of the room, two thrones were placed, one large and ornate, the other smaller and less ostentatious.

*　　*　　*

On their arrival at the palace, Zedekiah, the judges of the Supreme Court and the armed soldiers accompanying them were ushered into the prepared room. A senior officer directed them to their places; Zedekiah to the smaller throne; and the judges to the semicircular rows according to their positions as in the chamber in the courtyard of the Temple. The soldiers then stood to attention along the side and rear walls of the room.

A fanfare of trumpets heralded the arrival of Nebuchadnezzar, everyone bowing low until he took his seat on the larger throne at the head of the room. "Welcome to Babylon," he said curtly as he waved his hand to indicate they should be seated. Then he pointed to the senior judge and beckoned him to step forward.

"You are the people of the book," said Nebuchadnezzar. "The Torah you call it. Everything you do is controlled by your Torah. Especially the king. Where ever he goes, he carries the scroll of the Torah with him.

"Tell me! Is your Torah a civilised code? Does it respect the rights of others? Do kings have extra privileges? Do strangers to Judaism have rights?"

"Jewish kings have to be treated with honour," said the senior judge, "but a king does not enjoy privileges in law. As for strangers, our Torah has given us many commands concerning strangers. We are told to treat them with respect and justice."

"I would like to know more about this Torah of yours," demanded Nebuchadnezzar. "You, as senior judge, must know it better than anyone in Judah. Take Zedekiah's Torah and read it to me from the beginning. I wish to know all about Jewish Law."

The puzzled judge, unaware of the danger facing him and his colleagues, had no choice but comply with Nebuchadnezzar's demand.

He took Zedekiah's Scroll of the Torah, rolled it out to the beginning and slowly read out its holy words. Every now and then he stopped to look up at the Babylonian king. Each time, the unsmiling face gave no hint of the end of his ordeal.

The judge completed the reading of the first three books of the Torah and started the fourth book, Numbers. He had been reading the Torah for well over three hours and wondered to himself what possible interest Nebuchadnezzar had in the ancient records of the numbers of the children of Israel when travelling in the desert.

"And Moses spoke to the heads of the tribes . . . ."

As the judge commenced reading the chapter near the end of the fourth book, Nebuchadnezzar at last broke his silence.

"That last sentence you just read. About a person not breaking his word. Read it again!"

"He shall not break his word. According to everything that issues from his mouth, shall he do."

"So a Jew is bound by his vows."

"A Jew is duty-bound to honour his word. He has a legal obligation to do so. He can be punished if he breaks his word."

"If a Jew finds his vow impossible to keep? What happens then? Is a vow irrevocable? Can a vow be annulled?"

"In some cases. If keeping the vow creates immense personal hardship."

Nebuchadnezzar introduced a different element into his questioning. "If a vow was made at the request of another person? Can such a vow be repealed?"

"If the vow was made at the request of another person, then such a vow cannot be instantly repealed. One should obtain permission from the other person to repeal the vow. "Tell me if I've understood you correctly." Nebuchadnezzar's voice was as hard as steel. "If a vow is made to another person. Can that vow be repealed—without the permission of the other person?"

The judge hesitated. "Normally not," he replied guardedly.

Nebuchadnezzar threw back his words. "Normally not! But when the king of Judah makes a vow to the king of Babylon it can be repealed. In such a case only the interests of the king of Judah are considered. The interests of the king of Babylon are ignored. The king of Babylon is given no rights in your Torah." Nebuchadnezzar's looked coldly at the judge. "Do you call that civilised behaviour?"

The judge remained silent.

The shrewd Nebuchadnezzar was fully aware of the Supreme Court's motive in granting an annulment to Zedekiah's oath. They had been seeking to create a split between Zedekiah and Nebuchadnezzar in order to stir up a rebellion against Babylon. Zedekiah was not wholly to blame for seeking an escape from his oath. The Court should have turned down his request.

Nebuchadnezzar addressed the senior judge. "You were responsible for the annulment of the oath Zedekiah made to me. You will therefore bear the consequences. But I am a merciful man and I will permit you to return to Judah. However, you will not return directly to Jerusalem. First, you will go to Lud. Then we shall arrange a different form of transport for the last part of your journey."

Nebuchadnezzar then turned to Zedekiah. "As for you, Zedekiah at this moment you're too valuable an asset to dispose of. I still have need of your services. This is your final warning. Do not cross me a second time. Otherwise, I swear to you that your punishment will be without compassion. And the day will come when your eyes will regret the scene they saw in my palace."

*   *   *

Nebuchadnezzar exacted a frightful revenge upon the judges of the Supreme Court. After journeying in comfort to Lud, they were tied behind horses and dragged on the ground to Jerusalem.

Inevitably, the desecration of the Divine Name generated by Zedekiah's broken promise led to the destruction of Jerusalem, the loss of the Temple and the decimation of the Jewish nation.

As for Zedekiah, in the eleventh year of his reign after finally being persuaded by the Jewish warmongers to rebel (unsuccessfully) against Nebuchadnezzar, he and his family were taken as prisoners, in chains, to Babylon. His sons were put to death in front of his eyes. Then he was blinded and cast into prison for almost the rest of his life.

HIS OWN EXECUTIONER

Silver goblets overflowed with wine. Ivory tables groaned under the weight of roast ox, wild fowl, sweetmeats and baked delicacies. Nobles and ladies reclined on white leather couches. Minstrels, jesters and clowns sang, joked and cart wheeled on a speckled marble floor.

In the vast banqueting hall of the royal palace, Babylon celebrated the defeat of the Persians and Medes; the victory of their king Belshazzar.

Belshazzar, his eyes gleaming in triumph, relished his moment of glory. Finally, he had emerged from under the shadow of his father Nebuchadnezzar. His crushing of Persia and Media made him the undisputed ruler of the world. 'Now,' he said to himself, 'the people will honour me more than Nebuchadnezzar. Nebuchadnezzar is dead. My enemies are destroyed. The world is mine!' He waved his hands towards a group of clowns near his table. "Perform a play to celebrate my victory. Show us how we defeated the Medes and the Persians."

Four clowns came forward and bowed reverently in front of Belshazzar. Three were dwarfs, all less than three feet high. The other was a giant, about seven feet tall. "Your Majesty!" the giant said, "we present 'Belshazzar's Victory.'"

"Belshazzar's Victory," repeated the dwarfs, bowing once more to the king. "An epic story of bravery, courage and strength. Here is the first character in our play."

Two dwarfs stepped backward and the third began to dance and sing. "Darius the Mede I be, I rule over land and sea. I, I, I . . . ."

The giant interrupted his song. With one massive hand he picked up the dwarf by his collar and held him suspended over the floor. "Put me down!" squeaked the dwarf to the delight of Belshazzar. "Put me down! Do you know who I am?"

"You little worm! Who are you?" the giant roared.

"Darius the Mede I be. I rule over land and sea. I . . ."

"Silence!" thundered the giant. "Do you know who I am?"

"Well, you're bigger and stronger than me."

"So who am I?"

You're Belshazzar, the most powerful ruler in the whole world. Ooh! I don't like it up here. Don't hurt me. Please! Put me down!"

"Your majesty," the giant now addressed Belshazzar. "What shall I do with this little worm?"

"Kill him," laughed Belshazzar. "Crush him. Trample him under your foot."

"Your majesty, it shall be done." The giant tossed the dwarf in the air, caught him deftly on his foot, then lowered him gently on to the floor and pretended to stamp the life out of him. Belshazzar shook with uncontrollable laughter.

The second dwarf stepped forward and began to dance and sing. "Cyrus the Persian I be. I'm king over much territory. I, I . . ."

Once again the giant interrupted the song and, to the great amusement of Belshazzar and his guests, treated him in the same way as the first dwarf.

The third dwarf stepped forward, and an intrigued Belshazzar awaited the announcement of his identity. "Who can it be?" he asked himself. "What other opponent is worth mentioning? Who is there left for me to conquer?"

The dwarf bowed in all directions, flexed his muscles and performed an intricate dance. He bowed once more to Belshazzar and began to sing. "The God of the Jews I be, Emperor of all royalty. I . . ."

"Wait!" interrupted Belshazzar rising, somewhat unsteadily, to his feet. "Tonight I will show you who is ruler over the world. Like Cyrus and Darius, the God of the Jews is crushed and powerless."

"Your majesty!" Belshazzar's Prime Minister clutched the king's arm. "Be careful."

"Be careful!" slurred Belshazzar, turning to his Prime Minister. "You dare to question my words. I, Belshazzar need to be careful? Go to my treasure house. Bring out the gold vessels taken from the Jewish Temple in Jerusalem. We shall celebrate our victory over the God of the Jews."

"Your majesty, your father Nebuchadnezzar instructed the Temple vessels were not to be used."

"My father Nebuchadnezzar is dead. His bones have been taken from his grave. They've been scattered throughout the land. No power on earth, or heaven, can bring him back to life. Nebuchadnezzar can no longer dictate to Babylon. He can no longer dictate to Belshazzar. I command you! Bring out the gold vessels from Temple."

"But the prophecy, your majesty. Jeremiah's prophecy cannot be ignored."

"Jeremiah's prophecy? His prophecy is an empty threat. His God is a toothless tiger. The seventy years he prophesied until redemption have already passed. They have still not been redeemed?"

The raised angry voices of Belshazzar and his Prime Minister carried the length of the banqueting hall. Before long, all the guests were listening to the argument raging between them.

"Perhaps we made a mistake in the calculation of the seventy years."

"A mistake!" roared Belshazzar. "A mistake! There's only one mistake I've ever made. I should never have appointed you Prime minister. Do as you're commanded. Fetch the Temple vessels. Fill them with good strong Babylonian wine." Belshazzar raised his goblet high in the air and looked round the hall at his guests. "While we're waiting for my Prime Minister to bring the Temple vessels, we shall drink a toast. To Babylon! May Babylon live for ever!"

*   *   *

Thirty minutes later, a fanfare of trumpets announced the return of the Prime Minister from the royal treasury. The twenty-foot high cedar doors at the right hand side of the banqueting hall swung open and an army of servants, with the Temple vessels in their hands, entered the hall. They split into two columns and took up positions along the walls behind the guests.

The head-servant, his hands stretched out rigidly in front of him, carried a magnificent golden goblet on a blue velvet-covered tray. Conscious that every eye in the hall was following his movements, he walked stiffly towards Belshazzar.

"Your majesty," said the head-servant, bowing as low to the ground as possible, "this goblet was used by the High Priest himself. It is the choicest of the Temple vessels."

Belshazzar took the goblet from the tray and held it lovingly in his hand. "The workmanship is exquisite. It is a work of art, fit for a god. And it is fit for the king of Babylon."

Belshazzar looked round the hall and raised his voice. "Lords and nobles of Babylon! We have started a new era in the history of Babylon. The God of Israel is vanquished. We are the heirs to his kingdom. Take the Temple vessels. Fill them with wine. Drink with me to Babylon—and to the gods of Babylon."

From all sides of the hall, the servants moved forward and offered the Temple vessels to Belshazzar's guests. Immediately other servants filled them with wine. Then, to the sound of couches scraping the marble floor, the assembly rose and bowed reverently to the gold and silver idols around the banqueting hall. "To Bal! To Baalzebub!" they shouted out, raising their goblets high in the air. "To Belshazzar!"

As everyone drank thirstily from their goblets, Belshazzar held up his hand for silence. "Lords and ladies of Babylon, Babylon has many gods to thank for its victory over the God of Israel. We shall drink to Ish . . . ."

Belshazzar never completed the sentence, the last word remained suspended on his lips. He stood frozen to the ground, staring with disbelief towards the other end of the hall. His hand shook uncontrollably. Wine cascaded from the goblet on to his clothing. The colour drained from his face. Every bone in his body trembled with fright. "What is happening? What is it?" he wanted to say. But his tongue hung limply through his gaping jaws.

As one being, everyone in the hall swung round to face the other end of the hall. Lords, ladies, acrobats, clowns, musicians and servants; all turned to stare at the sight that had unnerved Belshazzar; a human hand of flesh, bone and sinew, hovering by the plaster wall at the other end of the banqueting hall. In full view of the horror-stricken audience, the hand began to write, in blood, on the wall.

"Where did it come from? What does it want? What is it writing?" Belshazzar, finally recovering some of his senses, managed to express some of the thoughts racing through his mind. "Sages, sages," he called out wildly, looking towards the table where the sages sat as confused as the rest of his guests. "What is happening? What is the meaning of the writing on the wall?"

Belshazzar turned to his Prime Minister and barked out an instruction that sent him scuttling away to confer with the sages. After two anxious minutes he returned. "They do not know your majesty. They cannot help you. They do not even know the language in which it is written."

"Wise men, you call yourselves?" Belshazzar raged, shaking his fists at them. "You're nothing but fools. Who knows what it says?" he shouted out. "Whoever reveals the message of the writing on the wall will be well rewarded."

A wall of silence greeted his request and Belshazzar felt compelled to seek the advice of his sages again. "Surely there must be someone in my kingdom who can advise me? Is there no one who can read this strange language?"

The chief sage rose to his feet. "Your majesty," he said, with all the respect and humility he could muster, "I'm certain the writing is in the Hebrew language. It must be a rarely used dialect. Allow me to consult with the Jewish sages."

"The Jews!" roared Belshazzar. "How can I rely on them? We've just insulted their God. They won't give me a good interpretation."

"Your majesty." A soft, gentle voice sounded in Belshazzar's ear. "Pray listen to me." In defiance of court custom, Belshazzar's queen had entered the banqueting hall and gone over to her husband. Royal ladies did not attend mixed functions and some years later Vashti, Nebuchadnezzar's daughter, would refuse the command of Ahasuerus to appear at his feast in Shushan, Persia. Only the urgency of the circumstances compelled Belshazzar's queen to violate the strict royal code of discretion and modesty. "We have little choice in the matter. Let me consult with one of the Jewish sages. Your father often sought his advice. It was always to the benefit of Babylon."

"My father is dead. Nebuchadnezzar and his policies are buried. I do not wish to see a Jewish sage."

"Your majesty," the queen begged. "This man is no ordinary Jew. It is the sage Daniel, the wisest man in your entire kingdom. He is the only person who can explain the meaning of those words. I beg you. Summon him. Reward him well. He will give a true interpretation."

Belshazzar clutched tightly at the table in front of him. "Very well, summon him to appear before me."

*   *   *

Before Belshazzar became emperor over Babylon, his father Nebuchadnezzar had repeatedly punished Judah's attempts to defy his authority. Eleven years before destroying the Temple and reducing Jerusalem to rubble, Nebuchadnezzar had swooped on Judah, seized its Torah scholars, nobles and artisans, and exiled them to serve in the royal palace in Babylon. One of these exiles, like Joseph in the court of Pharaoh, remained steadfast to his heritage and culture. And like Joseph, his wisdom, insight and integrity earned him the respect of both Babylonian and Jew. He advised Nebuchadnezzar on affairs of State; and together with Ezra and Mordecai, was a member of the men of the Great Synagogue. Before long, Belshazzar would also be a witness to the extraordinary powers of the Jewish sage, Daniel.

*   *   *

Daniel entered the banqueting hall, bowed low to the ground and offered his services to Belshazzar.

"Are you really Daniel the Jew whom my father brought out of Judah?" Belshazzar had heard that Daniel was a strict vegetarian and observed a demanding daily programme of fasting and prayer. He looked with amazement at Daniel's vigorous, upright figure. "I have heard that the spirit of God is with you; that you are filled with wisdom and understanding. My wise men are unable to interpret that writing on the wall. If you can tell me its meaning, you will be well rewarded. I will clothe you in scarlet, place a chain of gold around your neck and appoint you as a third ruler in my kingdom. What do those words mean?"

"I have no need for your gifts. You may give them to someone else. The meaning of the words is clear. You have sinned grievously." Daniel, although speaking with respect, did not flinch from rebuking the king. "Your father Nebuchadnezzar was appointed by God to be king over Babylon. God gave him a kingdom and majesty; glory and honour. But when Nebuchadnezzar became vain and proud, God took his kingdom away from him. Your father was driven from the sons of men and became like a beast. For ten years, he ate grass like an ox, and his body was covered with dew.

"Yet your father humbled himself and God restored him to the throne. Because of this, God gave your father the authority to punish Israel, the authority to destroy our Temple.

"As for the holy vessels of the Temple, God only appointed him as their custodian. God did not give him the authority to abuse them. These holy vessels were to be kept in trust until Israel would be fit to use them once more.

"That trust you have abused," Daniel accused a white-faced Belshazzar. "You have not humbled yourself. You have used God's sacred vessels for unclean purposes. You, your lords and their wives have drunk wine in the holy vessels of God. You have praised gods of silver and gold, gods of brass, iron, wood and stone. You believed that after seventy years of Babylonian rule you could defy the wishes of the God of Israel, the God in whose hand is the very breath of your life.

"Now God has sent part of that hand to write on the wall of your palace. Listen carefully to the words and their meaning.

"MENE, MENE, TEKEL UPARSIN.

"MENE, MENE—God has numbered your kingdom and finished it.

"TEKEL—you have been weighed in the balance and found wanting.

"UPARSIN—your kingdom is divided and given to the Persians and the Medes."

Belshazzar's conceit and pride did not allow him to fully appreciate the scale of his transgression against God. Foolishly, he believed that his wealth and power could still save him from the hand of fate. He, therefore, sought to find favour with God by offering gifts and honour to His loyal servant Daniel. "You are indeed a wise man, Daniel. You shall be well rewarded for your services. You shall be clothed in scarlet, and wear a chain of gold around your neck. I shall appoint you as a third ruler in my kingdom."

Daniel bowed low before the king. "I seek neither fame nor fortune. I seek only to speak in the name of God. With your permission, your majesty, I must refuse your generous gifts."

Belshazzar, ignoring Daniel's protests, waved his hand towards his Prime Minister. "Escort the sage Daniel from the banqueting hall and see he is well rewarded for his services. Then return to me immediately." He turned to his deputy Prime Minister. "Inform my guests, the party is over."

*   *   *

Four words, in blood, challenged Belshazzar's vision of power and fame. Yet he was determined to outwit the hand of fate. In the privacy and security of a well-guarded chamber in his palace, he conferred with his Prime Minister. "I will overcome the God of Israel," he said, pacing backwards and forwards in nervous excitement. "He has declared war against Babylon. But I shall defeat Him."

"Defeat the God of Israel?" the Prime Minister said guardedly. "Your majesty, do not underestimate His power."

"His power is over. His Temple is destroyed, His people are exiled. No Jew lives in His promised land. He cannot be a God without a country, without a nation, without sacrifices in his Temple?"

"Your majesty, be careful. The deeds of the God of Israel go back to the early mists of time. Pharaoh defied him. And he and nation were destroyed."

Belshazzar dismissed his Prime Minister's arguments. "The past is dead. The God of Israel is old and feeble. Our gods are young and strong. They defeated the Medes and Persians. They will protect us against the Jewish God."

The Prime Minister, realising he could never persuade Belshazzar to abandon his pagan beliefs, now felt compelled to support him. "Your majesty is right. Daniel told us the meaning of the writing on the wall. The God of Israel is telling us our days are numbered. But why warn us? Why did He not strike us direct? Why should a God that wiped out the first-born of Egypt give us a written warning? It doesn't make sense."

"It does make sense and at last you're seeing sense. As I've already said. His power has waned. Now tell me! After you washed down the wall, what happened? Did the writing return?"

"No, your majesty, it did not return. You're right. He has lost most of his supernatural powers. He is trying to frighten us, He wants us to panic. He no longer has powers over the forces of Nature. He is now forced to use human agencies to destroy Babylon. Did not Daniel say he used Nebuchadnezzar to destroy His Temple. So who can He use now? He is forced to use Cyrus and Darius to carry out his threat.

"Your Majesty, as long as they live they will be a threat to your kingdom. We must take the initiative and destroy them."

"In the meantime," said Belshazzar, "before we attack, we must defend. Remember this. I shall hold you personally responsible for any gaps in our defences. Throw an iron curtain around the palace. Stop even a fly entering. Go!"

As the Prime Minister rose from his seat to leave the chamber he was stopped by a command from Belshazzar. "Wait!" he called out suddenly. "How will the God of Israel give my kingdom to the Persians and the Medes? An old God has no strength. He must have something else. There is only one way in which He can defeat me; by cunning and by trickery. He will use cunning to find a traitor in my palace." His eyes gleamed wildly at his Prime Minister. "There is a spy in the palace. Find him. Bring him to me."

"Your majesty, I know of no spies among your guard. Your men are loyal to you. Rest assured. I'll see no stranger is allowed in the palace."

"But someone might get in by a trick." Daniel's ominous prediction was unnerving Belshazzar. The image of the writing on the wall was too deeply seared in his memory to be so speedily dismissed. 'MENE MENE—God has numbered your kingdom and finished it.' The words spun around and around in his mind. "What sort of trick? He might even pretend to be a friend of the king. He might even pretend to be the king himself."

"Your majesty . . . .," began the Prime Minister

"Summon the captain of the guards," Belshazzar screamed out hysterically. "Tell him he will be well rewarded. Give him careful instructions. Tell him to let no one in the palace. No matter what they say to him. Even if they pretend to be the king himself. I will fight cunning with cunning."

"Your majesty," the Prime Minister said. "I will carry out your instructions personally." He bowed low to the ground and retired from the chamber.

*   *   *

Alone in the chamber, the seeds of panic began to germinate and grow in Belshazzar's mind. He felt isolated and afraid. He kept taking shallow breaths and turning his head rapidly in all directions. He could not rid himself of the image of a hand mysteriously materialising out of thin air. At any moment, he expected the hand to materialise again. Only this time, the hand would not write on the wall. It would be holding a dagger. It would plunge swiftly towards his heart.

Outside, a scratching noise in the corridor sent him leaping to his feet. He drew his sword from its scabbard and held it up in front of his face. His knuckles whitened with the strength of their grip on the handle. He whirled round making sure there was no one behind him. "I will defeat the God of Israel," Belshazzar shouted out. "Whoever betrays me will pay dearly for their treachery. Who's there? Identify yourself."

"Your servant, Beshak, your majesty," was the reply.

"Stand guard quietly. Listen out for any intruder. Do not leave the chamber unattended. Stay at your post until your relief comes. Make sure he is loyal to Babylon. Do you hear me?"

"Yes, your majesty."

"Yes, your majesty, no, your majesty," mimicked Belshazzar. "The fools have no minds of their own? How can they fight against the cunning of the God of Israel? How can I rely on them?"

Belshazzar, his face a mask of anguish and fright, suddenly looked towards the far corner of the room. This time he spoke softly to himself. "The only wise thing my father Nebuchadnezzar ever did. I'll inspect the guards myself."

*   *   *

Thirty-seven years earlier, Nebuchadnezzar had constructed a secret exit at the rear of the private chamber; a two hundred foot long tunnel descending through layers of rock and soil to the grounds of the palace. The exit, camouflaged as part of the wall covering, was opened by pressing three sections of the wooden panelling. Belshazzar had accidentally discovered the secret when a workman, unaware anyone was present, tested the opening of the door.

A few weeks after his discovery, the young Belshazzar, in pursuit of excitement and thrills, had slipped quietly into the room, entered the secret passageway and closed the door behind him.

The sudden darkness terrified him. He turned back to get a torch but the sound of voices stopped him.

Two men had entered the room and, in graphic detail, one was instructing the other to cruelly torture and then execute an enemy of

Babylon. Belshazzar instantly recognised the chilling, nasal tones. It was his father Nebuchadnezzar.

Fifteen minutes passed before one of the men left and Belshazzar could contain himself no longer. Particles of cold dust had entered his nostrils and he sneezed loudly.

"Who's there?" Like lightning, Nebuchadnezzar drew his sword and flashed across to the entrance. "Throw your sword onto the ground and come out slowly."

"It's me father," came a whimper. "It's me, Belshazzar."

"Come out at once."

Belshazzar emerged from the darkness and blinked heavily to adjust to the light. He never forgot the cold, pitiless look on his father's face. He never forgot his words. "Never, ever reveal the secret of this tunnel to anyone. My life may depend on it. Your life certainly will."

*   *   *

'MENE MENE TEKEL UPARSIN.' With the words of doom racing through his mind, Belshazzar pressed firmly on the three panels. Immediately, a long vertical crack rippled down the wall but the door did not open fully.

For years, the exit had remained unused and Belshazzar, using all his strength, had to repeatedly push against the edge of the door before breaking down the coating of rust on the hinges.

Finally the door creaked open.

Belshazzar paused briefly to recover his breath. Then, with a sword in one hand and a lighted torch in the other, he plunged into the gloom of his father's secret passage.

Slashing with his sword at the thick cobwebs all round him, Belshazzar first cautiously descended a flight of fifty stone steps. Then, after walking more quickly along a gently sloping path, he reached the door leading to the grounds of the palace. He placed his torch in a ring on the wall and slowly opened the door.

To Belshazzar, the creaking of the hinges sounded like a clap of thunder but, to his surprise, it was not heard by the group of soldiers in their sentry box about sixty metres to the right of the concealed exit.

He was furious. "Just as I thought," he said to himself. "They're fools. They didn't even look round. I'll have them executed for negligence. But first, I'll show them. I'll show them how easy it is to get through their defences."

He waited for a sentry to finish patrolling the stretch of ground directly in front of him, then crouching low, sprinted towards the edge of the garden. He stopped by a small stone wall and climbed over it.

Belshazzar was now outside the main line of defence of his palace. Yet despite the full moon in a cloudless sky, no one had seen or heard him.

Belshazzar was livid. He climbed back over the wall and walked openly towards the sentry box. "Who is in charge here?" he shouted out loudly to a sentry. "Which fool is in charge of this area of the palace?"

"Who are you?" the sentry demanded. "What are you doing in the palace grounds? What unit do you belong to?"

"How dare you question me? I am your king. I am the king you were ordered to protect."

Belshazzar's words triggered a detonator in the mind of the sentry. 'Let no one through, even if he claims to be the king himself. We are fighting an enemy who will use cunning to enter these grounds.' Those were the instructions of the supreme commander of the Babylon forces. They came directly from the Emperor Belshazzar himself. 'Let no one through, even if he claims to be the king himself,'

"Who are you?" the sentry demanded again. "Identify yourself!"

"Fool!" thundered Belshazzar. "I am your king. Your ki . . . Aaah!"

Belshazzar, gasping at the sudden pain shooting through him, looked disbelievingly at the sentry's sword protruding from his body. Then he fell lifelessly to the ground.

*   *   *

Inevitably, Belshazzar's clumsy attempts to defy the God of Israel and outwit 'the writing on the wall,' ended in his own execution. This paved the way, some generations later, for Darius, son of Ahasuerus and Esther, to become king over Persia and assist in the rebuilding of the Temple.